WITHDRAWN
UTSA LIBRARIES

Mobilizing Resources in
Latin America

Mobilizing Resources in Latin America

The Political Economy of Tax Reform in Chile and Argentina

Omar Sanchez

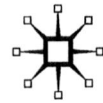

MOBILIZING RESOURCES IN LATIN AMERICA
Copyright © Omar Sanchez, 2011.

All rights reserved.

First published in 2011 by
PALGRAVE MACMILLAN®
in the United States—a division of St. Martin's Press LLC,
175 Fifth Avenue, New York, NY 10010.

Where this book is distributed in the UK, Europe and the rest of the world, this is by Palgrave Macmillan, a division of Macmillan Publishers Limited, registered in England, company number 785998, of Houndmills, Basingstoke, Hampshire RG21 6XS.

Palgrave Macmillan is the global academic imprint of the above companies and has companies and representatives throughout the world.

Palgrave® and Macmillan® are registered trademarks in the United States, the United Kingdom, Europe and other countries.

ISBN: 978–0–230–11446–3

Library of Congress Cataloging-in-Publication Data

Sánchez, Omar, 1974–
　Mobilizing resources in Latin America : the political economy of tax reform in Chile and Argentina / Omar Sanchez.
　　p. cm.
　ISBN 978–0–230–11446–3 (hardback)
　1. Taxation—Chile. 2. Taxation—Argentina. 3. Chile—Economic conditions—1988– 4. Argentina—Economic conditions—1983– I. Title.

HJ2535.S26 2011
336.200982—dc22   2011002897

A catalogue record of the book is available from the British Library.

Design by Newgen Imaging Systems (P) Ltd., Chennai, India.

First edition: July 2011

10 9 8 7 6 5 4 3 2 1

Printed in the United States of America.

Library
University of Texas
at San Antonio

Para mis padres,

Olga Sibony y Lorenzo Sanchez

por su incondicional amor y apoyo

Contents

Acknowledgments	ix
Introduction	1
1 Post-Pinochet Chilean Tax Policy (1989–1995): Finding Resources to Build a Social Democracy	17
2 Chilean Tax Policy Tested by New Political and Economic Conditions: 1996–2001	55
3 Argentine Tax Policy under Menem I (1989–1994): The "Tax Revolution"	89
4 Argentine Tax Policy under Menem II and De La Rua (1995–2001): Politicization, Firefighting, and Decay	127
5 Institutional Correlates of Tax Reform Consolidation: Success in Chile and Failure in Argentina	163
6 Conclusion	191
Appendix: Elite Interviews	207
Notes	209
Bibliography	217
Index	241

Acknowledgments

This book constitutes a modified version of my PhD dissertation at St Antony's College at the University of Oxford. It would not have seen the light of day without the important role of a number of special individuals.

I would like to thank two professors who had a marked influence on me as a graduate student at the Edmund Walsh School of Foreign Service at Georgetown University. Renowned Latinamericanists Arturo Valenzuela and Eusebio Mujal instilled in me a passion for comparative and Latin American politics that shall never fade. In particular, Eusebio showed me, via his impassioned teaching, the relevance and beauty of political science as a field of study. Unbeknown to him, he is probably the main reason I became a scholar and political scientist. I have always admired his encyclopedic knowledge, his contagious passion for teaching, his unassuming nature, and the lengths to which he goes to tend to his students. I am honored to count him as a friend today.

I owe a debt of immense gratitude to my two thesis supervisors at Oxford University: economic historian Rosemary Thorp and political scientist Laurence Whitehead. I feel privileged to have had the luxury of having learned from and been guided by two such world-renowned experts on Latin America. Laurence provided incisive insights and comments on my preliminary written work both while I was doing field work in South America and once I was back in Oxford to finish the final draft of the dissertation. Rosemary helped me navigate with aplomb the long years it takes to finalize a doctoral dissertation. She encouraged me to work through several drafts of every chapter, giving me copious written advice on how they could be enhanced. The final product is clearly improved because of it.

I am grateful to all of the forty Argentine and Chilean scholars, public officials, and policymakers who opened their doors to me and granted me lengthy interviews for this project. I especially want to thank former Chilean deputy finance minister Manuel Marfan for his generosity and time in granting me two long insightful interviews.

I want to make mention of a number of friends at St Antony's College from whom I learned a great deal about politics and economics and who made my stay at Oxford immensely enjoyable. They include Niaz Asadullah, Monica Pachon Buitrago, Reuben Wong, Alejandro Quiroz, Kunle Owolabi, Luciano Ciravegna, Francois Mann-Quirici, Patrick Iman, and Gregory Vincent. They are now successful academics, technocrats, and entrepreneurs. I feel lucky to count them as some of my best friends.

My childhood friends from Madrid (most from the school I attended as a child, *Colegio Guadalupe*) are exceptionally special to me, simply irreplaceable. Their lifelong friendship has always enriched my life in ways that cannot be described. They know who they are, so I will not list them by name.

Last and most importantly, I want to thank my family. My exceptional parents, Olga Sibony and Lorenzo Sanchez, have been a steady source of encouragement at every step of the way. This book could not have been written without their unrelenting support and unconditional love. To know that they are proud of me and my undertakings in life fills me with emotion and has always been very important to me. My mother has always encouraged me to dream and reach for goals that once seemed unattainable. And so has my father. As an economist and experienced European Union diplomat in two Latin America countries (Costa Rica and Guatemala), he helped to spark my intellectual interest in the region and taught me much about its political and economic dynamics. My sister, Olivia Sanchez, is a successful educator in her own right and now mother of two beautiful children. My brother, Oscar Sanchez, is a rising academic historian from whom I have learned and continue to learn a great deal. Four other special family members to whom this work is dedicated are my loving aunts Ilia Sibony and "Nany" Sanchez, my late grandmother Nelly Gallardo, and my 103-year-old grandmother Encarnacion Garcia, whose positive energy, agility of mind, and zest for life are an inspiration for all of us.

I would also like to thank the following individuals for their input: Michel Jorrat, director of research, Servicio de Impuestos Internos; Rosana Costa, economist, Instituto Libertad y Desarrollo; Ricardo Ffrench-Davis, economist, CEPAL; Ricardo Martner, director, Fiscal Affairs Division, CEPAL; Pablo Serra, professor of economics, Universidad de Chile; Jorge Trujillo, Direccion de Grandes

Contribuyentes, SII; Roberto Fantuzzi, president, ASEXMA; Andres Concha, general secretary of SOFOFA, Lunes; Franco Brzovic, tax lawyer, advisor to business associations; Felipe Larrain, economist, Universidad Catolica de Chile; Guillermo Larrain, Banco Central; Jose Yanez, professor of economics, Universidad de Chile; Oscar Cetrangolo, tax economist, CEPAL; Daniel Artana, senior economist, FIEL; Oscar Oszlak, professor and former DGI high-raking official; Jorge Macon, tax economist; Jose Maria Fanelli, senior macroeconomist, CEDES; Pablo Sanguinetti, economics professor, Universidad Di Tella; Jorge Sereno, AFIP, high-ranking official; Horacio Castagnola, current director, DGI; Ricardo Fenochietto, professor UBA, tax economist; Juan Carlos Torre, political sociologist, Universidad Di Tella; Jorge Schvarzer, economist, U. San Andres; Ricardo Cossio, former DGI director; Mario Teijeiro, fiscal economist; Ricardo Barris, AFIP, national director, Department of Fiscal Analysis; Carlos Acuna, political scientist, San Andres U.; Marcos Novaro, political scientist/sociologist, FLACSO; Marcelo Cavarozzi, political scientist, U. Nacional de San Martin; and Sergio Berenzenstein, political scientist, Universidad Di Tella.

Introduction

The Importance of Taxation in Latin America

The importance of taxation to the economic development of Latin America can hardly be exaggerated. Economist Albert Fishlow (1990, 62), one of the foremost experts on the economies of the subcontinent, does not go astray when he writes that "*the* principal economic problem confronted by the countries of the region [Latin America] has been a fiscal shortfall, not massive inefficiency problems resulting from misallocation of resources" (my emphasis). The low tax effort of most nations in the region has historically proven very damaging to their ability to successfully manage their economies. The inability of governments to rely on a solid and adequate source of domestic revenue has severely constrained policy choices, and often forced them to choose between the Charybdis of foreign debt and the Scylla of the inflation tax as sources of state finance. Fiscal inadequacy has made it more difficult for countries in the region to adjust effectively to changing external economic circumstances. No less importantly, it has constrained them from making the crucial public investments that are essential for economic development—from education to infrastructure.

Historically, it is the inability to generate sufficient public resources that ranks as the greatest malaise of tax systems in the subcontinent. Tax expert and adviser Nicholas Kaldor (1963, 7) eloquently explained in the 1960s the negative repercussions of low tax levels for development. His words resonate as forcefully today as they did five decades ago:

> The importance of public revenue from the point of view of accelerated economic development could hardly be exaggerated. Irrespective of the prevailing ideology or the political color of particular governments, the economic and cultural development of a country requires the efficient

and steadily expanding provision of a whole host of non-revenue yielding services—education, health, communications systems, and so on, commonly known as "infrastructure"—which require to be financed out of government revenue. Besides meeting these needs, taxes, or other compulsory levies provide the most appropriate instrument for increasing savings for capital formation out of domestic sources.

What are the most appropriate taxes that can be relied on for maximum revenue? The question does not admit of any general answer in the widely varying conditions of underdeveloped countries. The only feature that is common to them is that they all suffer from a shortage of revenue. This is partly because they have a low taxation potential—which may be defined as the maximum proportion of the national income that can be diverted for public purposes by means of taxation. But more important is the fact that the taxation potential in such countries is rarely fully exploited. (Ibid.)

The influence of the British economist's thinking remains very powerful indeed, and shall remain so for as long as Latin American nations continue to display low levels of tax effort.

Once the importance of taxation is established, the obvious questions are elicited: to use Kaldor's language, why do some countries "learn to tax" and others do not? Why do some countries exploit their taxation potential and others not? And, why does taxation reform consolidate in some countries and not in others? The importance of these queries cannot be exaggerated. Because taxation is at the heart of state-building (as well as economic development), understanding why some developing countries are able to permanently move toward a more solid fiscal foundation (higher-yielding and more efficient tax systems) while others are not is of great importance. This book compares and contrasts two countries at similar levels of economic development in order to shed light on this question. Social scientists have understandably been interested in explaining taxation levels (tax burden as a percentage of GDP) across countries. A host of factors have been identified. However, the standard explanations—political regime, level of economic development, economic structure, tax morale, and so on—are all too often found to be inadequate or incomplete to account for tax outcomes. Explaining successful fiscal state-building in the developing world deserves a closer examination from an institutional viewpoint. Until rather recently, scholars considered studying institutions in the developing world as irrelevant because these were discounted as weak and ineffectual, the empty superstructure of more powerful forces at work. Some still hold such views. They either dismiss the causal impact of institutions or assume uniformity in the level of institutional fortitude across developing countries, as well as across state institutions within each country. Au contraire, it is precisely because the nature and *strength* of national institutions differs quite widely across the developing world that institutions can and must be tapped more intensely for potential explanatory power.

Research Objectives

This book steps into that territory. It delves into the politico-institutional underpinnings of reform efforts to shed a different light on the taxation quandary. It tracks the evolution of tax policy in Chile and Argentina to understand why their efforts to build fiscal capacity in the 1990s succeeded or failed. Building fiscal capacity can be defined as consolidating a higher-yielding (in revenue terms) and reasonably stable tax system within the framework of an improved state-society fiscal pact. It follows a chronological and inductive approach to describing and analyzing tax policy, providing a unique window into the nature of the revenue policymaking process in two Latin American nations. In the process, broader insights can be gained into the larger question about why Chile has become the "tiger economy" of the region while Argentina has been such a persistent economic underachiever for so long.

In 2005, the Inter-American Development Bank dedicated its flagship publication, the *Annual Report on Economic and Social Progress in Latin America*, to the theme of political institutions and their influence on public policy outcomes. While the present book's underlying research predates the IADB Report (*The Politics of Policies*), it shares in its spirit and academic lens.

The Argument

This study seeks to expand analytically on standard institutionalist accounts of taxation by bringing into the explanatory framework the importance of institutional *strength* (not just design). Second, it seeks to also expand analytically on standard institutionalist studies by highlighting the importance of *informal* institutions (in addition to formal ones) for tax reform. Empirical evidence is presented to show that informal institutions have had important consequences for taxation outcomes in both countries.

This work posits that *the ability of a country's formal and informal institutions to aggregate and mediate conflicting societal interests crucially affects the probability of success and consolidation of state-building tax reform. What lies at the core of such ability is the level of institutional strength.*

Dissimilar institutional conditions in Argentina and Chile have decisively shaped the ability of each polity to devise and consolidate a reasonably coherent, reliable, and stable tax system. The institutional variables analyzed in this study include: state strength (degree of stateness), the level of institutionalization of the party system, civil society's interest aggregation structure, and institutions that foster macroeconomic and fiscal discipline. Informal institutions analyzed here include the presence of *politicas de estado*, the prevalence of patrimonial/clientelistic politics, and regularized patterns of decision-making (consensual versus unilateral). In Argentina, the confluence of these variables has led to hyperactivity and executive unilateralism in tax policy, while in Chile it has translated into relatively stable and predictable tax policymaking. The strength and nature of nation's institutional configuration decisively shape prospects for tax reform consolidation.

The Political Economy of Tax Reform

Few economic issues are as eminently political as tax reform. Fiscal systems constitute a basic pact between state and society. Major tax reforms are therefore important political watersheds. Nevertheless, despite taxation's centrality in political and economic development, there is a scarcity of studies on the politics of tax reform in Latin America. This paucity becomes particularly obvious when compared with the relatively abundant literature on the political economy of other structural economic reforms—including trade liberalization, privatization, and others. The general politics of first-generation economic reform have been analyzed in considerable depth (Nelson 1990; Bates and Krueger 1993; Haggard and Webb 1994; Dominguez 1997; Teichman 2001).

The bulk of the theory explaining tax reform has been based on case studies drawn from the developed world (Resse 1980; Peters 1991). However, the relatively scarce case study literature on developing countries has grown (albeit slowly) in recent years (Gillis 1989; Tanzi 1991; Bird 1992a; Carciofi, Barris, and Centragolo 1994; Perry, Whalley, and McMahon 2000; Brautigam, Fjeldstad, and Moore 2008). Other works have considered tax changes along with the broader package of neoliberal reforms (Williamson 1990; Perry and Herrera 1994). There are also a limited number of studies of tax reform in Latin America focusing on the role of political variables (Elizondo 1995; Berensztein 1998; Eaton 1998; Bergman 2003; Sanchez 2006, 2009a). Mahon (2004) assesses the political and economic determinants of tax reform in Latin America by way of a large-N study.

I now briefly review some of the main existing theoretical paradigms social scientists have used to explain taxation and state-building. These approaches are not necessarily exclusive of one another; indeed scholars often partake in a theoretically eclectic approach to explore taxation. The aim here is to situate this book's theoretical lens (institutionalism) within that literature.

Economists' Explanations of Tax Reform

Because economists have dominated the study of tax reform, the literature has traditionally ignored its political, historical, or institutional underpinnings. Some authors (Ascher 1989; Bates 1989 have usefully made explicit the deficiencies of such studies: these do not hold much explanatory power when accounting for the timing or the political fate of tax reforms. Economists have focused on normative issues of tax policy; that is, they have aimed at spelling out what constitutes "correct" or "first-best" tax policy given certain a priori objectives. Predictably enough, a serious limitation of the literature developed by economists rests on the assumption that economic and technical factors alone are responsible for inducing tax policy change. Burgess and Stern (1993) provide a typical economist's account of why tax reform occurs in the developing world. Their work posits that tax reform is the inevitable result of a number of pressures that build over time, including overreliance on particular tax sources (trade or natural resources), narrow bases such as income tax that create loopholes and evasion, weak administration, and others. These hypotheses, however, constitute no more than a description of typical shortcomings in developing country tax systems. It is all too often taken for granted that the economic pressures emanating from an inadequate tax system (insufficient revenue, economic inefficiency) will be enough to foster its reform. The political arena is sidestepped as inexistent. Traditionally, economists have portrayed politics as an obstacle to overcome, rather than an arena in which interests are articulated and the reformer may be able to enhance the long-term viability of the policy innovation through negotiation and the accommodation of various interests.

Moreover, the prescription for tax reform success offered by this literature is rather simplistic. In one typical recipe, the requirements are deemed to be: good planning and design; a resourceful team of experts; consistent macroeconomic policy; and reliable administrative structures (Gillis 1989). These factors may well be important in shaping economic success or failure but they do not tell us why some countries that fulfill these conditions have consistently failed to reform, or why reform does indeed take place when it does in a given country.

The body of literature developed by economists attributes a country's overall tax effort to structural economic factors. Economists have traditionally argued that a country's "taxation potential" varies according to factors such as per capita income, income inequality, and the sector composition of an economy (i.e., relative importance of agriculture, mining, foreign trade, and cash crops). Fiscal economists have found a general and robust association between tax levels and income per capita among a wide sample of countries. This is indeed a long-standing tenet in the field of public finance. What this line of analysis suggests is that the deeper, underlying causes of tax reform can be found in the long-standing inadequacy of the economic structure to provide sufficient revenues for the secular rise in public expenditure needs. While true, this borders on a tautology. To understand why and when reform takes place, we obviously need to probe deeper. Inadequate revenues to cover spending needs may be a necessary but hardly sufficient determinant of tax policy innovation.

Fiscal Contract Models (Rational Choice Theory)

Rational choice theorists have developed fiscal contract models that frame taxation as a collective action problem: governments wish to maximize revenues while taxpayers want to minimize payments (Levi 1988). The broadest political interpretation for explaining tax reform is centered upon the concept of the *fiscal contract* (also called fiscal pact or fiscal covenant), a "basic socio-political agreement that legitimizes the role of the State and establishes the areas and scope of government responsibility in the economic and social spheres" (ECLA 1998, 1). This contract involves the exchange of state-limiting and law-providing institutions for fiscal resources. Seen through such lens, the unending need to change tax codes reflects the structural fragility of the fiscal covenant in Latin America. This perpetual reform effort also points to the "poor quality of the political solutions arrived at through the renegotiation process" (89). In particular, there has been a permanent disagreement between the contracting parties (society and the state) about the horizontal and vertical incidence of taxes: the tax levied on similar economic activities has differed markedly, while some groups have shouldered an excessive share of the overall tax burden. Moreover, tax revenues have usually fallen well short of the level needed to fund public expenditures, rendering the system suboptimal. In the ever-lasting effort to prop up fiscal revenues and reduce chronic fiscal deficits via conventional means, states have continuously resorted to ad hoc statutory changes in the tax system—in the process leaving no societal group satisfied.

To understand why fiscal contracts are only rarely consummated, it must be understood that in Latin America few states have fulfilled their end of the bargain: few have developed bona fide institutions of fiscal accountability and the rule of law. Meanwhile, taxpayers at large have faced obstacles of collective action in demanding an effective, accountable state. As Mahon (2001, 3) points out,

> effective representation of taxpayers...has always been rare, for a variety of reasons: they might be numerous and geographically scattered; their collective identity and organization might be weak or absent; existing parties serve as vehicles for patronage; and a permeable executive, unable to resist the petitions of powerful resource providers, weakens the incentive for a fiscal contract that would serve the collective interests of all such providers.

Latin American states have been seriously constrained in their ability to demand more resources from society in no small measure because they have not accepted enough institutional self-constraints and effective representation to satisfy taxpayers. This includes guarantees of property rights and of institutionalized control over how public money is spent. Undoubtedly, that history of institutional failure has acted as a formidable impediment for undertaking revenue-enhancing tax reform.

Some rational choice theorists, prone to methodological individualism, posit that the political feasibility of tax reform hinges on individual rational benefit-cost calculations (or more accurately, subjective evaluations) of different tax policies. Because taxes remove revenue out of the private sector, tax reforms change the mix of private and public goods that people consume. Therefore, faced with tax policy innovations, individuals can be expected to compare the changes in public consumption with changes in private consumption. Following this logic, the study of tax reform cannot focus solely on taxes levied (the cost); it must also consider the services provided by those taxes (the benefits). This explains why new taxes are often earmarked to a particular government expenditure program, so that taxpayers can more readily gauge what they are paying for. It also explains why tax reforms are often packaged with other reforms, again reducing the ambiguity and uncertainties about the benefits associated with tax reform.

This simple picture, however, is complicated by the fact that taxation is a public good. Because public goods are nonrivalrous in consumption and nonexcludable in supply, individual actors have an incentive to free ride, enjoying the benefits of government expenditure but seeking to minimize their contribution (payments). Rational actors will seek to transfer the costs of public goods to others. As Bates (1989, 480) explains, this reality yields an important insight:

> Basic and elementary properties of public goods ensure that rational actors will, to put it bluntly, lie, cheat, and steal, and that governments that seek to allocate the costs of government will overtax some while under-taxing others, thereby fueling political discontent...this gives us insight into why tax reform is demanded...For each taxpayer possesses an incentive to claim that under the existing system they are overtaxed. And each possesses an incentive to seek reform, hoping thereby to shift the tax burden to others while consuming the benefits of public programs.

This does not imply that interest groups are constantly drawing up tax proposals and lobbying for their implementation. In practice, historical experience shows that interest groups seldom initiate tax reform proposals; they usually come at the initiative of governments. What Bates' comment does highlight is that once a tax proposal reaches the stage of democratic deliberation, the public good nature of taxation renders the bargaining process a highly political affair.

Societal Factors: Culture and Values

The cultural paradigm holds that a government's ability to collect taxes depends on people's willingness to pay them, which is mediated by their values, culture, and levels of interpersonal trust. There are two strands to the cultural paradigm. One emphasizes culture as exogenously determined, independent from the quality of state-society relations (Levi 1988; Putnam 1993). Religious traditions that inculcate a sense of moral obligation or a strong ideological belief about the merits of a large welfare state are variables that can affect a country's taxation potential. These are intrinsic societal traits. The other strand holds that public attitudes toward taxation are informed by society's interaction with the state. Perceptions of the fairness of the tax system (horizontal equality), the effective application of the tax law, overall government legitimacy, or the destiny of public expenditures financed with tax revenues are variables that taxpayers evaluate and that shape taxpayer behavior (Slemrod 1992; Andreoni, Erard, and Feinstein 1998). Governments thus have leeway to enhance tax morale by affecting such societal perceptions via concrete actions. Anchored in the cultural paradigm, Bergman (2009) has undertaken an important study focusing on the impact of deep-seated norms on tax behavior in the two countries studied here, Chile and Argentina.

The Institutionalist Lens

Because institutions comport the rules of the political game, they are necessarily important in the determination of public policy (Cox and McCubbins 2001; IADB 2005). The idea that a country's institutional configuration can bias public policy outcomes has a long pedigree in political science. E. E. Schattschneider (1960) suggested in his classic *The Semi-Sovereign People* that "organization [institutional configuration] is the mobilization of bias." Understanding a country's economic policy outputs requires understanding its policy-making process. The institutionalist paradigm holds that no country's reform performance and policy output can be understood without reference to the main features of its policymaking process, that is, its institutional configuration. Invariably, poor institutional environments with high political transaction costs translate into inefficient public policies (Dixit 1996). Not only do institutions stack the deck of cards in favor of some interests over others, they also provide the context in which groups and individuals interpret their self-interest and define their policy preferences. Institutions combine preferences and ultimately alter them.

Important features of public policy (such as stability, adaptability, or coherence) depend crucially on the ability of political actors to achieve cooperative outcomes, that is, their ability to strike and enforce intertemporal political agreements. Some institutional environments facilitate the striking of such political deals while others hinder them. In short, what determines whether a country's policymaking process aids or obstructs the achievement of stable and coherent policy reforms largely rests on the features of its underlying institutional infrastructure. What formal institutions affect public policy outcomes? Among the most important are those that dictate the division of constitutional power (presidentialism, federalism, bicameralism); the electoral system; the nature of the party system (degree of fragmentation); and the characteristics of the state bureaucracy, among others. In studying the connection of institutional variables to the workings of policymaking processes, Spiller, Stein, and Tommasi (2003) have advocated a systemic or general equilibrium approach, wherein the combination and interaction effects of the main institutional configurations are mapped out.

Sven Steinmo's *Taxation and Democracy* (1993) remains perhaps the leading scholarly work defending the idea that institutions crucially shape tax systems. The study shows that among established capitalist democracies tax systems differ significantly in objectives, structure, and effectiveness because of differences in the design of political institutions. Constitutional differences set the stage for dramatically different politics. He shows, for instance, how U.S. institutional arrangements provide many veto points as well as entry points into the political system, resulting in a tax system plagued with loopholes, subregimes, and exceptions that suit special interests. In conclusion, the design of institutions decisively shapes tax outcomes. Institutions matter in shaping taxation outcomes not least because they shape the type of relationship the state establishes with civil society. This includes two aspects: first, the initial degree of consensus that the reform commands among members of society; second, the degree to which the tax law is enforced in practice (Bird and Casanegra 1992). In order for civil society to make a positive contribution to the initiation of the reform, the state needs to allow for the incorporation of societal demands in the reform program (Sikkink 1991, 2).

Tax reforms have been posited to face different success ratios according to the particular objectives they pursue. "Potential simplification and greater horizontal equity are strong selling points in favor of a tax reform. Gains in economic efficiency and vertical equity, on the other hand, are much harder to sell…efficiency arguments are not well understood by the public and vertical equity is very much a matter of personal judgment," writes fiscal economist Wayne Thirsk (1997, 65). But such statements about the political feasibility of particular reforms are hardly set in stone or independent of context. Institutions mediate both "easy" and "difficult" reforms. Therefore, in some countries virtually any reforms may be difficult to enact and sustain, while in others even politically thorny reform initiatives see the light of day and achieve consolidation. The feasibility of a particular reform initiative cannot be studied in isolation from the institutional framework in which it is introduced.

The Importance of Institutional Strength
Perhaps the main deficiency of the institutionalist literature when applied to the developing world is that it assumes that institutions do not vary in terms of strength, and that therefore a given institutional arrangement will have the same or similar output effects anywhere in the world. A growing body of literature demonstrates that formal institutions produce different outcomes in different political settings. Students of developing country politics have only recently problematized the notion of institutional strength as a variable in its own right and one with crucial implications for public policy. Institutional strength can be disaggregated into two components: enforcement and stability (Levitsky and Murillo 2009). Enforcement is the degree to which formal or written rules are complied with in practice, while stability refers to the degree to which institutions survive not just the passage of time but also changes in underlying political conditions. Weakly enforced institutions may be created intentionally or unintentionally. In the former case, window-dressing institutions may be a response to international demands or expectations, or may be created in the pursuit of domestic legitimacy. In the latter case, creators of formal institutions may lack the power to make them binding. Low bureaucratic capacity limits the ability of state actors to monitor rule-infringing behavior (O'Donnell 1999; Soifer 2008). Weakly enforced institutions can also result from a disjuncture between those actors with the formal authority to make the rules and those that truly command power in a given polity. Another source of weak enforcement emanates from varying levels of societal compliance, which tends to be lower when rules are widely perceived as unjust.

It is difficult to overstate the consequences arising from institutional weakness. When institutions are not stable or enforced, actors cannot assume that others will play by the formal rules or that the current rules will endure in the foreseeable future. This shortens time horizons and enhances uncertainty, which, in turn, reduces cooperation and trust among actors. In such settings, players enjoy greater discretion than in settings where rules are stable and enforced: they choose both institutional and extrainstitutional options in rather unpredictable ways. Pervasive distrust and unpredictability inform the decisions of all players and collective action dilemmas are multiplied and magnified. The ability to sustain intertemporal agreements is consequently limited. The impact of such institutional environments on taxation and other public policy outcomes is enormous. Tax policymakers are inevitably hampered in their ability conduct revenue policy and to erect a robust, reliable tax system. Similarly, constant changes in the rules of the game as well as their intermittent enforcement seriously erode, over time, the solidity of the fiscal pact between state and society—fostering higher tax noncompliance.

Studying formal institutions without taking into account their *strength* can lead analysts astray. Simply put, similar institutional designs can lead to dramatically different outcomes depending on the level of enforcement and stability.

The Importance of Informal Institutions

Informal institutions can be defined as socially shared rules, usually unwritten, that are created, communicated, and enforced outside of officially sanctioned channels (Helmke and Levitsky 2004). Informal institutions must be distinguished from weak institutions. The mere fact that formal institutions are weak does not necessarily mean that informal institutions are present. In some cases no stable or binding rules exist, in which case noninstitutional behavior primes. Many regularized patterns of behavior cannot be classified as informal institutions. Only when such behavior is rooted in widely shared expectations among citizens and public officials, and there are costs for deviating from that conduct, can an informal institution be said to exist.

Studying informal institutions matters most in settings where formal institutions only structures some, but not most, political behavior. Consequently, acknowledging the role of informal institutions is of particular importance in the developing world. These institutions matter because in some settings the real incentives and constraints that underlie political behavior are not accounted for by formal institutions. Therefore, to understand why political actors act the way they do it is necessary to discover and account for rules that are transmitted outside of officially sanctioned channels, that is, outside of constitutions, laws, regulations, courts, legislature, or bureaucracies. In some settings, informal institutions can account for the bulk of political behavior—as in neopatrimonial regimes, for instance. In most settings, both formal and informal rules concurrently shape political outcomes (Taylor 1992). Thus, focusing only on formal rules and organization risks missing much of what motivates political actors to act in the way they do. Bringing informal institutions into the center-stage of political analysis matters for at least another powerful reason: they can modify the way formal institutions actually work, such that outcomes are quite different (or even opposite) from what the analyst could conclude from a strict interpretation of the system of incentives provided by those formal institutions. For example, a strict constitutional reading of the prerogatives and powers of Chilean presidents leads one to conclude that because Chile possesses one of the most powerful presidencies in the world, Chilean policymaking would be characterized by presidential dominance. Empirically, however, this is found not to be the case. The reason is that there is a set of informal institutions (as documented in this book) that limit presidential power and veers Chile toward multilateral, consensus-oriented policymaking. Some informal institutions are complementary, such that they effectively reinforce the work and incentives of formal institutions; other informal institutions are accommodating, in that they create incentives to behave in ways that alter the effects of formal rules, but without directly violating them; still others are competing, in that they are incompatible with the formal rules and effectively undermine them; and yet other informal institutions are substitutive, because they achieve what formal institutions were designed to do but fail because they are weak.

Book Outline

In what constitutes the bulk of the thesis, chapters one–four analyze the evolution of tax policy through time in Chile and Argentina, embedding the process in inherited and evolving political, economic, and institutional conditions. The country chapters proceed chronologically and cover the 1989–2001 period. In each country, the account begins with the antecedents of tax policy and administration needed to understand that country's starting points in regard to taxation and the strength of its state-society fiscal pact.

In the case of Chile, the tax reform process (as well as the overall economic reform effort) dates back to the mid-1970s, when the "Chicago boy" economists working for the Pinochet dictatorship overhauled the existing tax system and moved it in the general direction that later informed tax reform efforts in the rest of Latin America: a much more simplified system (reduction in the number of rates, brackets, and exceptions), and one based on indirect taxation (with the Value Added Tax as its center-pillar). The changes of the 1990s did not fundamentally alter the tax system inherited from the dictatorship. However, reform projects, which sought to increase the overall tax level in order to invest more resources on poverty-reducing social programs, ran counter to the minimalist-state ideology of the Chilean Right. Yet, a preoccupation with broader issues than tax pressure per se or the size of the state made agreements possible and reform consolidation a reality.

The Argentine tax "story" is qualitatively very different. Even a cursory study of Argentine economic history shows that the state has lacked autonomy, coherence, and efficiency. Long-standing political instability and a populist political environment have undermined economic rationality. Unlike their Chilean counterparts, Argentine generals did little to streamline or enhance the extractive capacity of the tax system during their rule (1976–1983). The new Argentine democracy inherited a dire fiscal panorama, which president Alfonsin's economists knew had to be addressed in order to attain a measure of economic governability. Yet, Alfonsin's own lackadaisical attitude toward economic issues, coupled with the majority status the opposition Peronist party enjoyed in Congress, doomed fiscal reform during the 1980s. Only a traumatic economic development such as hyperinflation (present during much of the 1989–1990 period) shuttled fiscal reform to the top of the presidential agenda. President Menem's exceptionally strong political position—given by his strong electoral mandate, the honeymoon provided by a crisis situation, and a Peronist majority status in Congress—allowed his third minister of economics, Domingo Cavallo, to inject the economy with strong policy medicine (indeed, shock therapy), as chapter three documents. Cavallo's currency board (*Plan de Convertibilidad*) provided a stable macroeconomic context in which economic authorities could begin to think about tax policy and tax administration reform. An economic boom lasting four years (1991–1994) enormously helped the tax effort, as well as the presidential scheme to combat evasion. On both fronts, high-profile initiatives were taken and implemented. As chapter four explains, both of these faltered and unraveled. The chapter elucidates the institutional, political and economic factors behind such a turn-around. The second half of the 1990s demonstrated in stark fashion that the previous tax policy and administration reform efforts were built on quicksand. Political considerations systematically trumped economic and tax policy rationality, as the political wing of the cabinet (and the president himself) increasingly encroached upon fiscal policy.

Chapter five aims to make analytical sense of the previous chronological chapters. What accounts for tax policy coherence and incoherence through time? Why have tax reforms been institutionalized in Chile and not in Argentina? A number of factors are adduced, relating to institutional strength and design. Because Chile enjoys an effective state and the prevalence of the rule of law, it can map policies onto outcomes rather easily. The convergence on economic policy among social and political actors in Chile helped in the development of informal institutions fostering stable and predictable fiscal policy. As regards formal institutions, Chile's structure of interest aggregation facilitates broad societal accords on taxation. This includes interest groups (labor unions, business associations) that are encompassing and can reach broad accords that incorporate much of society. This also includes a party system that is institutionalized, meaning that parties have deep roots in society, a stable pattern of interactions, are internally coherent, and showcase clear programmatic agendas. All of these characteristics are absent in Argentina, as the chapter explains, fostering policy unpredictability and economic irrationality, and rendering it difficult for tax policy reform to become consolidated.

The concluding chapter seeks to make the comparison between Chile and Argentina more explicit, by bringing together the theoretical discussion (chapter five) with the empirical content of the book. This final chapter also extracts some insights regarding Latin America's efforts at building tax states.

1

Post-Pinochet Chilean Tax Policy (1989–1995): Finding Resources to Build a Social Democracy

Introduction

Latin American tax systems throughout the post–World War II period proved dysfunctional for economic development. The Chilean pre-1973 tax system was no exception, displaying many of the deficiencies previously outlined: a bewildering number of taxes, special regimes, exemptions, and tax expenditures; a highly unstable system, with new taxes being created to cover particular revenue shortfalls; a system highly vulnerable to inflationary episodes; lack of horizontal equity or fairness; very inefficient in terms of resource allocation, and so on.

The Chilean military government bequeathed an essentially modern tax system to the civilian authorities, much in line with worldwide prevailing tenets in taxation. The transition to democracy raised worrisome questions concerning changes in policy thrust. However, the convergence in economic views between center-left and liberal economists presaged substantial continuity. The chapter outlines the ways in which the *Concertación* government sought to use fiscal policy to contribute to the irreversibility of democratic governance. This center-left coalition came to office with a broad conceptualization of democracy that included economic policy: "democratic" economic policies were those that served the interests of and incorporated the input from all social classes. Not only did the Aylwin government (1990–1993) seek to engage all relevant interest groups in decision-making but also to make the reigning neoliberal economic model serve the interests of all Chileans. It thus called its model one of "growth with equity."

The 1990 tax reform was at the heart of this endeavor, because it guaranteed the resources for financing an expansion of pro-poor and other social programs. By increasing the tax burden, the tax reform permitted the elevation of social spending for years to come. The second part of the chapter illustrates how, as the special circumstances of transition years receded into the past, economic conditions changed, and opponents of the revised tax structure gained political strength, the "growth with equity" model came to face increasingly formidable enemies and challenges.

Antecedents of Chilean Tax Policy

Chile has historically displayed a deficit-ridden public budget (Meller 1996). The inability or political unwillingness to rein in public spending throughout various administrations exerted constant pressure upon the tax system to yield ever-higher revenues to keep apace. Thus, the tax system came to be shaped through time almost exclusively on the basis of the revenue motif. New taxes were created or higher tax rates enacted simply to cover new, specific spending items. Rarely did governments resort to structural reductions in overall spending or to reallocation of expenditure among different items. As Ffrench-Davis (1973) has documented for the years 1952–1970, all governments throughout this period without exception introduced yearly modifications to the tax system in search of higher revenues that allowed economic authorities to attenuate the chronic fiscal deficits in public accounts. Public spending was already a relatively high proportion of GDP in 1952—about 18 percent—of which four-fifths were destined to current spending and the remaining 20 percent to direct and indirect spending (the latter including capital contributions to the *Corporacion de Fomento de la Produccion de Chile* (CORFO). In relation to other Latin American countries, Chile displayed a relatively developed tax system at the time. The income tax was the highest revenue yielding tax, accounting for a third of total revenues, then came the tax on imports (20 percent), and then the tax on production (18 percent). Copper's importance in the revenue picture becomes clear when it is noted that about 40 percent of all tax revenues were linked to copper exports—via taxes levied on the large mining sector and taxes on imports (ibid., 157). One of the main flaws of the Chilean tax system was that it did not incorporate any mechanism to deal with the inflationary phenomenon so as to palliate the revenue-reducing Olivera-Tanzi effect.

A number of misguided policies throughout the 1950s and 1960s worsened the extractive capacity, equity, and efficiency of the tax system. First, the government created a number of free ports exempted from taxes, beginning with Arica and a few northern provinces. Generous tax exemptions were also created for companies or sections of companies that were export-oriented, while tax privileges were also granted to the fishing sector and to imports of raw materials and capital goods. In the early 1960s, a number of tax exemptions were introduced with the purpose of fostering private investment, exemptions that in practice had a marked regressive effect with a dubious impact upon investment. This overall tax panorama prompted some years later the following remark from Pinochet's first finance minister Jorge Cauas (1974, 122): "we can say, without exaggeration, that general tax regimes constitute the exception, while regimes of exception constitute the general rule." There was no particular criterion to determine special tax treatment, with wide variations among regions and sectors. This intricate web of special tax treatments entailed a substantial loss of efficiency in the allocation of resources as well as large horizontal and vertical inequities. All of these tax privileges also provided a powerful stimulus for tax evasion—further undermining extractive capacity, efficiency, and equity. If the overall tax burden was maintained it was due to the creation of a myriad of new taxes and the increase in the rates of existing taxes. When a new spending program that required additional finance arose, a tax was usually levied on the consumption of a certain product. For many years, the objective of financing public expenditure was given primacy, so that a given tax was judged on its revenue potential alone, ignoring its effect on resource allocation. High-yielding taxes were often very distortive, dampening economic growth. Such an unwieldy fiscal picture was engendered by the *cortoplacismo* (short-termism) informing the elaboration of economic policy in general—including taxation and public budgets. Chile was slow to develop medium-term economic development plans and a forward-looking, dynamic approach to economic policymaking.[1]

To sum up, by 1970 Chile (not unlike other Latin American countries) displayed a bewildering number of taxes, deductions, exceptions, and so on that as a whole made for anything but a coherent system. In addition to inefficient resource allocation and substantial evasion, situations of double taxation were common, and tax collection was too inflexible, regressive, and vulnerable to inflation.

Tax Policy in the Context of the Neoliberal Transformation: 1973–1989

The Pinochet government inherited a precarious fiscal situation from the socialist Allende administration, which had drastically boosted public spending to implement its attempted economic and social revolution. The consolidated public deficit in 1973 was an extraordinary 11.5 percent of GDP, endangering economic stability (Ffrench-Davis 2002, 7). The immediate concern of the new economic authorities in the last trimester of 1973 was to stabilize an economy burdened by scandalous macroeconomic imbalances. The fiscal deficit's magnitude obliged the government to take measures to cut overall public expenditure as well as boost tax revenues. Because inflation had skyrocketed during 1973, it became imperative to adopt solutions to minimize its impact upon the tax system and upon tax administration.

After having somewhat rationalized the tax system (unifying a number of tax rates, eliminating discrimination between national and imported goods, etc.) the Pinochet regime was in a position to entertain a global reform of the tax structure. A comprehensive manuscript of liberal economic reforms known as *El Ladrillo* (the Brick) spelled out the fundamental objectives of tax policy espoused by Pinochet's economists:

> A. To obtain, in tandem with economic policy in general, the most efficient allocation of resources as possible from a social viewpoint.
> B. To provide the necessary resources to cover fiscal expenditure without generating a deficit—or a surplus that is not consciously sought in order to carry out anti-cyclical policy.
> C. To contribute to a better income distribution. Via taxation, particularly via progressive taxes on income, it is possible to partly correct existing inequalities. However, tax policy is not the only tool to achieve this; spending in education, health, etc. also contribute to a better income distribution. (CEP 1992, 103; my translation)

In practice, the third objective only proved a statement of good intentions and was discarded. The Chicago team was wedded to a trickle-down economics worldview, meaning that rapid economic growth would take care of poverty and inequality by itself. As *El Ladrillo* explained:

> The only real way to improve the income levels of the poor is by reaching a high and sustainable rate of economic development. A

real miracle can be had if, via rational economic policy, we can reach growth levels between 7 and 10% [of annual GDP growth], which is feasible for Chile...That is why it is indispensable to follow the economic measures we present in this study. These will make possible for Chile to reach the levels of growth other countries are displaying via a technical and non-political management of their economies. (144; my translation)

It is important to highlight this important aspect of the Chicago boys' economic thought, as it continues to inform the policy prescriptions of the greater part of the Chilean right today.

The main elements of the 1974 tax reform included the correction of inflationary effects, the creation of the value added tax, and the elimination of special tax regimes. To deal with inflation's effects on the tax system, a correction of the assets, liabilities, and income of companies was institutionalized, thereby reflecting real rather than nominal income; moreover, the brackets on personal income were indexed for inflation. More generally, all liabilities and credits that individuals and firms had vis-à-vis the national treasury came to be expressed in a new unit of constant purchasing power, the *Unidad Tributaria* (tax unit). Until 1975, the central pillar of indirect taxation was the so-called *impuesto a la compraventa*, a tax with a general 8 percent rate on the transference of goods and services applied to each stage of the productive process. The cumulative nature of this tax produced a "cascading" effect on the prices of products, so that those products that were the result of a greater number of intermediate transactions were levied with a greater tax burden. Predictably, the new economic authorities scrapped this tax and replaced it with the VAT, which was set at a rate of 20 percent and became the pillar of the new tax system. The VAT would be "the tool that leads to a coordination and harmonization of taxation with the other instruments of economic policy," according to the finance minister (Cauas 1974, 121–122).

It was predictable that the new authorities proceeded swiftly to eliminate many special tax regimes, exceptions, and assorted tax privileges to products, enterprises, sectors, and zones. Not only did this intricate tax code interfere in the optimal allocation of resources, it also curtailed public revenues substantially. Granting state privileges to certain economic agents or groups over others stood in stark contradiction of liberal economic tenets and, moreover, the government desperately needed to increase tax collection. This did not spell their complete elimination, but certainly their rationalization. "Unlike the anarchy which reigns in this field [of tax privileges], the new norms, being coherent and clear, will tend to have a significant impact on the pattern of growth," remarked Minister Cauas. A number of basic principles informed all so-called Development and Tax Exemptions Laws. No other measure contributed more to simplifying the Kafkaesque Chilean tax system than the elimination of the bulk of tax privileges. Overall, it is clear that the new tax system emerging for the decrees enacted in December 1974 was much more simple, efficient, and equitable.

In the obsessive pursuit of fiscal discipline, which had historically eluded Chile and had burdened it with much economic instability, the new economic authorities took advantage of the freedom of political maneuver the dictatorship granted them to decree a law (*Decreto Ley* 1263) that radically changed the financial institutional framework of the state (Arellano and Marfan 1987). The law defined precisely the responsibilities of the executive and legislative branch in the administration of the budget. In short, it essentially gave the executive (the Ministry of Finance and the Office of the Budget) the exclusive right to make expenditure proposals and to estimate public revenues, while the legislative branch was only allowed to either approve the budgeted overall expenditure or lower its level. In effect, this grants the executive the sole responsibility over the management of public finances. These changes were codified in the Constitution of 1980. The contribution of this new institutional architecture to fiscal discipline in subsequent decades cannot be overemphasized.

During the 1974–1983, period the regime enacted a number of tax changes much in line with the general goals informing the 1974 reform. Pinochet's economists, under the command of Sergio de Castro, sought a more neutral system so that economic agents' decisions would not be much affected by taxes. As concerns direct taxation, policymakers aimed at levying all income sources of a given taxpayer at the same rate, so as not to favor one factor of production or certain economic activities over others. In the same spirit, changes in indirect taxation were designed not to interfere with the relative prices of various goods as determined by the market (Cheyre 1986). These innovations, in line with strict textbook liberal economic philosophy—which postulates that taxes should be structured so as to interfere as minimally as possible with the market mechanism—coincided with the most orthodox period in economic policy observed during the seventeen years of authoritarian regime, namely from 1976 to 1982.

Despite all the worthy tax changes introduced, economic authorities had neglected the impact of the tax structure on savings and investment (one of many examples witnessed in this period illustrating the flaws of applying free market principles in strict, uncompromising fashion). It was the correction of this important omission that informed a new tax reform in January 1984, affecting personal income taxes (*Impuesto Único al Trabajo* and *Global Complementario*; Law N. 18.293). Tax code changes included the reduction of marginal income tax rates and a modification of the income tax base. For companies, a different tax treatment was given to income that was distributed and income that was reinvested. Furthermore, personal and company income taxes were integrated: taxes paid at the company level were now a tax credit against personal income taxes for those who received company dividends or profits. Effectively, the integration of income taxes acted to avoid double taxation, which was deemed to discourage savings and investment (Larrain and Vergara 2000). The 1984 tax reform was not intended to be revenue enhancing; it was simply aimed at improving efficiency by relying more heavily on indirect sources of revenue. In fact, throughout the 1980s, government revenues from taxation remained rather stable at around 20 percent of GDP even though the relative importance of different taxes changed considerably. The pursuit of a long-term secular increase in the amount of resources under the state's control was anathema to the Chicago worldview. For Pinochet's economists, keeping the size of the state small was an ideological end in itself (Delano and Traslavina 1989). The reform had an unambiguous effect on the importance of income taxation to government revenues, which decreased from 5.5 percent of GDP in the early 1980s to 2.9 percent in 1985 (Carciofi, Barris, and Centragolo 1994).

To summarize, the 1974 and 1984 reforms, taken together, decisively shaped the tax structure that exists in Chile today. It is quite an efficient tax system that puts the burden of taxation on consumption (in particular the VAT, about half of all revenues), has relatively few special regimes and tax privileges, and largely discards redistribution as a nominal objective. It is widely acknowledged that toward the end of the 1980s, Chile had an rather modern tax system.

The 1990 Tax Reform: Enhancing Extractive Capacity

Fiscal Antecedents

Accounting for the fiscal context of the latter years and months of Pinochet's regime is paramount in order to understand the nature of the first tax reform under the *Concertación* period. The period from 1985 to 1990 was one of fiscal austerity. This austerity was initially prompted by the need to deal with the 1982–1983 banking crisis, which brought high fiscal stress. The banking crisis, causing a staggering 12 percent drop in GDP in 1982 alone, prompted a modification of the regime's economic orientation. It moved from a strictly orthodox neoliberal textbook model to a more pragmatic neoliberalism, which allowed for greater government intervention in the economy and allowed for more input from society into economic policymaking. New economy minister Hernan Buichi, who was not a "Chicago boy," led this pragmatic orientation. The regime maintained remarkable fiscal austerity throughout the latter half of the 1980s in order to restore market credibility (Larrain and Vergara 2000). General government public spending declined from 32.7 percent of GDP in 1985 to 22.4 in 1990, contributing to transform a fiscal deficit of 3.7 percent of GDP in 1985 into a healthy surplus by 1987 (a state of affairs that lasted until the late 1990s).

In 1988, the Pinochet regime undertook expansionary monetary and fiscal policies, having in mind the crucial plebiscite to determine whether his rule was to be extended for another eight years or whether general elections would be summoned the following year, in accordance with the 1980 Constitution. The authoritarian regime sought to artificially boost the economy in order to gather support for the all-important plebiscite. The regime came to believe that its claim to power was based on "output legitimacy"—that is, on the prosperity brought about by its economic performance. It is noteworthy that the regime fielded its economy minister Hernan Buichi as its 1989 presidential candidate. Armed with this self-perception, the regime played the "economic card" to its very limit: it sought to generate (artificially) an economic mini-boom right before the plebiscite with the aim of influencing its outcome. Economic authorities provided a short-term supply-side economic stimulus by expanding the money supply, reducing the VAT from 20 to 16 percent, and lowering import taxes from 20 to 15 percent. It was to little avail. While the reduction in the overall taxation burden did not influence the outcome of the plebiscite, the tax cuts did come at a cost to the Chilean treasury of more than US $600 (Marcel 1995). The result of these expansionary measures was an overheated economy by early 1989.

Political Antecedents: The Campaign Platforms

Former Brazilian president Fernando H. Cardoso is fond of pointing out that the fundamental underlying issue surrounding economic progress is this: development for whom and for what purpose? It is in the fundamentally different answers to this question offered by the Pinochet regime and the democratic opposition that we can begin to understand the social and economic policy differences espoused by the Chilean center-left and the Chilean right. Finance minister Hernan Buchi represented the authoritarian regime, while the opposition—the *Concertación de Partidos por la Democracia*, an amalgam of parties of the center and the left united by their opposition to the military regime—was embodied by elder statesman Patricio Aylwin, a political heavyweight of impeccable democratic credentials. Their campaign platforms agreed on the substantive orientation of economic policy, reflecting a process of significant intellectual convergence during the 1980s between government and opposition economists in the realm of economic thinking (Puryear 1994). Both sectors made a similar diagnosis of the Chilean economy and proposed similar policy prescriptions. Neither of the two main contending electoral cartels offered to alter the outlines of the Chilean economic model. Both candidates proposed to maintain an open and internationally competitive economy, both advocated the use of market signals to guide economic decisions, both envisioned the private sector as the motor of growth, and both favored an overall framework that ensured macroeconomic stability and stimulated savings and investment (*Programa de la Concertación* 1989; Buchi 1993). The main differences rested in their approach to social and labor policy.

Although the liberal "Chicago model" of accumulation had been recognized by most relevant parties and sectors of Chilean society as very successful in generating overall economic growth, it did not come without costs (Ffrench-Davis 1991). The policies of the 1980s had as side effects a high rate of unemployment and depressed wages. Moreover, the lion's share of fiscal adjustments in this decade fell on the lower income groups. By 1987, poverty affected no less than 5 million Chileans, or about 40 percent of the population. With 72 percent of Chileans voting "no" in the 1988 plebiscite primarily for economic reasons and 38 percent choosing poverty as the reason for the need to change, economics was the key issue for the electorate (Drake and Jaksic 1991, 76). The implication of these poll numbers escaped no one. There were strong electoral incentives to embark on a campaign focusing upon the themes of redistribution and poverty alleviation. Indeed, both the right and the left reflected the electorate's concern with social justice in their respective campaign platforms. The official campaign proposals of both electoral cartels explicitly addressed ways to improve on the rampant inequality and increased poverty rates that had presided the Pinochet years—even if the stellar economic performance during the last four years of the regime (1985–1989) somewhat reversed the trend on poverty figures.

The *Concertación*'s overarching platform was one of national reconciliation for a country that had experienced at least two decades of deep and divisive political confrontation. Its objective was to give a voice to those social groups and social demands that had been ignored by the exclusionary policies of the military regime. This meant a decision-making process that sought to build consensus and political compromises among alternative, competing views. And this political philosophy extended to the economic realm as well. That is to say, it was not enough for all sectors of society to have a voice in the democratic political process: it was just as important that Chilean society as a whole share the material fruits of economic progress. The thinking went that only then would democracy grow strong roots in the soil of Chilean society.

The *Concertación*'s highest economic priorities, in the context of macroeconomic stability, were the reduction of absolute poverty and a more equitable distribution of income. After experiencing Latin America's worst one-year economic contraction in 1982 (a 12 percent decline in GDP), the dictatorship had recovered rapidly and was posting the highest growth rates in the region from the mid-1980s onward. Yet overall prosperity belied the reality of increasing income inequality. By 1990 no less than 44 percent of all Chileans lived under the official poverty threshold. Presidential candidate Patricio Aylwin campaigned on a "Growth with Equity" slogan. His coalition's message to the electorate was rather straightforward: it offered to maintain the pace of economic progress of the current regime while combining it with redistributive spending policies. This was a significant modification to the reigning neoliberal model in place, whose ideologues maintained that income redistribution would come from "trickle-down" economic growth. The *Concertación*'s emphasis on equity was not only grounded on a social-democratic ethical concern for social justice: it was also deemed a basic prerequisite for the consolidation of the new democracy. For Chilean Christian Democrats and Socialists alike, current and growing inequality levels imperiled the quality of democracy. It was imperative that all Chileans partake in the country's economic prosperity if liberal democracy was to flourish and build roots in society. This explains why the *Concertación*, true to its social-democratic credentials a la PSOE (Socialist party) in Spain, contemplated a boost in public funding for social programs in education, health, housing, and nutrition.

Public polls conducted in the late 1980s were unambiguous in showing a widely shared concern among Chileans about economic inequality and the precariousness of social conditions. The *Pinochetista* regime, all too cognizant of the electoral weight of such polls, could not fail to address them. This is how the Right's campaign platform read: "the modernization of our economic and social system is incomplete. It must be deepened in order to improve the living conditions of Chileans, along with a social policy that presents equal opportunities and eliminates the economic restrictions on those who are not reaping the benefits of progress." Yet, the actual policy proposals to address the "social debt" bequeathed by the Pinochet dictatorship were rather nebulous. The Buchi promise was the creation of one million jobs over the 1990–1994 period through growth of 5 percent a year, which would also purportedly generate fiscal resources to finance social programs aimed at alleviating extreme poverty. This was supply-side economics at its most rudimentary: it was held that tax cuts would augment the economy's growth rate, generating additional fiscal revenues over and above the shortfalls generated by the lower tax rates. As the right's rhetoric had it, tax policy was to play a role in enhancing social equity via its effects on growth. The policy prescription was a reduction (again) of the overall tax burden, in line with the thrust of taxation policy changes implemented throughout the latter half of the 1980s. Moreover, a new wave of privatization would provide additional fiscal resources. On labor matters, the Buchi candidacy did not advocate any change in legislation. It was argued that raising the minimum wage would raise labor costs above productivity, imperiling Chile's competitiveness. In sum, the right did pay lip service to the social debt problem, but its actual policy proposals sought to address this problem via indirect means. The clear and exclusive beneficiary of the Buchi program was the private sector. In more ways than the

Buchi team dared admit in public, the program represented straight continuity with the economic policy thrust followed since 1985.

Raison d'etre for the Tax Reform

Because the advent of democratic governance by definition changes the societal balance of power by giving political voice to previously voiceless social groups, regime transitions inexorably give rise to new demands on public resources. Because the Chilean transition to democracy (1988–1990) came later than most others in Latin American, the Chilean political class had the benefit of hindsight, the benefit of bearing witness to the politico-economic successes and pitfalls characterizing other regime transitions in the subcontinent. One of the stark lessons to come out of these experiences was that, in the absence of adequate public revenues,, Latin American governments often made recourse to economic populism to attend to popular demands. In country after country, authorities had succumbed to a populist cycle of unsustainable (debt-financed) public spending and rising fiscal deficits, with very negative economic consequences. Few had been able to successfully sort out the fiscal tension arising from the simultaneity of low tax levels and powerful spending pressures. The new Chilean government considered that failure to manage the fiscal conundrum successfully could well unravel the transition to democracy itself. As finance minister Alejandro Foxley (1990, 11) wrote before entering office, "in good measure, we will be successful or we [the *Concertación*] will fail depending on what happens during the first year. We have to avoid at all costs the traditional political economy cycle so common to Latin American countries, one that we have experienced [here in Chile] ourselves."

The fiscal challenge facing Chile was exacerbated by the serious budget constraints left over by the military: the steady lowering of tax rates and thus of fiscal revenues since 1984, the public debt contracted to rescue the financial system during the 1982–1983 banking crisis, and the virtual end of fiscal proceeds from the privatization of public enterprises, most of which had been sold off by 1989. The new authorities were walking a fiscal tightrope. If taxes were raised substantially to attend to social problems, the government risked alienating the business sector and the right, giving credence to the allegation made by the Pinochetista *Union Democrática Independiente* that the *Concertación* would act to undermine Chile's successful market economy—and thereby summoning the ghosts of the Allende period

(1970–1973). On the other hand, if the new government did not sufficiently increase social spending, democracy itself may well be put at risk, as the relegated sectors of society would be betrayed. This would be fertile soil for social conflagration. A third scenario, leaving taxes untouched and resorting to fiscal deficits to finance new government social programs, risked recreating the Latin American populist syndrome—as well as spoiling Chile's growing international reputation in solid macroeconomic management. The 1990 tax reform had as its overarching raison d'etre the financing of a social program that would allow the government to reconcile economic stability with social peace. It was an astute "middle way" that allowed authorities to steer a course different from any of the three aforementioned dilemmas. Tax reform was to "buy" social peace by financing a number of initiatives that constituted the backbone of the *Concertación*'s electoral offer to Chileans: to improve the operational capacity of public hospitals; to provide primary health services for free; to increase the food rations given to schoolchildren of low-income families; to restitute a 10.6 percent readjustment in pensions that had been suspended by the military government in 1985; to increase minimum pensions; to augment the low-income family subsidy; and a few others (*El Mercurio*, March 15, 1990). All of these measures were to come into operation as soon as the tax reform was approved. From a narrower technical viewpoint, the reform had three objectives: income redistribution, tax administration rationalization, and revenue enhancement.

Tax Reform Content

The government aimed to collect an additional $600 million or about 2 percent of GDP to finance its announced social programs. The bill sent to Congress increased the rates of the two highest-yielding taxes in Chile: the VAT from 16 to 18 percent and the corporate income tax from 10 to 15 percent. The personal income tax bracket structure was also changed, keeping the minimum exempt level intact as well as the marginal rates, but in effect increasing the burden on the higher income earners. Moreover, important modifications were effected in the income tax system that applied to the agriculture, mining, and transportation sectors, by changing the tax base from *renta presunta* (presumed income) to *renta efectiva* (actual income). There was also an amalgam of tax code changes that made tax avoidance via the creation of new companies impossible. Finally, a special tax credit was created for companies' productive investments.

After the *Concertación* published its government program, a tax reform committee was established in mid-1989. The work for the elaboration of a coherent design fell mainly on Manuel Marfan and a team of fellow highly trained economists at the renowned *Corporación de Investigaciones Económicas para America Latina* (CIEPLAN). The committee reported to a team of *Concertación* senior politicians, headed by Alejandro Foxley and Carlos Ominani, who were shadow ministers of finance and economy, respectively. Patricio Aylwin brought an impressive group of economists to his team. The most important figures came from the CIEPLAN. Patricio Silva (1996) has argued that the "CIEPLAN monks" represented straight continuity with the Chicago boys of the military regime. This has to be qualified. While both groups shared a technocratic discourse and graduate training experiences in the United States and Europe, there were important political and ideological differences. While CIEPLAN economists valued democracy as a vital, indispensable priority, many Chicago boys saw economic development as a more important goal whenever these two clashed. As concerns economic thinking, many Chicago-trained economists espouse an orthodox monetarism, while many CIEPLAN monks have a structuralist viewpoint linked to the CEPAL tradition. CIEPLAN economists are generally not adherents of crude versions of "trickle-down" economics, and believe that equality needs to be pursued with proactive economic policies, while right-wing liberal economists are simply not concerned with the goal of equality as an outcome of policy.[2] These differences, however, may be less important than the overarching coincidences: the role of the market as the preferred mechanism to allocate resources and an open economy to spur productivity and growth.

Political Negotiations between the Concertación and the Right

The tax reform bill, introduced to Congress in March 1990, represented the first litmus test of the "politics of consensus" approach. The *Concertación* had the political backing necessary to approve the tax bill with a simple majority, but this was deemed insufficient. A much broader political accord was explicitly sought with the purpose of endowing the new tax structure with stability and credibility. Moreover, because this was the first major piece of legislation introduced by the new government, it inexorably set a political precedent that shaped the political climate for the future.

Because of the distribution of political power (biased in favor of the right) at the time of transition and the restrictions of the 1980 Constitution (Siavelis 2000), the new government was all too aware that a maximalist posture regarding political or economic reforms threatened to unravel the transition to democracy. From the outset, Aylwin and his cabinet chose to pursue a *política de acuerdos* ("politics of agreements"), ensuring that every important piece of legislation was broadly discussed with the opposition and with the relevant interest groups. There was, in short, a conscious and calculated decision to leave behind the absolutist, winner-takes-all conception of politics that had characterized Chilean political history (Loveman 2001; Collier and Sater 2003). Tax reform would be no exception. The main tax reform negotiator for the government, economist Manuel Marfan (PS), saw the reform as a long-term measure to be erected upon three pillars: first, macroeconomic equilibrium, duly recognizing the fiscal needs that accompany a transition to democracy; second, a structural commitment to an open economy, as commercial and financial exchanges were seen as opportunities; and finally, an active role for the state, with a duty to address social deficits (Marfan, interview).

It must be noted that the *política de acuerdos* approach was also followed within the seventeen-party ruling alliance itself. Predictably, there was no consensus within the broad coalition about proposed tax changes. In particular, the Socialist party and sectors of the leftist *Partido por la Democracia* (PPD) opposed the increase in the VAT on grounds that it was a regressive reform insofar as it diminished the purchasing power of the poor and the middle class. To understand why policy differences within the coalition did not escalate, two factors must be borne in mind. First, a strict hierarchy of decision-making was established, in which the president and the ministers would make decisions largely in isolation from political pressures. In all policies significantly impinging upon the economic realm, minister Foxley was given strong authority over all other ministers in the conviction that the macroeconomic coherence of the government's project was paramount for the transition to be successful (Landerretche, interview). Foxley made sure that institutional arrangements reinforced his control over government spending by heading both the Committee of Economic Ministries and the Committee of Social-Sector Ministries (Giraldo 1997). Moreover, not only did he enjoy firm presidential support, he also had a coherent economic team—made up of economist colleagues he had brought on board from the ranks of CIEPLAN. Second, all members of the left-wing coalition willingly delegated decision-making to President Aylwin, with the understanding that the government needed to project unity in purpose in order to be effective. In short, the coalition consciously acted as a unified political party.[3]

The hard-line right-wing *Union Democrática Independiente* (UDI) chose to marginalize itself from the process of tax reform negotiations. The UDI's approach remained much more aligned to old-style Chilean politics: uncompromising in its principles and its global project and an absolutist, win-lose conception of politics. Its leadership argued that the tax project proposed would inexorably lower investment and growth. This was also the view of the business class, many within *Renovación Nacional* (RN), and even some sectors of the *Concertación*. As minister Foxley (1995, 90) reminisced years later: "when we came to power the 'conventional wisdom' amid the Chilean political class and the international community was very influenced by Reaganism, the basic notion that a rise in taxes inevitably meant a reduction in investment, a retraction of the private sector in the process of capital formation, and thus a self-defeating policy."

The RN, on the other hand, took the political lessons stemming from its electoral defeat seriously: it recognized that the center-left platform had been widely endorsed and legitimated by the Chilean electorate. Such popular endorsement included tax reform to finance social programs, as this proposal had been made explicit and had figured prominently in the campaign. This placed limits on the extent to which the right was able to oppose new taxation legislation, lest its self-styled future development as a mass-based party be compromised. RN president Andres Allamand (1999, 245) years later described (in his memoirs) the political calculation made by his political formation:

> To challenge the new government [on tax reform] did not come for free. If we confronted them we would be unable to negotiate the terms of the reform, and therefore, the most probable scenario would be that the *Concertación* would impose a reform at odds with the prevailing economic model. Politically, taking this avenue [of confrontation] we would be granting the government an excuse to justify any deficiencies of its administration. We could almost hear what they would say: "those responsible for not having solved the problems of the poorest, which have been dragging for 17 years, are the Right and the Senate. Therein lay the villains!"

Indeed, the more moderate of Chile's two main parties of the right would have to pay a political cost in supporting a rise in taxes, and it would have to assume that cost in political isolation (given the UDI's self-marginalization). However, noncollaboration potentially carried an infinitely higher political price tag. What was at stake in Chile with this tax reform transcended the interests of the government, as the political developments of the first months and years of the new democracy would affect Chile's economic and political development for years to come. This reality escaped no one within RN.

But the moderate opposition's willingness to negotiate the reform was not simply based on a cold electoral calculation. Many of the party's leading figures were convinced that the Chicago boy economic model's greatest deficiency, and potentially the source of its undoing, was its lack of democratic credentials. Sebastian Pinera, the main tax negotiator for RN explains:

> Our thesis, within *Renovación Nacional* (and one that we defended in difficult conversations with the UDI) was that in order to fully consolidate and legitimize the model of economic development based on a social market economy two things were required. First, to demonstrate that this model could serve all Chileans, given that it was perceived as efficient but unjust; that is to say, it needed higher levels of solidarity in order to be legitimized. Moreover, the model presented one other weakness, which was that the great majority of people perceived that labor legislation had been imposed from above and did not have democratic legitimacy. These were the two flaws of the [economic] system. It was because of the above that, from the outset, we sought accords in the labor and tax realms. (Quoted in Marcel 1997, 61)

In short, the country's main political formations had a common interest in reaching accords on socioeconomic issues of major importance so as to consolidate both democratic governance and the existing free market open-economy model of development.

Engaging the Business Community

Chile has a tradition of "social corporatism" in which entrepreneurial organizations have had an important voice in the formulation of public policy, dating at least from 1933 (Rehren 1995). Indeed, business associations have been said to historically constitute a "political sub-system." During the authoritarian interlude (1973–1989), entrepreneurs had enjoyed a privileged business environment and many prominent businessmen came to hold important political posts, alternating between public and private duties. Their input in public policy was somewhat restricted by the highly technocratic nature of the regime and the ideological worldview informing policymaking. However, since Buchi's appointment as finance minister in 1985, their access to the executive was broadened (Drake and Jaksik 1991).

The transition to democracy was marked by mutual mistrust between business and the center-left alliance. This development was to be expected after seventeen years of authoritarianism during which big business had closely identified with the military government and was perceived by soon-to-be *concertacionistas* as an enemy of democratic governance. Both had legitimate reasons to be suspicious of one another. Business fear of democracy, and in particular of center or leftist governments, was rooted in the turbulent 1960s and 1970s. Nevertheless, finance minister Alejandro Foxley and his circle were all too aware that forging a good relationship between government and the entrepreneurial class was paramount. They understood all too well that even well-conceived policies could be rendered ineffective in the context of deficient state-society relationships. Chile's history showed in stark terms that the behavior of economic agents depends not only on actual public policies but also on their perceptions of, and their degree of trust in, government, as well as their expectations about the thrust of future economic policy. Ministers Foxley (1993), Ominami (1991), and Boeninger (1997) have given ample testimony of the *Concertación*'s overarching preoccupation with securing broad policy accords among the main social actors in order to foster trust, bury the ghosts of the past, and endow economic reforms with stability. In that vein, the new government set out to engage in direct negotiations with the country's largest peak business association, the *Confederación de Producción y Comercio* (CPC).[4]

On their part, entrepreneurs entered the transition to democracy in a position of greater strength than right-wing political parties who had closely identified with the (electorally) defeated military regime. In spite of the very public efforts of many *Concertación* leaders to signal that they would pursue responsible and orthodox economic policies, many businessmen remained skeptical. Democratization represented a danger for the business community: it feared not just social destabilization as a result of excessive politicization but also the advent of populist economic measures—such as fiscal imbalance as a result of an explosion of spending demands, the reversal of privatizations, or the comeback of the "entrepreneurial state." Although Chilean business had backed the candidacy of Hernan Buchi, all relevant business associations publicly recognized the legitimacy of the opposition's victory, and steadily distanced themselves politically from the military regime. To be sure, business acquiescence to the new political reality was not based on a sudden conversion to democratic values. It was the institutional setting provided by the 1980 Constitution (authoritarian enclaves), and the political equilibrium between the right and the center-left in the senate (meaning that reforms had to be negotiated with the RN), which secured business' acquiescence to democratic governance. In short, Chilean entrepreneurs were ready to acquiesce to the "democratization of economic policy," in exchange for the maintenance of the rules of the economic game. As three prominent entrepreneurs and members of the new parliament put it, business' most important objective was to "defend a model in which the private sector has had a fundamental role" (Rehren 1995, 58). Their objectives coincided with those of the new center-left government, which in order to be successful (and fulfill campaign promises) needed to maintain the rate of economic growth experienced in the second half of the 1980s, augment the rate of private investment, and not least, endow their economic policy with social and political legitimacy. It escaped no one within the ruling coalition that business played a strategic role in the transition to democracy and that establishing a cooperative relationship with the sector was nothing short of essential.

The government took the CPC to be the interlocutor for the business community as a whole. Yet, it only approached the peak organization once negotiations with RN were successfully completed and passage of the reform was virtually a fait accompli. Given this political scenario, the CPC faced the option of exercising its veto power or accepting that this exceptional political juncture of transition to democracy required exceptional measures. It is not surprising that it chose the latter: the success or failure of the transition (which largely hinged on meeting social demands and concurrently maintaining macroeconomic equilibrium) would decisively affect the business environment. Political stability had also become an absolute priority for the entrepreneurial class. Vetoing a tax reform endorsed by a majority of Chileans at the voting booth risked threatening that stability.

The stipulated raise in the tax on corporations from 10 to 15 percent represented a sizable 50 percent increase, while the corporate tax base would also be augmented—from distributed earnings to total earnings. However, most analysts of Chilean economic policy are agreed that the tax increase postulated by the new government did not represent an intolerable burden on the private sector. In fact, it can be argued that the proposed reform simply reversed the tax reductions enacted by the military during the 1980s, in effect signifying a return to the tax scene of the early 1980s. Yet, this observation overlooks the historical and political significance of the 1989 tax proposal. Its importance rests on the fact that it represented a progressive economic reform (i.e., taxing the wealthy to benefit the poor) and was in that sense a sharp break with the revenue-reducing and regressive tax changes pursued during the Buchi period.

In order to win business acquiescence, the new government had to dismantle two sources of entrepreneurial concern: ideological and practical. Concerning the first, the business community (in alliance with the UDI) aired its deep reservations about a reform that it viewed as a signal of a return to economic statism. Some business quarters, with an eye on the Allende period, feared the reform could be the beginning of a number of measures that would increase the size of the state and reduce the scope of the market, in an effort to return to the old days of state-centered economic development. The practical objection was based on the argument that increased taxes on the private sector would hinder private investment and thus overall economic growth. As an alternative to finding increased finance for social spending, both business and the opposition proposed an increase in the VAT and the use of resources from the Copper Stabilization Fund).

In large part, entrepreneurs acquiesced to pay more taxes because the new government went to great lengths (in rhetoric and actions) to reassure them that it would maintain a vocation for free markets and an open economy. All in all, the entrepreneurial class understood that the economic legacy of the Pinochet years was being largely kept untouched and that the proposal of a higher tax burden had been legitimated by the December 1989 electoral results.

The 1991 Tax Reform: Sustaining an Open Economy

The economic adjustment measures taken to cool an overheated economy meant that economic growth for 1990 had been barely 2 percent of GDP, much below the potential growth rate of the Chilean economy. Yet, the alternative was "artificial, inflationary growth," as Minister Foxley had put it. The *Concertación*'s responsible management of the economy had contributed to a number of positive accomplishments during that perilous transition year, not least of which were the containing of inflation, the avoidance of a fiscal deficit, and the maintenance of high investment rates. But most importantly, the new government had set in place credibility and trust in its macroeconomic management. Given the historically rooted apprehension of the business sector toward the center-left, this was no small achievement.

After the foreign capital drought of the 1980s, the year 1990 saw a massive return of capital flows into the Chilean economy—mainly due to supply factors but also due to the new appeal and magnetism of so-called emerging markets (Ffrench-Davis and Grifith-Jones 1995). This caused a substantial appreciation of the peso and a deficit in the current account (trade balance) of the balance of payments. (The balance of payments reflected a surplus of 10 percent of GDP in the capital account and 2 percent deficit in the trade balance.) The inevitable consequence was a loss of degrees of freedom in monetary policy (Marfan 1998). A second problem was posed by the unrestrained growth in global (public plus private) expenditure—it had grown by 12.8 percent in 1989 alone—which was fueling inflation (21.4 percent in 1989 and 27.3 percent in 1990) and threatened to get out of control. Economic authorities needed to restrain global spending and cool down the economy, but there were no obvious ways to do it: fiscal austerity was deemed insufficient for the task (as much of the bulk of "excess spending" was private) and making an economic adjustment via increasing interest rates threatened to further attract foreign capital and thus foster the appreciation of the domestic currency. In short, it was the coincidental configuration of particular external and domestic economic conditions at the time that posed this policy conundrum. Policymakers sought to recuperate monetary autonomy, stem the appreciation of the peso, which was hurting exporters, and put a lid on the burgeoning trade imbalance. To these ends, short-term capital inflows were taxed and a four percentage point unilateral lowering of export tariffs was effected (from 15 to 11 percent). The four-point reduction in tariffs obviously carried a fiscal cost. Given the *Concertación*'s political commitment to enhance the extractive fiscal capacity of the state and satisfy unmet social needs, it was a foregone conclusion that such a fiscal sacrifice would be compensated with other tax measures. In that spirit, the base of the stamp tax was expanded, while a tax levying capital inflows was introduced. Together they compensated for two of the four-point reduction in tariffs. The remaining fiscal shortfall was filled via an increase in the gasoline tax.

Economic authorities, from the minister of economy down, pledged in repeated public statements that the government would not push a new tax reform during the remaining period of the Aylwin administration. Finance Undersecretary Pablo Pinera clearly laid out the rationale: "to maintain the rules of the game in governmental economic policy means that there will not be new tax reforms during this administration" (*El Mercurio*, September 27, 1991). Such rhetoric sought to allay business fears about purported new revenue-enhancing tax innovations. Aside from building trust vis-à-vis the business community, the government had to face down an active and aggressive political opposition. The RN and UDI unleashed a barrage of criticisms directed at the new government for its alleged inaction on acute social problems afflicting the country. The official response was firm, as exemplified by socialist deputy and member of the *Comisión de Hacienda* Armando Arancibia:

> sections of the opposition are beginning to engage in demagoguery with respect to social demands. We ask them that they approve the corresponding tax measures that will finance the resolution of those social problems... We stand ready to approve that expenditure as long as they grant us the sources of additional income for the task. (*El Mercurio*, September 19, 1991)

In short, the *Concertación* was making crystal clear its commitment to fiscal responsibility and the accompanying tax-and-spend model, and proved impervious to political pressure to modify that model in any way. This commitment extended to corporatist actors, including such unsuspecting defenders of fiscal rectitude as the country's largest labor union, the *Central Unitaria de Trabajadores*. Its president Manuel Bustos stated his organization's position thus: "I am not sure that right now the appropriate [political] conditions to propose a new tax reform exist in order to solve the problem of teachers and others... but what is certain is that the resources for it need to be searched for and I have the impression that the answer is via taxes" (*El Mercurio*, September 19, 1991).

Suggestions that the tax-and-spend model be discarded were met with an invariable response from government: Chile's socioeconomic ills needed urgent attention. It is in that spirit that Finance Minister Foxley provocatively announced with fanfare: "one in three Chileans lives in poverty." The statement, startling to many unfamiliar with the numbers, had the intended effect of raising consciousness among the populace, putting pressure upon the political class, and focusing the political debate upon the economic and social conditions of the lower strata of Chilean society. The minister was effectively paving the political grounds for further revenue-enhancing tax reforms in the near future.

The Tax Policy Debate Heats Up: Proposals and Reactions

In March 1992, Alejandro Foxley announced that the 1990 tax accord needed to be renegotiated in Congress the following year. "We still believe that social progress does not come for free, that it is not easy and that all need to contribute to solving the problem of poverty" (*El Mercurio*, March 24, 1992). With this declaration of intentions the government was making clear its commitment to deepen the social democracy model it defended in the presidential campaign and to take whatever tax measures were needed to finance it. It also signified a retreat from President Aylwin's explicit disavowal of new parliamentary negotiations aimed at making permanent tax changes that had been made temporary in the 1990 agreement. It had become increasingly obvious to Foxley's economic team that future social spending commitments would require a higher permanent tax burden.

The political right's answer to such intentions was rooted in its ideological position in favor of a small state (defined both in terms of degree of interference in the economy and fiscal weight), but arguments were couched in more sophisticated terms. The editorial comments of the conservative daily *El Mercurio* (April 7, 1992) exemplify well the right's recurrent panoply of contentions used to oppose an increase in taxation:

> A substantive element in civilized political interchange is to respect and make good on one's word. It damages the credibility of government to alter the terms of [the 1990 agreement]. The change in the rules of the game, and more than that, the insinuation that the government does not respect its formal and public compromises on issues as important as basic economic definitions, introduces elements of uncertainty that are very undesirable for the country's development. There exists a generalized agreement on the priority to be accorded to the fight against poverty and the alleviation of urgent social problems. However, it is not clear that the optimal solutions involve an increase in the tax burden

and state bureaucracy. Social programs need substantial resources in order to be effective, but there remains much to be done in augmenting their efficacy and improving the targeting of social public spending so that it effectively reaches those who most need it.

Finally, to round up the multifaceted argumentation, the editorial did not exclude the populist supply-side mantra by which lower nominal tax rates would be revenue-enhancing. Extra economic growth resulting from the tax cuts, the argument went, would bring added resources to the national treasury, which would cover social expenditure needs. That each additional percentage point in GDP growth brings much more revenue than virtually any single tax reform is strictly true. Yet this argument is intellectually flawed on at least two counts: first, there is little international evidence for the claim that lower tax levels foster higher long-term rates of growth (of course, they can be used as short-term reactivating measures); second, economic growth itself has a multiplier effect on expenditure needs through time. The right's position unrealistically took it for granted that spending needs are stable.[5]

In response, the government's leading economists left in the air an important and disquieting query for the business community and the right to answer: if the 1990 agreement to lower certain taxes to the status quo ante was kept, how would the ensuing $800 million financial hole be covered? In other words, which social programs would be cut? Indeed, under a framework of fiscal discipline, these queries were unavoidable and the answers far from obvious.

Moreover, the right's crude version of trickle-down economics found little empirical support in Chile's recent economic history. In fact, there was no better example than the Pinochet (1973–1989) period, which oversaw significant economic growth side by side with an increase in economic inequality (as measured by the Gini coefficient). On the face of it, recent Chilean economic history would presumably lend much intellectual credence to the economic philosophy of the center-left while it would work at cross-purposes for UDI/RN politicians and economists. However, the left and the right obviously gave very different *interpretations* to recent economic history—surely politically motivated accounts of the past (Landerretche, interview). However, Chilean economic developments since the 1990 tax reform clearly supported the government's point of view. The fact that private savings had doubled during 1992 and private investment had risen by about 30 percent, contradicting the dire predictions formulated by tax reform opponents, constituted powerful intellectual ammunition for the government. In fact, Aylwin's officials duly publicized and marketed these numbers in order to discredit the opposition's claims.

With regard to the VAT, the public concern was about the effect the high 18 percent rate could have on the purchasing power of the working classes, as well as its impact on inflation. Economic authorities considered that inflation was under control (it had come down from 30 percent in 1990 to 13 in 1992) and that the VAT was not having a discernible impact on the consumer price index (*La Tercera*, November 28, 1992). This reality, coupled with robust growth and attendant wage increases, more than compensated any effect of the increased VAT on purchasing power. In sum, the rosy macroeconomic picture gave the government the upper hand in the economic debate with the opposition.

What escaped no one within the Aylwin administration was that the later the new tax reform was negotiated (and the closer to the 1994 elections), the more it would become entangled in a political rather than a technical discussion, and it would be the legislature and the different presidential candidates that would be taking a position on the subject. The reform's politicization was surely not in the best interests of the Chilean economy. What *oficialismo*, the opposition, the trade unions, and the business associations all agreed upon was that there was nothing sacrosanct about the existing tax structure and that what was needed was to refashion it in a way that would serve a key objective: to augment public savings so that growth would be sustainable at the high rates of 1992, as well as to emphasize exports and employment in tax system design. This is another example of the degree to which political and social actors are forward-looking in Chile and their predisposition to agree to pacts whose benefits are reaped in the future and shared by all. Chile's strong institutional framework, facilitating intertemporal exchanges, can be credited for this. Jose Antonio Guzman, the president of the powerful business association *Confederación de la Producción y el Comercio*, echoed the sentiment of entrepreneurs when he declared that the CPC was prepared to negotiate tax changes on the basis that the state would contribute to finance more public spending via a more efficient administration of the public apparatus and the privatization of public enterprises (*La Época*, November 27, 1992).[6] It was the CPC's conviction that the public and private sectors should make a *shared* contribution of resources to finance indispensable expenditure. Clearly, the political soil was fertile for serious negotiations on consolidating the hitherto temporary tax structure.

The informal exchange of viewpoints between government authorities and the business sector made clear their respective starting positions. The Finance Ministry was open to the idea of reducing the income tax on individuals or *impuesto global complementario* (which Foxley admitted was "a bit too high" by international standards) from 50 to 40 percent or so, but it wanted to keep the rest of the tax rates intact. This would come at a cost of only $40 million. Entrepreneurs, on their part, advanced the concept of changing the base for companies' income tax (*Impuesto de primera categoría*) from total earnings to retained profits (*utilidades retiradas*)—effectively restricting the base—on the grounds that this would provide a stimulus to savings and investment, particularly for firms that were starting up or expanding activities and were characterized by high reinvestment rates. However, this change in the tax base came at a cost of around $500 million for state coffers, much more in fact than the $300 million entailed by the law's tax rate reduction from 15 to 10 percent. From the government's perspective this was a nonstarter. The CPC presented an interesting proposal: to allow companies that allocated resources to education to deduct income taxes. This would incite businesses to make a direct contribution to institutions or educational establishments involved in their issue-area or active in their geographic location and generally foster closer ties between education and business. Other issues informing the tax debate centered on how to refashion the tariff structure (export taxes) in ways to foster export competitiveness, as well as how to foster savings of individuals and families, which empirically contributed little to the country's aggregate savings effort. On this second point, the idea was to grant different tax treatments to families who saved and those who spent. Another issue permeating discussions was the item of double taxation of foreign investment. The taxes levied on international trade in services such as property rights on brands, patents for industrial activities and others ranked as one of the highest in the world. It was deemed that lowering them would stimulate investment in industries characterized by abundant know-how, and create positive externalities to foster a better insertion into the world economy. In sum, on a technical level, the Chicago-boy legacy of striving to create an efficient, investment-friendly tax system was very much alive—extending to all political actors.

Among political actors, the *pinochetista* party *Union Democrática Independiente*, continued to stand on the fringes of the tax discussion and kept an intransigent stance. Its discourse was profoundly ideological, as the claims made by prominent UDI economist Julio Dittborn attest: "the problem is that the *Concertación* government wants to augment the power of the state, and thus that of the political class that is in charge of it and controls society" (*La Época*, February 11, 1993). Political autism was not absent in the country with the most mature and responsible political class in Latin America. This political formation implausibly presented their low tax agenda as a pro-poor policy, and rhetorically posed as the champion of the poor. Notwithstanding political motivations, there was substance to Carlos Ominami's description of the UDI as an "irresponsible party that plays in the third division" (with the understanding that the *Concertación* played in the first league). The UDI seemed to tackle the relationship between taxation and secondary incomes in isolation, devoid of any reference to spending. Thus, it systematically criticized indirect taxation, for instance, as highly damaging for the poor without allusion to how those taxes were being put to use in social poverty alleviation programs. To be sure, secondary incomes are a function of both taxation and spending policies taken together. Only by considering both sides of the fiscal equation can state policies be judged as regressive or progressive in nature. For the UDI, taxes simply financed "a bureaucracy that paralyzes the individual creativity of Chileans" (ibid.). The *pinochetista* political formation displayed an unabashed, blind belief in the beneficial effects of an unfettered free-market economy. It was not infrequent for UDI legislators and economists to make a partial or outright spurious use of statistics to buttress their ideas.[7] While it was true that Chile collected in taxes a higher proportion of GDP than most other countries in Latin America, this was due to the comparatively lower levels of evasion. That is to say, the real tax burden was higher but the nominal tax burden was not high by Latin American standards. Moreover, Chile was already by the early 1990s one of the most developed countries in the region and therefore its spending needs were accordingly greater. The tax burden of 1991–1992 (19 percent of GDP) was not high, either by international or Chilean historical standards. In fact, it was in line with that of the years between 1980 and 1987, before the Pinochet government enacted a series of electorally motivated tax reductions.

Maintaining the 1990 Tax Reform in Place: The "Growth and Equity" Model under Threat (1993)

Back in 1990 the government contemplated tax reform as a permanent tool of governance, and it was only the lack of political support that obliged it to concede to the reform being temporary in order to secure parliamentary approval. It was foreordained that the *Concertación* would eventually press for the permanence of the new tax structure, not least because defending the new tax level was to defend the new "growth with equity" model the *Concertación* was politically and ideologically committed to. In 1993, the political stakes surrounding tax reform permanence were thus very high.

The government's leading economic policymakers, including Jose Pablo Arellano, Manuel Marfan, Carlos Ominami, and Foxley himself, raised the stakes of the taxation debate, when they presented the issue as one in which Chile's reputation in responsible macroeconomic management hung in the balance, not least vis-à-vis international investors and financial agencies. The issue at stake was to ensure the continuation of the macroeconomic equilibriums that had underpinned growth and price stability. Studies by the Ministry of Finance estimated that reducing the tax level to the 1989 status quo would generate a public deficit ranging between 1.4 and 2.1 percent of GDP in 1994, depending on different macroscenarios. Therefore, keeping the 1990 tax changes in place was a matter of national consequence, not to be toyed with by corporatist interests. Insofar as the dilemma was one of fiscal deficit versus fiscal equilibrium, there was much substance in the government's contention.

Moreover, the government construed a direct link between tax resources and social stability. It reasoned that hundreds of thousands of Chileans who were beginning to benefit from the 1990 tax changes would see their secondary incomes (i.e., incomes after tax and spending policy) fall, and the delicate state of Chilean hospitals and schools would remain unattended. The alleviation of Chile's "social debt" as well as the poverty and inequality inherited from the Pinochet regime required a sustained fiscal effort in time, certainly longer than four years, it was argued.

But Chile's political dynamics had changed inevitably since 1990. The political calculus that underpins transitions from authoritarian rule no longer applied in any strict sense. The RN was not easily be brought into the reform mould this time. Thus, the government turned to business first. The government's private dialogue with the most important business grouping (the CPC) had yielded important understandings on two fronts: that macroeconomic stability would be endangered by the tax reductions (improvements in tax administration and increases in public savings were deemed insufficient); and second, that reaching an accord to ensure tax policy stability for the medium term was to everyone's benefit. Such agreements were vitally important, indeed a sine qua non, in paving the way for a political negotiation with the leading party of the opposition, RN. While on principle business would always oppose a tax increase on their activities, its acquiescence to the 1990 reform revealed that its decision-making matrix was rather more complex than the Chilean right painted it. Indeed, economic and political stability ranked very high among business priorities. Moreover, there was little evidence that the 15 percent corporate tax rate was slowing down private sector activity. Minister Foxley revealed that "in private, informal conversations business sector leaders have confessed to me that the actual tax rates are reasonable, that they have already adapted to them and this has not impeded their companies' adequate functioning" (*El Mercurio*, November 25, 1992). Also noteworthy was the fact that 1993 was the first time in recent Chilean memory in which an electoral year (both general and parliamentary) had not had any discernible effect on basic macroeconomic variables, further validating the *Concertación*'s responsible management of the economy.

The continuing public disagreements about the appropriate tax level and structure for the country between the government on the one side, and the business associations and the opposition (UDI/RN) on the other was a sign that the consensus-seeking politics characterizing the transition was faltering. Minister Foxley spoke of the advent of the "grey color of democracy, that opaque color of everyday life that appears when the most urgent and painful problems seem to be resolved" (ibid). Indeed, sensing that the win-win political exchanges of the transition were in the past, "politics-as-usual" behavioral patterns seemed to be returning, whereby economic and political reforms were increasingly perceived in zero-sum terms. Yet the social challenges facing Chile remained enormous. To be sure, the background of the discrepancy reflected a long-standing Chilean public debate about the adequate size of the state.

It became increasingly clear that RN would not relinquish the transitory clause it had secured in negotiations three years earlier.[8] This prompted a radical change in governmental reform tactics:

Minister Foxley, in consultations with President Aylwin, announced a "national offensive" whereby the importance of keeping the tax reform in place were explained to the public at large—with Foxley undertaking a nationwide journey to personally act as educator on the matter. The *Concertación* government thereby sought to bring the political discussion to the level of the population at large, as it knew all too well that it enjoyed a continued overwhelming popular mandate to press on with yet more social spending. Polls showed that more than 60 percent of Chileans favored keeping existing tax rates on consumption and on companies (*El Mercurio*, April 23, 1993). As the finance minister put it:

> I need to present to Congress in September [of 1993] a Law of the Budget bill that is self-financing, and explain how I am going to balance the budget in the event [the opposition] cuts $800 million from tax resources, which will force cuts in expenditure. It is my responsibility as Finance Minister to tell ordinary Chileans why we are forced to cut spending in education, health, housing, roads, ports and airports... We are going to tell the truth and let people form their own opinion. I hope that this is not necessary. (Ibid.)

In a further sign of the political importance the *Concertación* attributed to the issue, President Aylwin also stepped into the fray: "we are ready to reach accords on taxation, but if these do not ensue within a framework by which the well-off sectors finance social policies, then it will be the people who decide. I will ask Chileans to take this into account when they cast their vote in December [of 1993]" (*La Nación*, April 25, 1993).

To be sure, the credible threat of throwing the tax issue into the terrain of public opinion put much pressure upon the opposition to reach an agreement before the electoral campaign was in full swing—unless it was willing to pay a large political and electoral price. Within a month, RN was engaged in negotiations with the government. The aim was not only to preserve fiscal balance, but also to beget a horizon of tax policy stability for the medium term that would reduce economic uncertainty and provide economic agents with a more propitious environment in which to save and invest. The specifics of the agreement reflected faithfully what had transpired in public discussion—namely, that the income tax on individuals was too high and that the income tax on businesses (15 percent) was still low by international standards and had not prevented sky-high investment rates.

Thus, the marginal tax rate on personal income was reduced from 50 to 45 percent over two years and the number of tax brackets increased (from six to eight) so as to enhance progressivity. It was estimated that this change would benefit around 130,000 middle-class taxpayers. The VAT was maintained at 18 percent for the first two years and lowered to 17 in the third, with the addendum that the president had the faculty to augment or reduce the rate by one percentage point depending on economic conditions (*La Nación*, April 27, 1993). The gradual nature of these changes was meant to avoid an abrupt change in tax collection from one year to the next.

While these constituted the core elements of the reform, a number of tax innovations were agreed to in order to fine-tune the tax system and adapt it to changing trends and needs. As concerns the financing of subsidized education, two modifications took place, the second of which granted tax benefits to companies that donated funds to educational establishments administered by municipalities and not-for-profit institutions. A second area concerned personal taxes. The concern that greater disposable income created by the reduction in marginal income tax rates would be consumed and would detract from savings provoked the introduction of a measure that made income saved on financial instruments tax-exempted. Finally, measures were taken to reduce international double taxation, thereby lowering an obstacle to greater foreign investment. Double taxation levied on Chilean firms with investments abroad was eliminated, which aimed at enhancing Chile's insertion into the international economy—particularly with neighboring Latin American nations.

The signatories to the accord agreed on a rapid treatment of the tax bill in the legislature so that the budget of 1994 could be discussed with the new tax structure already in place. The pledge was duly complied with, as Congress turned the tax initiative into law by September 1993. By adhering to this timetable, the government had made certain that the tax debate would not be excessively politicized, an objective that the business community also espoused wholeheartedly. Negotiations were informed by the overarching principle that taxes must remain predictable and stable in the medium term in order to facilitate growth. The reform set tax policy in stone for the next four years—that is, changes would be effective from January 1994 and be operative until the end of 1997.

In the end, both parties to the agreement made concessions and both attained some of their policy goals. RN senator Francisco Pratt echoed the sentiment of his political formation when stating that "this reform has advanced in the correct direction insofar as it is informed by the idea that economic growth is the best road to give the state more resources for social actions; that is what has been privileged" (*El Mercurio*, June 5, 1993). RN president Andres Allamand (1999, 246) later summed up his party's thoughts about the 1993 settlement thus: "the global result was valuable: another four years of tax stability. And the political signal was even more valuable: from now on, taxes would go down, not up." Trickle-down ideas had by no means been validated with this reform, but the goal of promoting savings and investments ranked high in its design. Likewise, the government could certainly contend that the reform reaffirmed the commitment to fiscal balance and that the "growth with equity" model underpinning their economic philosophy had been ratified. However, the government had ceded some ground: the reform implied a modest reduction in the country's tax level, from 19.1 percent of GDP in 1993 to 18.5 in 1996, which represented a restriction on public spending during the transition period and a lower rate of growth in tax collection beginning in 1996. It was clear that this lowering of the tax level would, insofar as fiscal equilibrium was kept, somewhat limit the growth of global public spending during the next few years. It would not, however, threaten any of the social programs on course.

But it was the RN that had traveled the greatest distance to meet the challenge of an accord. In fact, the starting position of the RN had not been different from that of UDI.

Official data undermined criticisms stemming from the 1990 tax reform's presumed consequences on economic indicators. The fact of the matter was that during the 1990–1993 period inflation, investment rates, national savings, employment growth, and productivity, all displayed improvements on a scale rarely seen over a four-year period in Chilean economic history. The evolution of the economy during the past three years gave much weight to the *Concertación* economic policy discourse, while opposition could not credibly resort to the alarmist arguments made in 1990 concerning tax reform.

The tax reforms undertaken under the Aylwin administration needed to be judged in light of their stated aim of improving social conditions. No one could reasonably deny that they had been validated by the impressive social achievements of 1990–1994: poverty was reduced from 38.7 to 27.5 percent, while extreme poverty (less than $1 a day) had been brought down from 12.9 to 7.6 percent. The next administration was inheriting an enviable economic picture: average growth of

7 percent, inflation of 17 percent and declining, unemployment under 6 percent, and savings around 24 percent of GDP.

Relative Tax Stability under a New *Concertación* Government

The December 1993 electoral contest catapulted to the presidency another Christian Democrat as head of the *Concertación*: Eduardo Frei Montalva. Frei's two overarching goals, as he laid them out in his May 1994 address to Congress, were modernization and defeat of extreme poverty. President Frei put education at the top of his agenda. The new finance minister Eduardo Aninat spelt out the details in his first annual address to the nation in August 1994:

> The specific goal of this government is to reach in less than 8 years a level in education spending that represents 7 percentage points of GDP, which means reaching the standards of Great Britain or Germany. This effort must be shared between the public and private sector. In the fiscal area, it is imperative to privilege gradually education spending within the national budget in a way that those resources increase more rapidly than the rest of expenditure items... In the 1990s the objective of President Frei is to improve the quality of our education, to foster equity in access to the educational system, and above all, its management. Four big tasks facing Chilean education in the next few years emanate from this grand objective. The first is curricular modernization, understood as tailoring the contents of the educative process to the necessities of the Chilean economy and society. The second is to increase significantly schools' effectiveness, that is, the capacity to generate better academic results given the socioeconomic characteristics of students. The third challenge is to increase the retention rates of students from low socioeconomic backgrounds. Finally, we need to improve the management of the educational system so that we can ensure an efficient use of disposable resources. (*El Mercurio*, August 30, 1994)

Such priorities were in line with Aninat's personal economic worldview (much attuned to frontier academic research), by which the state had to abandon its role in the area of production and assume an ever-more important role in the social sphere. Moreover, it was the minister's conviction that "investment in human capital is the key to development" (*La Época*, October 4, 1994). Echoing President Frei's famous remark to the effect that the country faced "a historic opportunity and we do not have a right to waste it," the minister made very explicit the new administration's continued commitment to fiscal balance:

> The historic opportunity before us will only materialize if we are able to take on the new challenges without undermining the economic pillars that we have built with so much effort in recent years. We cannot run the risk of altering our macroeconomic stability or derailing our public finances. This consideration along with the priorities here outlined [productivity, education, labor training, and infrastructure] will be our only disciplining factor [in the elaboration] of the upcoming Budget Law of 1995. (Ibid)

In November 1994, Socialist senator Sergio Bitar handed the *Ministerio de Hacienda* a proposal to eliminate legal loopholes in the tax code. Eliminating these opportunities for tax avoidance was estimated to add $160 million to state coffers. The document solicited the revision of: tax subsidies granted to first-time buyers of stocks; VAT exemptions on interest earnings; the Federal Tax Bureau's lack of information on rents earned on financial instruments; the VAT on the construction sector, only levied on first sales; the excessive number of tax exemptions on luxury items; excessive tax exemptions on earnings coming from Argentina, and a few others (*El Mercurio*, November 15, 1994). Undersecretary of the Treasury Manuel Marfan defended the proposal as an attempt to "advance the principle of horizontal equity" and thus one that had "merits as a whole." Although unstated, what economic authorities were effectively doing was getting around the dilemma of securing additional resources for the state while concurrently complying with the tacit agreement not to undermine tax policy stability. Predictably, some voices from the political right interpreted Bitar's proposal as a violation of that accord.

Increasing Consumption Taxes to Fund Pensions and Education

In his annual message to the nation in May 22, 1995, President Frei announced that the government would take specific measures to improve pensions and education. The idea was to increase taxes on gasoline and cigarettes in order to finance a 10 percent readjustment in minimum pensions (those under 100,000 pesos, at a cost of 43,820 million pesos) and a 5 percent increase in school subsidies that would benefit all children in schools administered by municipalities (at a cost of 18,600 million pesos). The tax on gasoline was estimated to yield 39,800 million pesos, the tax on cigarettes 13,500 million, and the planned rationalization of the tax system another 9,300 million—a total of about 150 million dollars. There were another nine social programs at a cost of an additional 150 million dollars, including the extension of the family subsidy to students between fifteen and eighteen years of age, an increase in the number of scholarships, the introduction of a labor training program for the young, and a special handout to pensioners over sixty-five years of age who received minimum pensions. These would be financed by a rearrangement of the fiscal budget, the improvement of tax administration efficiency and an added emphasis on fiscal austerity. In addition, the government would obtain additional resources from eliminating some legal holes that allowed for tax avoidance among high-income sectors. Taken together, the measures would help over one million pensioners and two-and-a-half million children and young students. Improving pensions had been a political staple of RN; however, it was the manner in which it was financed that drew criticism.

Critics from the business association and the political right jumped to the political fray with well-rehearsed accusations: this was one more initiative to increase the size of the state that would damage economic activity; moreover, they argued, the tax increase would largely fall upon the poorer classes. While resources were being extracted from increases in consumption taxes that are by definition regressive, 84 percent of gasoline was consumed by the upper 20 percent of income earners, which would therefore be funding 84 percent of the new social expenditures. Second, the critics conveniently ignored that the recipients of these social funds would be more than one million Chileans pertaining to the lowest strata of society. Moreover, one-fifth of the revenues came exclusively from high-income earners. All in all, the intended reform was eminently redistributive. Minister Aninat justified these measures "because we cannot have a country growing at 6 percent with inflation under control and pensions as low as the state is handing out" (*El Mercurio*, May 22, 1995). A technical argument was also made to tax consumption to yield needed resources, as economic authorities deemed that with total consumption growing at rates of 6 percent and higher, it needed to be restrained. It was the belief of many interest groups and opposition politicians that financing for social initiatives should come from fiscal savings or the sale of state assets. Others maintained that economic growth of the order or 5 percent (or higher) was enough to finance the scheme.

Compensating for Assorted Revenue Losses: Maintaining the VAT at 18 Percent

Minister Aninat announced in August 1995 that he would recommend to the president to keep the VAT at 18 percent, making use of the executive prerogative to set the rate at anywhere from 16 to 18 percent for 1996 and 1997, as agreed with the opposition in 1993. The revenue associated with each VAT point was not minor, amounting to about 70,000 million pesos ($184 million). This position was publicly justified on the basis that direct taxes on individuals and companies had been falling as a percentage of GDP during the past two years. Second, it was asserted that various international trade agreements negotiated with third countries had caused significant revenue losses for the treasury; third, maintaining the VAT rate intact was needed to ensure adequate financing for the administration's eleven social expenditure projects.

Although the decision over the VAT, in this particular case, fell exclusively within the domain of responsibility of the executive, Aninat's intentions stirred up intense opprobrium from political opponents. RN president Andres Allamand was the most visible figure among critics of the measure, which he deemed unjustified given the surplus budgetary stance of the nation and the fact that resources were not being efficiently spent. The finance minister was confusing his role as the chief administrator of the country's progress and modernization with his role as the chief collector of taxes, contended Allamand. The coalition of right-wing parties *Union por Chile* showed figures indicating that between 1990 and 1995 tax collection had increased from $4,000 million to $12,000 million, and that this spectacular growth had not had a sizable impact upon the creation of new social programs, pointing out that between 1990 and 1993 the country had experienced a $240 million increase in state bureaucracy in order to administer the augmented public resources. Moreover, the right-wing establishment alleged that social spending targeting was highly deficient, on account of the fact that the very poorest quintile of Chileans received only 18.5 percent of social spending while 39 percent was directed at the highest two quintiles (40 percent) of society. Thus, it was claimed, the new state resources had become trapped in an intricate web of bureaucracies. Such arguments had substance. They pointed to perhaps the greatest conceptual weakness afflicting the *Concertación*'s approach to battling poverty and inequality: the idea that money alone suffices to cure such ills.[9] At the end of the day, the background of the fiscal discussion in Chile reflected different conceptions about the adequate size of the state. At the most profound level, it was an eminently political debate, although both sides couched it in "scientific" or technical discourse.

Conclusion

This chapter has argued that the successful enactment of the all-important 1990 tax reform owed much to the unique political and economic circumstances surrounding the transition from authoritarian rule. Predictably enough, defending the "growth with equity" model in subsequent years was not to be easy for the governing *Concertación*, not least because both business and the political right were wedded to a "growth only" philosophy. No other area of economic policy in Chile illustrates better this clash between two conflicting politico-economic conceptions. The temporary nature of the 1990 agreement (valid for three years) meant that renegotiation of tax policy in 1993 signified a litmus test of the *Concertación*'s overall policy orientation. But several factors played in the government's favor that worked together to keep the reform in place. Its highly orthodox and responsible management of the macroeconomy, outstanding economic results (in terms of overall economic growth, low inflation, high investment rates, etc.), and social outcomes (in terms of poverty reduction) gave much credence to the compatibility of pro-growth policies with an active pro-poor and social agenda. Moreover, the *Concertación* forged a constructive working relationship with organized business, took its input seriously, and granted entrepreneurs ready access to the main economic policy ministries. The Chilean business community's instinctive distrust of center and center-left parties was greatly assuaged as a result. In addition, the numerous international accolades bestowed upon the Aylwin administration and its model performance endowed the *Concertación* with an independent source of legitimacy for its policies.

But an important part of the puzzle that allowed for the maintenance of the 1990 tax changes was the steadfast commitment to fiscal balance and the manner in which government was able to legitimize the inviolability of this unwritten rule. Both the Aylwin and Frei governments credibly peddled fiscal equilibrium as a fundamental element underpinning the Chilean economic boom. Chilean finance ministers successfully sold the idea that such a sturdy fiscal position allowed the economy to better handle external economic shocks and as it differentiated Chile from other Latin American countries. The nearly sacrosanct status of the fiscal equilibrium rule meant that any conceivable reductions in the tax level advocated by the political opposition had to go hand in hand with reductions in social expenditures, which was a politically risky proposition. Whenever the growth with equity model was put in peril by the actions or policy positions of RN, the government intuitively shifted the tax debate to the court of public opinion, where it invariably scored a resounding success. More often than not, the government successfully linked taxation policy to the fight against inequality and poverty. The year-to-year economic outcomes on growth, inflation, and poverty figures consistently supported the contentions of the government while they undermined those of an intransigent *Union Democrática Independiente* and some recalcitrant sectors of RN.

The first half of the 1990s also set in place the consensus among all political and social actors on the importance of tax stability—that is, the avoidance of continuous changes in the tax structure. By and large, the *Concertación* fulfilled its promises to maintain the main tax rates and bases intact after reaching a broad accord on them, thereby building credibility. However, the need to find additional sources of revenue to cover new spending commitments (on pensions, education, etc.) and revenue losses accruing from lower trade tariffs would sooner or later pose a quandary for the center-left ruling coalition: how to meet the new spending needs without altering tax rates or bases and without compromising the fiscal balance tenet. The *Concertación* government responded creatively by rearranging the budget, improving tax administration efficiency, raising taxes on specific consumption items, and eliminating legal loopholes allowing for tax avoidance. To be sure, all of these actions were challenged by an ever-more vociferous political opposition, and (as the transition receded into the past) the expected emergence of "politics as usual" in Chile. This is the political and fiscal backdrop that would shape the tax policy debate during the latter half of the 1990s, the subject of the following chapter.

2

Chilean Tax Policy Tested by New Political and Economic Conditions: 1996–2001

Introduction

The second half of the 1990s provided a number of significant challenges to the survival of the "growth with equity" socioeconomic compromise, the seeds of which can be discerned from the previous chapter. These came not only from business and the political right, but also from the left. Entrepreneurs made much noise in their opposition to tariff reductions that were to be fiscally compensated by tax raises, arguing in terms of loss of competitiveness. The political right also called for a reduction of social expenditure, so as to allow for a lower overall tax burden that would not compromise fiscal discipline. However, the *Concertación* doggedly and systematically rejected any suggestions to embark on a direction different from the overarching one it first devised in the 1990 campaign. This chapter will show how astute political management, as well as features proper of a highly institutionalized political setting allowed the government to deflect pressures to deviate from fiscal policy tenets inherent to the "growth and equity" model.

The Failure of Aninat's Brainchild: A Global Tax Reform

As the expiration date for the 1993 accord (valid for three years) approached, the *Ministerio de Hacienda* received more than a dozen formal tax reform proposals from business associations and parties of the right. Most of the reform proposals advanced to the government tended to be revenue decreasing in nature. In particular, a high-profile joint proposal by the PPD, RN, and UDI focused on the need to level the income tax rate levied on individuals with the income tax rate levied on companies—thereby following the tendency observed in the developed countries. Other blueprints simply advocated a lower overall tax burden, in light of the fiscal surplus observed in 1995. The Finance Ministry invariably rejected such requests with allusions to the numerous acute problems facing the country in the areas of health, education, justice, housing, and poverty and the need to continue shifting the structure of the budget toward social expenditures. Finance Undersecretary Manuel Marfan remarked: "the point is that there does not exist a sufficient degree of [political] consensus to modify the existing tax reform accord [dating from 1993] and we are not ready to accept one that reduces the resources of the public sector" (*El Mercurio*, March 4, 1996). The government had good reasons for disavowing any talk of reductions in the overall tax burden on the economy: crunching out the tax and expenditure numbers for the short- and medium-term horizons spelled an upcoming "fiscal squeeze." The incorporation of Chile into the MERCOSUR free trade area as an associate member implied a reduction in trade tax revenues of $119 million for 1997, $153 million for 1998, and $198 million for 1999 (*Comentarios sobre la Situacion Economica*, 1996–1997). There was a possibility that the VAT rate would be reduced from 18 to 17 percent—in accordance with the flexible VAT scheme introduced—signifying an additional loss of $300 million. On the expenditure side, the government would be facing rising bills. Due to demographic trends, social security outlays were projected to increase by 4 percent annually, whereas education subsidies would experience a growth not lower than that of GDP. Public sector wages were also expected to increase around 4 percent, in line with overall economic productivity, so that the gap between public and private sector salaries would not be widened. Moreover, there were government commitments on the horizon that did not come for free: the educational reform, via greater spending on school subsidies, would cost an additional $300 million annually, while the reform to justice administration came with an annual $80 million price tag attached. These factors clearly constrained the government's ability to initiate any revenue-reducing tax reform.

Economic authorities also had macroeconomic considerations in mind in not lowering taxes. Given that total spending had grown at 13 percent during 1995 and the economy at 8 percent, reducing taxes would have exacerbated such disequilibrium. Moreover, legislative bills to be considered during 1996 already had negative implications for tax collection, such as a number of international trade agreements and plans to eliminate situations of double taxation. Despite the number of tax reform proposals, all political actors agreed that the permanent public discussion of tax innovations was counterproductive for economic performance.

In August 1996, however, Minister Aninat startled fiscal policy observers and economic agents in general by proposing a "large, unique, and stable" tax reform with a time horizon of "ten, fifteen or twenty years" (*El Mercurio*, August 10, 1996). Such an ambitious project, the minister declared, would be discussed in 1997 and would constitute the only comprehensive tax reform to be enacted during the Frei administration. Its design would be informed by three overarching objectives: overall simplification of the tax system, incentives to save and invest, and finally, vertical and horizontal equity concerns.[1] In seeking a global tax reform with a long time horizon, Aninat was following in the footsteps of the 1990 and 1993 agreements: namely, the pursuit of tax stability. The upcoming tax reform was inserted in a discussion about a unilateral reduction of tariffs. Minister Aninat explained that the reform would go beyond a simple compensation of revenues, as had been the case in 1991: "It is not only about agreeing to a gradual road of tariff changes and a concomitant road of equivalent tax compensations [in revenue terms]; we would like to reexamine the design and general structure of the tax system" (ibid.). Aninat's public statement was prompted not simply by a personal conviction, but by the increasing pressure exerted by political parties of all colors and by the entrepreneurial community in favor of business-friendly tax innovations. As the new chief of business interests (president of the CPC) Walter Riesco noted, echoing the finance minister, "a modification of the tax scheme must be sought, looking for long term stability in order to avoid changes every year" (*La Epoca*, January 5, 1997). The relative inaction in taxation matters between 1993 and 1996, however, would mean that many pent-up demands by disaffected sectors would presumably have to be addressed, and somehow reconciled with the economic authorities' own views about the flaws of the tax system and the need for its adaptation to new, ever-changing economic realities. The looming negotiation over tax policy promised to be fierce, not least because of the magnitude of the changes the government had in mind and the time elapsed since the last comprehensive tax reform (1990). While most political parties and business associations expressed the view that the tax system needed to be revamped, there was disagreement about objectives as well as their optimal instrumentation. Yet, widespread agreement about some of the deficiencies of the tax system boded well for the materialization of an accord. Notably, everyone agreed that the income tax on individuals was too high and that there were many low-yield taxes that were superfluous and dispensable—such as those levied on luxury items, stamps, automobiles, and alcoholic beverages, to name a few. The discussion on whether to keep the VAT at 18 percent or to lower it (as the government had informally committed to) promised to be more contentious.

President Frei also stepped into the taxation fray and signaled that tax reform ranked high among government priorities for 1997: "The current tax accord has a shelf life of four years; therefore, in the course [of 1997] we will initiate a profound debate vis-à-vis the country involving all the affected sectors" (*El Mercurio*, January 7, 1997). From a technical, economic, and administrative viewpoint, a global overhaul of the tax system so as to render it more efficient and simple and to take taxes out of the political discussion for a number of years was a laudable enterprise. But what promised to be Minister Aninat's greatest legacy was not to be. Comprehensive tax reform was frozen in time by a myriad of environmental factors. First, the crushing defeat of Frei's education reform in Congress— not least due to the executive's intention to keep the VAT at 18 percent during 1998—had polluted the political climate between the executive and the opposition. Second, the country had undergone a recent economic adjustment and many economic agents worried about its continuation. Third, the imminent change of *Renovacion Nacional*'s political leadership (via elections) as well as the scheduling of a number of executive initiatives (such as the project to eliminate designated senators), among a number of other factors, made it exceedingly complicated for the parties to focus attention upon something as time-consuming as comprehensive tax innovations. But the most important obstacle was posed by the political calendar for the year, with parliamentary elections scheduled for December 11. Despite the Ministry of Finance's wish to direct and oversee a new tax reform, its timing was entirely determined by political circumstances. Finance Minister Aninat, under instructions from President Frei, soon adopted a lower profile on the taxation issue and assert that "the government does not want to pursue a great revolution of the Chilean tax system," but simply to postulate changes in the composition of existing taxes in order for the treasury not to lose public resources (*El Mercurio*, January 18, 1997).

There was another, structural factor that convinced the executive to postpone tax reform: political polarization between the *Concertación* and the opposition. As the years of the transition from authoritarianism receded, the RN increasingly adopted a more rigid and intransigent negotiating stance. Such political dynamics spilled on to a number of economic issues, taxation included, that were being approached in a more politicized manner. Although unstated, leaders of the political right (including Andres Allamand, Evelyn Matthei, etc.) held the view that any tax reform ought to be revenue-decreasing. Favorite items for the right included the reduction in VAT and in personal income tax marginal rates. For its part, the government was willing to seriously entertain these ideas only on the condition that they were fiscally compensated. This was anathema to the right, who wanted an overall reduction in the tax burden. Ironically, in a historical twist of fate, it was the center-left governing coalition that stood as the firmest defender of equilibrium in the public accounts, rather than the right. No *concertacionista* economist was oblivious to the fact that fiscal policy had played a fundamental role in ensuring macroeconomic stability and had been a useful feature distinguishing Chile from neighboring countries in the eyes of the international investors and financial institutions. It was understandable that the government should not be willing to sacrifice fiscal rectitude. In the traditional October annual address to the Congressional Budget Commission, Budget Director Joaquin Vial Ruiz-Tagle was able to give this glowing assessment of fiscal policy over 1990–1997:

> From 1990 until now [late 1997], the Chilean economy has evolved in a framework of macroeconomic stability. The economy has grown 6.8% a year on average, while inflation was reduced from 27% to a single digit, and unemployment has dropped from 9.5% to 5.9% over the same period. Likewise, we have been able to maintain stability in our external accounts. Fiscal policy has played a key role in attaining these results. In fact, the maintenance of a global fiscal surplus of 1.8% over the 1990–1996 period shows the contribution of the government to macro stability. From a macro viewpoint, the government has made efforts to keep high and stable rates of public savings, which has been possible due to the control of current spending, which has remained around 17.5% of GDP in the 1990s. In this context, fiscal savings has turned into the most stable component of national savings, alongside social security savings.

The high level of public savings has allowed for the increase of public investment, thus generating the greater infrastructure required for sustaining a higher rate of economic growth. The fact that the rising public savings has allowed for the steady replacement of foreign indebtedness as a source of public investment has meant not only a reduction in the financial burden that this generation of Chileans bequeaths to their children, but also to reduce the dependency [of the economy] upon financial and real external economic cycles. Thereby we have significantly enhanced our economic autonomy. (Vial Ruiz-Tagle 1997)

In spite of structural obstacles and the inherent difficulties posed by a busy electoral calendar, the tax reform was still described by top Ministry of Finance officials as a "national priority for Chile's competitiveness." Given the wide agreement among parties and interest groups on the need to change the tax system—albeit with different objectives in mind—its negotiation seemed no more than a matter of time.

Reducing Trade Tariffs: The Battle over Fiscal Compensation

Concertación governments were more than rhetorically committed to extending and deepening the open trade regime implanted by the Chicago boys. (Consolidating an open economy is one of the objectives that elicited the widest agreement among Chilean economists.) The Aylwin government had already reduced import tariffs unilaterally from 15 to 11 percent, with the objective of reducing the import cost of capital goods and other inputs, thus making Chilean exports more competitive worldwide. The Ministry of Finance was convinced of the need to deepen trade integration with the rest of the world if Chile's economy was to keep roaring ahead. Aninat proposed to reduce import tariffs a further three percentage points in a gradual fashion over three years. While the government and the business community saw eye to eye on the importance of opening up the economy, they disagreed on whether the revenue loss represented by the tariff reduction needed to be fiscally compensated by increasing other assorted taxes. The treasury stood to lose $430 million. To compensate for lost revenues, economic authorities were considering four measures: a rise in the tax on gasoline; the widening of the stamp tax base; a reduction in tax evasion; and last, the elimination of export reimbursements. Virtually all of the major business associations—including the CPC, SOFOFA, AXESMA, and others—maintained that fiscal compensation formulas, however designed, would reduce the competitiveness of the industrial sector. For instance, the government's plan to increase fuel taxes, which would provoke a rise of 6–10 percent in fuel prices, was deemed by SOFOFA's secretary general Andres Concha to be clearly "a tax on competitiveness insofar as it increases the cost of transportation and the use of energy in all productive sectors" (*La Epoca*, July 17, 1997). Fierce opposition also ensued over the elimination of export reimbursements (which represented around $140 million). Many leading entrepreneurs argued that the export sector was already in a delicate situation because of the lower real exchange rate; thus, they argued, the tariff reduction needed to be treated as an issue of resource allocation rather than a fiscal matter. They also rehearsed the standard argument that fiscal compensation measures were unnecessary because the economy could grow at a faster rate as a result of tariff reductions, thereby canceling the fiscal losses arising from the trade reform.

It thus became increasingly clear that both sides were on a collision course. Aninat made it clear that for the government, fiscal compensation was a non-negotiable issue:

> I will not sacrifice even one centimeter of fiscal savings, which allows us to deal with situations of shocks and disasters, situations we have faced and the government has dealt with successfully. Neither is it in the interests of the government to forgo social spending, an issue [social conditions] in which Chile still has many deficiencies. (*La Epoca*, August 26, 1997)

Although the business community, whose own commissioned studies indicated widespread benefits and positive externalities from the reduction of tariffs, eventually signaled its willingness to accept the concept of fiscal compensation (as long as it had a say in the design of the "tax menu"), *Renovacion Nacional* adopted a hard-line stance. They proposed a reduction in fiscal savings by reducing social spending. It was the parliamentary elections of December that created this paradox and led to the indefinite freezing of tariff reduction plans. The episode was further proof of the *Concertación*'s unwavering commitment to fiscal balance and to keeping social expenditures growing. Once again, the intense pressure from the business sector (to enact the reductions to trade) and the political opposition (to cut fiscal spending) had failed to make a dent on the *Concertación*'s "growth and equity" model. The government was ready to lose medium-sized battles in order to keep laboring on what it deemed the larger war against social debt, poverty, and inequality. As Aninat summed up: "there are battles and battles" (ibid.).

In late 1997 the executive signaled its intention to send a tax reform bill to Congress in April 1998. Because 1999 was again an electoral year political timing dictated that any reform would have to be agreed in 1998 in spite of the fact that starting positions on the tax issue were as far apart as ever. The imminence of a new tax system naturally provoked a number of academic and technical proposals on the subject, the most notable and publicly discussed of which was one elaborated by economists Bernardo Fontaine and Rodrigo Vergara (1997) from the think tank *Centro de Estudios Publicos*. In essence, they advocated efficiency and investment-promoting reform that kept the overall burden intact. The study proposed to lower the maximum tax rate on personal income from 45 to 20 percent, and to make a differentiation between tax rates applicable to profits (*utilidades retiradas*), to be set at 20 percent, and rates levied on reinvested earnings, to be set at 5 percent. The VAT would be kept at 18 percent. Questioning one of Aninat's most cherished goals, income redistribution, these economists maintained that empirical evidence gathered from recent Latin American economic history showed conclusively that the pursuit of redistribution objectives via the tax system had proved a failure.[2]

What most of these proposals to fashion a new tax system had in common was the prioritization of economic growth in their design. Most Chilean economists deemed it necessary to eliminate those taxes that discouraged savings and investment (such as the income and luxury taxes) and to replace them with savings-neutral taxes. The pursuit of neutrality (efficiency) was in line with the thrust of tax system reforms since 1974, and reveals the wide agreement in Chile about the relevance of this objective above all others. In particular, the income tax was (and is) considered to be both inequitable and inefficient. It is inequitable due to the many deductions and exceptions with which it is burdened; it is inefficient because it is rather complex, entails substantive indirect (compliance) costs for taxpayers, and distorts savings and investment decisions.

Dealing with a New Enemy: Economic Crisis (1998–)

Starting in mid-1997 a financial crisis detonated in Asia, when a number of countries in the region faced the consequences of their high levels of short-term dollar-denominated debt. This had a very negative impact upon Chilean export performance, given that one-third of exports are destined to Asia. The lower demand coming from this key region in the global economy also translated into lower prices. Most worryingly, the price of copper, Chile's main export, fell from 103.3 c/lb in 1997 to 76 c/lb in 1998. This inauspicious international environment led to a rapid increase in Chile's trade deficit. A strong acceleration of internal demand, led by an unexpected rise in private consumption, only compounded the deficit in the current account— estimated to reach $5,300 million in 1998 (Marcel 1998). Whereas the structural strengths of the Chilean economy allowed for the financing of this deficit for that particular year, the economic authorities reckoned that in the context of a negative and uncertain external economic climate, such a deficit needed to be corrected as quickly as possible so as not to imperil the economy's prospects. Thus, the Central Bank undertook a restrictive monetary policy, while the government enacted successive reductions in the national budget.

The deterioration of international markets and the lower economic growth partly emanating from the process of economic adjustment inevitably had a significant impact upon public finances and upon tax revenues in particular. First, the lower price of copper translated into lower revenues via the transfer of CODELCO earnings to the national budget and via the lower income tax collection from private copper firms. Similarly, lower economic growth obviously meant lower yields from the income tax, the VAT, and other assorted taxes. This new panorama could not help but affect the politics of the fiscal policy game. The fiscal straightjacket imposed by the external economic environment meant that the government would have a more difficult time keeping all political factions of the *Concertación* content over tax and spending decisions.

It is in this context that one of the most powerful political operatives in the Frei government opened a Pandora's box. Secretary of the Presidency Juan Villarzu created a large controversy when he said publicly that what Chile needed to solve its pending social problems was an increase of the overall tax burden from 18 to 25 percent. Villarzu's candor constitutes more than a mere curiosity because it exposed in public the economic worldview of a (left-wing) sector of the Chilean political class—hidden as this was from public political discourse. Villarzu's comment was also revealing because of the political reactions it created. It raised the specter of what some perceived to be the true intentions of the *Concertación* (a large state presence in the economy with the objective of redistributing income) and drew an instant, powerful rejection and denunciation from entrepreneurs and right-wing politicians. Predictably, Villarzu's idea was promptly dismissed by governmental operatives, who labeled it as "purely academic." "The government's plans have never included and do not include a tax reform that generates massive new public resources to be spent by the state," clarified the president's spokesman (*El Mercurio*, February 10, 1998).

The financial turbulence coming from the Asian crisis prompted economic authorities to prioritize predictability and stability in economic policy above all else. Not surprisingly, the government announced the exclusion of the taxation issue from its agenda "due to the complex international economic panorama" and declared that tax reform should be debated only from 2000 onward. The year 1998 marked the onset of a period in which a particularly sharp tradeoff arose between the pursuit of policy stability and the pursuit of social equity and justice. Some felt social expenditure needed to be increased further to meet the government's various commitments; others felt that the unstable international economy called for the postponement of changes in fiscal policy. Even the executive proved incapable of speaking with a unified voice on this dilemma. In fact, during the first trimester of 1998 there were conflicting messages from various governmental spokesmen concerning the taxation issue, fostering a sense of restlessness and uncertainty among economic actors. These conflicting messages reflected, in no small measure, honest differences of opinion within the *Concertación*.

In November 1997, the government had signed an accord by which public sector wages was to be readjusted by 6 percent and the pensions of 800,000 retirees (with incomes under 50,000 pesos) improved, implying an increase in the tax burden of one or two percentage points (from the existing level of 18 percent). Many inside the coalition reckoned that such commitments could only be ignored at the *Concertación*'s peril. Yet, it stood to reason that many key technocrats would not have the stomach for such an increase at this juncture, given the electoral schedule and the unstable economic panorama. Chirstian Democratic senator Jorge Lavandero's words reflect the tense climate apropos of such matters: "within the government there are two views: those of *principistas* [or governed by principles], who believe in solidarity, in popular participation in economic life, and in social justice; and others who have come here to utilize power to defend the interests of large economic groups" (*El Mercurio*, February 17, 1998). Within the left (PS and PPD), a distinction is made in Chile between a sector of *autocomplacientes* (the "complacent") and a sector of *autoflagelantes* (the "self-flagellants") (Marfan; Landerretche, interviews). The former have adopted the free market wholesale; the latter have tolerated the neoliberal policies under previous Christian Democrat governments as a necessary, but transitory, evil (Fontaine and Vergara 2000). They propound some ideas that hark back to the Allende period, but in general, it can be said that they are in search of an identity as well as a set of ideas. These are politicians who defend social justice at all costs and envision themselves as fighters against those social forces that defend the economic status quo—in what is, in effect, a static view of economic processes. It was the *autoflagelantes*[3] (senator Lavandero is a prime example) who were leading the charge in favor of more social spending. That technocrats espousing economic prudence and orthodoxy easily won this battle over left-wing politicos again demonstrates that in Chile economic considerations override more political ones when these come into sharp conflict. This confirmed once more that economic stability had acquired sacred status in Chile.

The Debate over Fiscal Discipline Revisited

Figures showed that for the first time since the late 1980s tax collection in 1998 had failed to increase from the previous year in real terms (in fact, it fell slightly from 17.9 to 17.7 percent of GDP, about a 4.4 percent fall), a consequence of economic stagnation and developments in the international economy. There was, however, no sign of an increase in evasion levels, as is often the case during economic downturns, corroborating Chile's strong tax culture as well as the efficiency of its tax bureau. It was the belief of many observers of the economy that tax collection of basic items such as VAT and income taxes could very well continue to fall in 1999 due to lower productive activity and higher unemployment. If the political soil for the approval of a global tax reform had proved infertile in 1998, the prospects were exceedingly low for an electoral year such as 1999. Yet, the fiscal debate was far from dormant. One of the themes of political discussion centered upon the real danger that public accounts might display a fiscal deficit in 1999 (given the low growth expected), in light of which many considered the government should reduce public expenditure sooner rather than later. Economic authorities responded to this challenge by maintaining that such fiscal measures would endanger the possibility of economic reactivation, particularly because better international economic conditions were expected. The government also reiterated its firm commitment to fiscal surpluses. As Frei's director of the budget Joaquin Vial wrote,

> This commitment [with fiscal surplus] is not a whim or a vogue, but is borne out the conviction that the fortitude of our fiscal finances is one of the pillars that has underpinned this decade of stable, noninflationary growth. It is also one of the factors that explains why Chile, one of the economies most affected by the international economic crisis, is one of the very few that has completed its adjustment in its external accounts and is initiating the road to reactivation. (*El Mercurio*, March 21, 1999)

Predictably, the perilous state of economic activity prompted many suggestions on how to oil the wheels of a rusty economy. The president of the powerful *Confederacion de la Produccion y el Comercio* Walter Riesco formally proposed a temporary reduction on the income tax levied on firms, a suggestion that was promptly discarded on grounds that tax reductions had already been effected in the first trimester. The sacred tenet of fiscal discipline was again invoked. During these turbulent months only a minor tax reform concerning luxury automobiles was approved.

Economic data for the first half of 1999 showed a virtually stagnant economy, which took economic authorities by surprise. A restrictive fiscal policy and high interest rates were partly to blame, but the prime culprit was the climate of business uncertainty (aggravated by Pinochet's detention in London), which explained a 13 percent fall in private spending. In the face of such an economic panorama economic authorities sought, in the words of finance undersecretary Manuel Marfan, to "send a signal that will normalize aggregate expenditure." The government resorted to well-conceived supply-side tax policy. One of the ways devised to kick-start the economy and create jobs was to reinvigorate activity in the construction sector. In that vein, the government proposed a number of tax incentives for buyers of so-called DFL-2 houses with the aim of selling about 20,000 houses in stock. While the business community warmly received the initiative, its discussion in the Chamber of Deputies was not exempt from opposition. The UDI stood as the main opponent on grounds that the project was inequitable, as it benefited relatively richer homebuyers who could discount a greater part of their taxes. Such rhetoric was clearly influenced by electoral concerns and also formed part of the UDI's political strategy to refashion itself as the party of the middle classes. Their contentions were not heeded. At the end of the day, what was hailed as one of the most attractive reactivating measures being discussed was approved in both chambers of Congress with substantial support.

During 1999, fiscal policy was deliberately expansionary to try to palliate the economic downturn. It is important to note that the government's ability to engage in countercyclical policies rested on the state's solid financial situation, because for countries afflicted by structural fiscal deficits (many in Latin America) this possibility did not even exist. Where economic authorities proved most vulnerable to economic criticism was in the area of monetary policy. There was widespread consensus that the president of the Central Bank Carlos Massad had been far too aggressive in increasing interest rates (up to 14 percent), unnecessarily prolonging and deepening the recession. Were it not for the sky-high interest rates, some government economists considered that the economy could have grown at 2 percent during 1999, and this was the reason why this came to be labeled by some as the "Massad recession." This clear failure in economic management resuscitated a debate about the need to have more tools of macroeconomic adjustment.

But the potentially most damaging criticism made by the political opposition was the claim that increases in public resources directed to social spending had not led to improvements in the areas of education, health, or housing. Of course, such allegations struck at the heart of the *Concertación*'s overarching political agenda—"growth with equity." While some improvements in social services had indeed ensued from the doubling of social spending effected between 1987 and 1998, the inescapable reality is that the opposition's claims had real substance. In fact, there was widespread discontent among the populace about the quality of service in housing, education, and health policy, to name three areas. Independent studies indicated that poverty reductions were largely the result of overall economic growth rather than social expenditure, and that only a relatively small fraction of public spending reached those in need, while a large portion of resources were diluted in financing the cost of bureaucracy. Social spending per poor person had risen from 250,000 pesos in 1990 to 719,000 in 1996, an increase of 187 percent. However, as economist Jose Yanez pointed out, "the question is whether the poor's welfare has risen proportionally or, rather, spending has become increasingly ineffective due to the impossibility of reaching the poor as poverty levels are reduced" (*Comentarios sobre la Situacion Economica* 1997–1998, chapter 5). All independent diagnoses pointed to the urgent need to improve the targeting and management of social spending.

Cognizant of the country's still unfulfilled social debt, two of the country's most prominent voices in economic matters, DC senator Alejandro Foxley and CEPAL economist Ricardo Ffrench-Davis, called for a plebiscite on (revenue-enhancing) tax reform. A plebiscite, they reckoned, would be the basis of a "participatory debate" and circumvent the infertile political terrain for such a discussion during an electoral year. These two figures embodied the conviction of many sectors within the *Concertación* that Chile needed to advance more decisively in so-called second-generation reforms (education, health, justice) and that this necessitated an increase in state resources. "The country must debate seriously and in depth each of the policies that it wants to implement, and then consider how it is going to finance those policies via the tax system" (Foxley, *El Diario*, August 3, 1999). In Ffrench-Davis' opinion, more investment in human capital (education, labor training, health) was crucial in order for the "poorest to get somewhat closer to the opportunities faced by higher income groups" (ibid.). While both economists did not belittle the importance of improving the efficiency of public spending, they argued that, at the end of the day, more state resources were needed.

The Steady Erosion of the "Politics of Consensus"

If these important economists were calling for changing the venue in which tax and expenditure issues were discussed, it was clearly because fiscal reform was losing impulse among political parties themselves. A decade after the transition to democracy the "growth with equity" compromise rested on a weaker political footing. Less willing to compromise, the RN and UDI had systematically rejected calls for any meaningful rise in taxes, regardless of their intended use. (The overall tax burden had not budged from around 18 percent of GDP for some time.) Party strategists came to conclude that their electoral fortunes were increasingly linked to their ability to differentiate themselves from the other parties, to offer a visibly different message and policy recipe to the electorate. Playing the so-called *politica de acuerdos* (consensus politics) yielded ever fewer votes at the ballot box. Thus, "politics as usual" came to dominate the political scene more and more. The replacement of consensus-seeking Andres Allamand as president of *Renovacion Nacional* in 1997 was important in this regard, partly caused by the aforementioned political trends. Allamand had staked the party's political future on a steady pilgrimage toward the center of the political spectrum, a strategy based on reaching agreements with the *Concertación* and distancing the RN from the Pinochet legacy. The figures that took over the RN very much opposed this political project. The fortunes of the pinochetista *Union Democratica Independiente* best illustrate the new Chilean political dynamics. Its strategy remained unchanged since the transition to democracy: an uncompromising, non-negotiating stance on virtually all issues while publicly deriding political accords and consensual decision-making. This clearly differentiated it from all other parties. As Chileans became disgruntled with politics and the political class in general, this antipolitics approach of self-marginalization gave the UDI a new allure. Its steady rise in voting intentions, culminating in the 1997 parliamentary election and a very successful 1999 general election performance (in which it almost landed the presidency), spoke volumes. It is not coincidental that the UDI candidate Joaquin Lavin had achieved remarkable political success by portraying himself as an outsider above party politics, as someone who was simply effective in "getting things done." His widespread political appeal shows that many Chileans had grown weary of traditional politicians, notwithstanding the remarkable economic performance during the 1990s. Indeed, parties enjoyed very low levels of public esteem by the late 1990s, with the number of respondents that did not sympathize with any party growing from 32 percent in 1990 to an unprecedented 47 percent by mid-1997 (Siavelis 2002, 231). As two noted analysts of Chile observed, during the latter half of the 1990s "there was evidence that indifference and hostility to the political system was increasing" (Angell and Pollack 2000, 359). Indeed, it was the evolving ideological convergence across the political spectrum (i.e., a marked decrease in polarization) that was largely responsible for this trend. The new popular lack of interest in political affairs can be interpreted as an inevitable corollary of Chile becoming a "normal" country in political terms. Indeed, "the decline in interest in politics in Chile is parallel to that in most countries where the issues at stake are not posed in sharp ideological terms" (360). For all economic accomplishments under democratic rule, there was a worrying and surprisingly high level of dissatisfaction with democracy's fruits (i.e., low levels of output legitimacy), with only 52 percent of Chileans agreeing in 1997 with the assertion "democracy helps Chile solve its problems," down from 84 percent in 1990.

This sociopolitical dynamic certainly generated increasing political strains within the *Concertación* alliance, as the Socialists, Christian Democrats, and PPD members hardened their views and policy positions. Only thus would they be able to carve out a separate identity from their coalition partners and prop up their flagging electoral appeal. Not surprisingly, reaching consensus became a more difficult enterprise, as parties sought to highlight and accentuate their uniqueness vis-à-vis the public. The inevitable result was reduced legislative output, particularly on substantive matters.

The Lagos Government: Financing its Political Project by Tackling Evasion (2000–2001)

The 1999 presidential election pitted Socialist heavyweight Ricardo Lagos (representing the *Concertación*) against UDI's young and ambitious Joaquin Lavin, mayor of Las Condes, a rich district in Santiago. During the presidential campaign none of the two main candidates had promised to lower or increase taxes. However, Lagos was explicit in arguing that massive tax evasion had become a serious problem in Chile and he vowed that his government would battle evasion, close loopholes facilitating tax avoidance, and improve tax administration. He vowed to use the added revenues thus collected for a number of social programs, in what constituted perhaps the key proposal of his campaign. The election, which was the most closely contested in Chilean history, did not bestow a ringing endorsement to Lagos' program; rather, it reaffirmed the rise of the UDI as the single largest political force in the country.

The *Concertación* leadership knew all too well that the prospect of a Socialist party president would unnerve some sectors of the business community. Lagos, himself with a Duke PhD in economics, moved quickly to reassure local business and international financial markets by selecting liberal and technically gifted members for his economic team. The new finance minister, Harvard-trained Nicolas Eyzaguirre (PPD), was a former director of research at the Central Bank and executive director for the southern cone at the IMF. The new minister of the economy, energy, and mining, Jose de Gregorio (PDC) had an MIT doctorate, was a former advisor to Minister Aninat, and also had worked at the IMF. All in all, the group of economists brought on board the new administration was just as qualified and technically brilliant, if not more, than that of the Frei government. Lagos's rhetoric constantly sought to dispel any lingering questions about his government's management of the economy. With a view to distancing himself from the Allende government he served, President Lagos promised "not a second Socialist government but a third Concertacion government." In referring to his political platform as the "third way," Lagos asserted: "We accept the market as a system to allocate resources. But the state has a lot to say about how to organize society as regards to the kind of social services that should be available to everybody. I refer in particular to education and health" (*Institutional Investor*, March 1999). There was little evidence that the new president intended to enact any significant change to the free-market economic model. A generally liberal economic policy direction was assured. Yet, Lagos's personal commitment to equity was beyond doubt, following the Socialist party line:

> I want to improve income distribution, provided that the tools I use don't take us back to inflation or zero economic growth or major economic imbalances. You have to demonstrate that democracy is compatible with sound and responsible economic policies. But if we don't have a more equitable society, we are not going to be able to compete abroad. In the short run it may be that I will need social expenditures to reduce poverty levels in Chile. Societies that succeed in the world economy have some degree of social cohesion. (Ibid.)

Political logic dictated that the government's economic policy could not simply reflect the views of the economic team but also had to weigh the priorities and worldviews of Socialist congressmen and party cadres, to whom Lagos was politically accountable. Lagos could not afford to completely alienate the so-called *autoflagelantes* within his own party. Although the Socialist party had long renounced nationalization or economic planning (Roberts 1998; Hite 2000), many within it had priorities that clashed with those of business, including adjusting social spending (via higher tax burden), giving the state a larger role in health and education, and tackling extreme poverty with tools other than "trickle-down" economics. Renovated socialists espoused neostructuralist economics. While neostructuralism shares many of the key elements of neoliberalism, it advocates mild industrial policy to generate competitive advantage in manufactures, a stronger role of the state in the governance of markets and a key role in redistributing income. Equality is, in their view, a key condition for the attainment of *substantive* (as opposed to procedural) democracy. These and other ideas worried Chilean big business.

In fact, the restraint and pragmatism that had characterized state-business relations during the first two *Concertación* administrations was to be broken under the Lagos presidency. To be sure, both the decline in the electoral fortunes of the Christian Democrats and the change in the center of gravity of the ruling coalition toward a left-pole is part of the answer. However, two other conditions explain this souring of relations (Silva 2002). One was the loss of power of the *Concertación* in favor of conservative parties, and the shift in power relations among business associations toward more intransigent factions (in particular, the ascendancy of the Sociedad de Fomento Fabril). The rise of the UDI as the main party of the right also spelled trouble for reaching accords on tax and economic policy in general. Undoubtedly, the context of economic slowdown gave business a stronger voice in economic policy. All of these factors meant that the Lagos government began its term from a position of weakness.

A significant source of business apprehension was the specter of a fiscally irresponsible "tax and spend" government that led to macroeconomic instability. Furthermore, business confidence in the *Concertación*'s management of the economy had faltered during the last two years of Minister Aninat's tenure, which saw a deepening economic crisis and a fiscal deficit for the first time in fifteen years (Yanez, interview). It was in order to restore lost business confidence and exorcise past ghosts of fiscal profligacy that Mario Marcel, a key member of Lagos's economic team and shadow director of the budget, proposed during the campaign the idea of institutionalizing a structural fiscal surplus of 1 percent during the Lagos administration (2000–2005).[4] This was enthusiastically received by Lagos and his key advisers (ibid.). An official Ministry of Finance document spelled out the characteristics and the purported technical merits of the measure thus:

> The government of President Ricardo Lagos has proposed to reaffirm and intensify the commitment to fiscal responsibility, conducting public finances on the basis of a policy rule. This rule consists of the

generation of a structural surplus of 1% of GDP as of the year 2001. Having this rule will help orient the expectations of economic agents, promoting the benefits of a future fiscal policy; it will strengthen fiscal discipline and make it possible to refocus on the fiscal aggregates of macroeconomic relevance. The Structural Balance makes it possible to orient fiscal policy for effective performance of its counter-cyclical role, maintaining the stability of public finances. In this regard, the separation of the structural component from the cyclical component of the Actual Balance makes it possible for the so-called "automatic stabilizers" of the budget to operate fully, avoiding unnecessary neutralization of movements of fiscal accounts that respond to the typical dynamics of the economic cycle and help to reduce the instability of the economy throughout the cycle.

In addition, Structural Balance is a tool that makes it possible to strengthen fiscal discipline. Meeting the stable goal of a structural surplus of 1% of GDP every year assures a constant fiscal balance throughout the cycle, guaranteeing the operation of the budget's automatic stabilizers will not lead to risky fiscal deficits. The structural budget is a key tool, in this regard, to assure a sound financial position, permitting the deterioration of the fiscal balance in the recessive phase of the cycle to be compensated by the strengthening of the balance during the expansive phase. (Ministerio de Hacienda 2000, 7)

As important as the foregoing was, perhaps the more vital consideration was, as the same document stated, "the undeniable fact that fiscal policy in Chile plays a symbolic role, representing the Government's commitment to macroeconomic equilibrium" (ibid., 8). What the Lagos executive sought with the announcement and creation of the surplus rule was to reduce economic uncertainty by formally institutionalizing fiscal discipline and reduced fiscal policy discretion, thereby giving business a guarantee of macroeconomic stability. In a real sense, it was a signaling device as much as a substantive measure. The structural surplus measure was born to guarantee economic credibility in the context of a Socialist president (Ffrench-Davis, interview). However, it was not a measure discussed and digested among political parties or technical cadres. It simply arose out of an individual initiative. The measure had not been discussed with the Socialist party itself (surely because it would have opposed such a constraint on state activism). This was sure to generate political squabbles over fiscal policy between the executive and Socialist congressmen.

The Lagos government was faced with the age-old dilemma of being burdened by many social commitments (amounting to $8200 million) and lacking sufficient resources to carry them out. Given that 1999 had been mediocre in terms of revenue collection and the business cycle had not yet decisively turned around, the new administration needed to find resources from somewhere without endangering the commitment to fiscal balance. The new authorities duly admitted that economic growth alone would be insufficient to fund proposed social programs. Because the political climate was inauspicious for tax increases, the government used its political capital on the one issue that enjoyed widespread agreement among all parties as a way to enhance public resources: battling evasion. Tax evasion levels had stabilized around 24 percent since 1994 and tax administration authorities had not been able to make a further tangible dent on the problem. For this reason, SII director Javier Etcheberry had for some time been advocating for more resources to be devoted to the tax agency along with some legal reforms in order to battle evasion. In particular, Etcheberry put the emphasis on the need to increase the number of personnel in tax control and administration functions, enhance the SII legal powers in a number of areas where it lacked teeth, and coordinate tax payment procedures with the Treasury. He warned that without substantial legal and institutional changes affecting the functioning of the SII, tax evasion could well surge from the existing level of $4,000 million to $5,000 million a year. One month into his tenure, Finance Minister Nicolas Eyzaguirre let it be known publicly that the problem was on the government's radar screen:

> One the one hand we have a problem to solve, which is to give the *Servicio de Impuestos Internos* more resources so that it can better carry out the administration of taxes. That is what we are going to do. In the medium term, we need to effect changes in the tax regime to inhibit elusion... given the complexity of the issue we need to reach a consensus about what is the most appropriate course of action. I can say already that one of the points we are necessarily going to have to talk about is the possibility of seeking convergence between the income tax on firms, which stands at 15% and that on individuals, now at 45%. (*Senales Economicas*, April 14, 2000)

The presidential message of May 21, 2000, featured the reduction of evasion as the first priority of Lagos's *sexenio*. In that speech the president announced a *Plan de Lucha Contra la Evasion de Impuestos* (Plan for Battling Tax Evasion), which contemplated the restructuring of the Tesoreria General as well as the SII. A special commission, made up of Director of the Budget Mario Marcel, SII director

Etcheberry, and General Treasurer Gianni Lambertini, was set up to restructure public sector tax administration. The bill to be submitted to Congress included measures to strengthen the SII administrative capabilities, endow it with greater legal attributions, and increase its personnel. Another facet of the *Plan de Lucha* focused on closing loopholes in the tax code that allowed for tax avoidance. A third aspect included in the bill concerned SII access to taxpayers' bank accounts, following in the footsteps of developed countries, where tax agencies have powers to control the siphoning off of tax resources. If approved, the project was expected to yield $200 million in extra tax collection during 2001; once in full operation, it would bring in an additional $800 million annually from 2005 onward, at current levels of tax burden (17.5 percent) (*El Mercurio*, May 23, 2000). There could be little doubt that the enterprise was ambitious in scope, as it sought to reduce evasion levels to a fifth of theoretical tax collection (from 24 to 20 percent of total revenues).

To counter its critics, government operatives were keen to point out that this antievasion/antiavoidance project would not affect taxpayers that complied with their tax obligations, and that it was directed at large evaders or those that had the technical capacity to exploit all of the loopholes provided by the tax law to pay less in taxes. Thus, it was aimed at large enterprises. If the antievasion project were successful, it would allow for the alleviation of the government's budgetary problems. However, to accomplish such a task required resolving a paradoxical situation: in order to avoid a diminution of public resources, the tax agency needed a larger budget. According to the 2000 budget, inherited from the Frei government, the SII resources had been cut by 3,000 million pesos (a substantial 7 percent reduction) as part of the general economic adjustment ordeal. Another five institutions important for tax administration purposes, including the *Contraloria General*, had experienced similar reductions.

Legislative discussion of the antievasion project soon revealed that the opposition would not object to granting more resources and personnel to the SII. What proved a sticking point was the proposed assault on tax avoidance. The business community reacted promptly and vigorously to what they considered "a change in the rules of the tax game." The new president of the *Confederacion de la Produccion y del Comercio* Ricardo Ariztia put the business viewpoint thus:

> Whereas in common language evasion and avoidance are used as synonyms, in tax jargon they are quite different terms. The former is not

only an illegal but also immoral act, via which taxes due by law are not paid. Tax avoidance, on the other hand, is an ethical conduct, consisting in using all the instruments provided by the law in order to alleviate the tax burden a person or a company faces. The government's project incurs in the mistake just alluded to, in its intention to combat both. The bill has an anti-investment bias because it eliminates mechanisms that allow for the moderation of the negative impact upon investment produced by taxes, and substantially increasing the tax burden befalling on Chilean taxpayers. (*El Mercurio*, May 30, 2000)

Minister Eyzaguirre had a very different view: "tax avoidance is not illegal, but it is an abuse consisting of using all of the loopholes of the law to pay less in taxes than should really be paid. (ibid.). While the government contended that this project was not truly a tax reform because neither rates nor bases were being altered, businessmen countered that closing loopholes allowing tax avoidance was in effect a widening of the tax base. Whereas tax avoidance is not illegal, from an economic viewpoint it is comparable to evasion because it diminishes revenues without attaining any economic policy objective in return (such as equity, simplicity, etc.). Moreover, it produces inequity because not all taxpayers have the knowledge or capabilities to make equal use of legal loopholes. Tax avoidance is associated with the use of *franquicias* (special tax regimes) or tax exemptions that were introduced in the tax code with a specific economic policy purpose and are not exploited in the spirit in which they were conceived. Therefore, if economic authorities decided to launch an attack against evasion, there were no good economic or technical reasons not to tackle avoidance as well.

Simply put, the semantic discussion disguised an old-fashioned battle over resources between the public and the private sectors. A more substantive argument from Chilean entrepreneurs was that the initiative was particularly inconvenient because of its timing, in the midst of a difficult and uncertain process of economic reactivation. In fact, this view was shared by many powerful figures within the governing coalition, who thought, like senator Foxley, that "what needs to be done now is simply to look for the reactivation of investment, and for that, the more stable the rules of the [economic] game the better. (*Estrategia*, April 18, 2000). The powerful president of the Senate's Finance Commission, socialist senator Carlos Ominami, shared this opinion. It was this deep ambivalence about the timing of the project that delayed its treatment for months. It would not be retaken in earnest until mid-2001. The Lagos government's overwhelming priority in the short term was to inject confidence in the economy. Only once reactivation was underway would the evasion project be introduced in Congress.

A key reform that, all observers reckoned, would help fight tax evasion and avoidance was the eventual merging of the income tax rates on business (15 percent) and on individuals (45 percent), by increasing the former and lowering the latter. Senators Foxley, Sergio Bitar, and Eduardo Boeninger came out with a proposal along these lines: they proposed that the corporate income tax rate be reduced from 45 to 35 percent and the personal income tax rate be raised from 15 to 18 percent. The defenders of the proposal had powerful intellectual ammunition in a number of objective facts: the marginal income tax rate on firms was certainly among the lowest in the world; the marginal tax income rate on individuals was very high by international standards; finally, the tendency in developed countries was to seek a convergence among all income tax rates. In the words of the sponsors, "the measure must be understood as a stimulus for a sector, the middle class, that is usually slighted by government and that, in the current economic circumstances, would give high value to this tax reduction as a signal of future welfare and income expectations" (*La Tercera*, October 15, 2000). In short, the measure aimed at stimulating private consumption. Once more, in the context of economic stagnation, a proposal in the tax realm had a supply-side flavor.

What surprised many was the force with which the Boeninger-Foxley initiative erupted on the national agenda and the rare degree of consensus it generated within the *Concertación*, the business community, and the political right. A key reason for this broad agreement lay in a happy coincidence: business, UDI, and RN were ideologically inclined to lower taxes on individuals, whereas many *concertacionistas* deemed the measure as ideal to reactivate consumption, as well as lowering evasion and making tax administration easier. Not only did the Boeninger-Foxley initiative have a powerful technical rationale, but it also had obvious political appeal. Minister Eyzaguirre gave the green light for it if two conditions were met: that it enjoyed political consensus and that it did not threaten fiscal balance.

During the last trimester of 2000, with a still sluggish economy, policymakers looked for ways to foster private spending. In that context, the Foxley-Boeninger proposal made more economic sense; the idea of significantly reducing marginal income tax rates in order to augment people's disposable income gained political momentum. The promoters of the measure held that, because a rate reduction would lead to greater tax compliance (i.e., lower evasion and avoidance), only a modest increase in the income tax on firms (from 15 to 16 or 16.5 percent) was needed to guarantee that the reform would be revenue-neutral, rather than revenue-reducing. The government welcomed the proposal, which it promised to study and perhaps include in the antievasion bill that was being discussed in the chamber of deputies. Many calculated that the inclusion of this proposal would contribute to change the center of gravity of the tax debate and improve the political odds for passage of the law against tax evasion, which remained a high priority of the Lagos administration. However, priority did not entail urgency in this case. Minister Eyzaguirre repeatedly asserted that only under conditions of economic reactivation and on the basis of a wide political accord would the executive send a tax reform project to parliament. These conditions were not met throughout 2000. The fact of the matter was that, as the memory of the elections of 1999 faded and the day-to-day reality of seeking ways to reactivate a sluggish economy took hold, tax initiatives with equality-promotion objectives were brushed aside. Indeed, the economic growth debate that the business associations and right-wing think tanks wanted placed at political center-stage won the day. The message was that the equity discussion could only be meaningfully raised when growth was high (say, around 7 percent). That this dictum became hegemonic even during a Socialist-led government speaks volumes about the high degree of consensus that it commands among Chilean economists, as well as a critical mass of the political class—*concertacionistas* and *aliancistas* alike. This is not to say that this "holy" dictum goes unchallenged. In fact, many Socialist party legislators sternly objected to such views and demanded that the government fulfill its promises on the social expenditure side, regardless of the state of the economy.

In November 2000, SOFOFA, the association representing Chilean exporters, grabbed the political spotlight by making a formal proposal to the executive on a plan to reactivate the Chilean economy: the *Agenda Pro-Crecimiento y Empleo* (Pro-Growth and Pro-Employment Agenda). The initiative sought to expand economic activity via an amalgam of microeconomic reforms. It received the immediate endorsement of President Ricardo Lagos. The U.S.-trained economist was all too aware of the urgent need to exit the mediocre post-1998 economic performance if his administration's most cherished social programs were to be fully put into operation, thus fulfilling campaign promises. No less than twenty-eight commissions were created to work on the elaboration of the Agenda, consisting of a close group of more than one hundred experts from the public and private sectors working on five subject matters: stimulation of savings and investment, coordinated by the Finance Ministry; promotion of competitiveness, entrusted to the Economy Ministry; the modernization of and reform of the state, in the hands of the Ministry of the Presidency; employment creation and improvement of human resources, coordinated by the Ministry of Labor; and the promotion of corporate social responsibility, a task entrusted to the SOFOFA itself. The resulting document was one without precedent in content and conception. The importance of the *Agenda pro-Crecimiento* lay in its encapsulating a new way of elaborating modern economic policy, with entrepreneurial leaders eschewing localized interests working in tandem with governing politicians who understood all too well that employment was generated by firms operating in competitive and open markets. Few Latin American countries, if any, could boast of having such a fruitful and symbiotic government-private sector partnership.

Tensions over Fiscal Policy within the Socialist Camp

Responsible fiscal management on the part of Lagos's economic team had allowed the Central Bank to apply a more expansionary monetary policy in seeking to stimulate the sluggish Chilean economy. While this was applauded by broad sectors of the business community, Chilean entrepreneurs encouraged the government to move more assertively and urgently on a number of issues. Ricardo Ariztia, the head of Chilean business, made public a formal proposal by his *Conferacion de la Produccion y del Comercio* for six measures "needed to recuperate a 7% rate of GDP growth." Among them: the closing of the tax and labor discussions; the signing of a Free Trade Agreement with the United States; advances in the modernization of the state, including privatizations; the improvement of a deteriorated political climate; the end of Mapuche violence; and reform of the domestic capital market. Without urgent action on these themes, the CPC argued, the prevailing politico-economic environment would fail to instill confidence among entrepreneurs and delay investment and economic resurgence. Congress approved the antievasion bill, the most emblematic Lagos project in the economic realm, in May 2001. This was one of the most significant successes of the Lagos administration to date, not least because it was one of the electoral promises made by the *Concertación* candidate during 1999. Minister Eyzaguirre made the following assessment of the eight-month ordeal to have the measure approved:

> I would say that, at the end of the day, the animal [the antievasion project] was not as ferocious as it was portrayed. In this I do not seek to apportion blame; maybe the government had a share of responsibility [in its delay] in that we were not able to explain from the beginning what was the extent and nature of these measures and maybe there is responsibility on the part of those who had to vote [the opposition] in that they politicized the issue. (*La Tercera*, May 31, 2001)

Much in line with the objective not to ruffle economic agents in the context of a delicate economic environment, the minister wanted to dispel any uncertainties about the future of tax policy under the Lagos administration:

> there are no plans to increase the tax burden, to raise taxes in a general manner. There is always the possibility of tax rationalization in the sense of extending some taxes and eliminating others. I will aim not to make changes unless they are fully consensual, for generating noise [in the economy] with taxes is harmful. (Ibid.)

Moreover, key political operatives within the Lagos cabinet wanted to attenuate political divisions within the ruling alliance (and with the opposition) over taxation. The government stood to lose much by exacerbating the more confrontational political climate that followed the 1999 elections.

While the government remained predisposed to consider the Boeninger-Foxley income tax reduction project, the increasing political noise and tension surrounding the proposal (particularly over its intended method for fiscal compensation) boded ill for a number of other governmental pieces of legislation—including the antievasion project, whose legislative delay effectively cost the government hundreds of millions of dollars in nonmaterialized extra revenue. Therefore, the government was keen to avoid negative spillovers from one project into the other, and did its utmost to keep them separate. "Let us finish with the evasion project and then we will talk about other things. Today, the main issue is evasion," clarified President Lagos (*La Segunda*, March 13, 2001).

The main detractors of the Boeninger-Foxley project were found in the Socialist party, which considered it socially unjust and regressive in nature and thought that it would not reactivate economic activity as most taxpayers would not receive any type of tax benefits (70 percent of Chileans do not pay any income tax, as their incomes are below the minimum established threshold). In fact, this position reflected larger tensions over fiscal policy within the governing coalition. Political heavyweights within the Socialist party, led by Senators Carlos Ominami and Jaime Gazmuri, wanted greater fiscal expenditure than Minister Eyzaguirre was willing to contemplate in order to tend to politically sensible sectors including health, education, and pensions. These had been somewhat relegated during the economic recession and the concomitant need to keep public spending in check. This preoccupation with inequality, a deep-seated malaise that post-1990 governments had not been able to improve upon, had been growing within the Socialists since the mid-1990s. Writing toward the end of the Frei administration, two prominent *Concertacionista* economists Oscar Landerretche (PS) and Jose de Gregorio (1998, 152) asserted that

> the debate [on inequality] reveals a broader preoccupation with the insufficient integration characterizing the process of economic development in [Chile]. It reveals dissatisfaction with the possibility that a profoundly divided society may be consolidated, in which opportunities and the fruits of progress are concentrated in reduced sectors of the population, while the rest advances very slowly. Among important sectors of the governing coalition one can observe a growing degree of impatience and discontent with the pace of change, particularly as it refers to the redistribution of income and opportunities. And because the government defends its administration and aims to promote trust and stability needed for good economic performance, discontent with the government's discourse has also augmented, which is perceived by some as a concession to neoliberal self-adulation.

Official figures showed that the 1.5 percent fiscal deficit of 1999 had given way to a 0.1 percent surplus in 2000. The *autoflagelantes* argued that fiscal equilibrium had been restored at the cost of excessive spending cuts. Second, they criticized what in their view was a low level of fiscal activism during 2000, which did not allow for solving the unemployment problem.

These criticisms were debatable at best. Improvement in the public finances had been largely due to increased government resources with respect to 1999, chiefly from privatizations, the income tax, and the higher price of copper. Second, it is doubtful that greater public spending could have "solved" the employment quandary, given that the private sector represented four-fifths of the economy and an even higher proportion of employment. This fiscal policy dispute within the *Concertación* was anything but trivial: it was, in effect, a litmus test of the post-1990 commitment to fiscal balance. Many Socialists openly advocated a purposeful temporary fiscal deficit in order to finance special proemployment programs and attend unmet needs in the health, pensions, and education sectors. In their view, given current economic circumstances, a Keynesian-type expansionary fiscal policy would be reactivating. But in essence, party figures were troubled by what they deemed as an insufficiently progressive Socialist-led government, whose lack of activism on the social front to date was betraying the principles, values, and programmatic agenda of the party. At the time, the Socialist party commanded particular political strength from their strong showing in the latest parliamentary elections, and obviously, the fact that they nominally commanded the presidency. The power of the *autoflagelante* sector of the party rose accordingly. Consequently, the pressure to have their views accommodated was intense, obliging president Lagos to devote his full political capital to the delicate balancing act of appeasing the burgeoning tensions within his alliance and keeping all sectors reasonably content. Minister Eyzaguirre and fellow key economic policymakers within the government proved inflexible in their opposition to Socialist designs. Their standard (academic) response is well encapsulated in the following piece authored by Director of the Budget Mario Marcel:

> The fundamental condition for a fiscal deficit to generate more activity and employment in a sustainable way is for this deficit not to put upward pressure upon interest rates; otherwise, the rise in the cost of credit will reduce consumption, private investment, activity and employment. This condition only applies under very special circumstances, which certainly do not apply to Chile today. Discipline in the management of public finances is considered nowadays as a key aspect of economic management in so-called "emerging markets" and a guarantee of future stability. This is what endows Chile with one of the lowest country risk ratings and cheapest access to external credit, what allows for lower long-term rates of interest and more flexibility for the Central Bank to conduct monetary policy. To abandon this discipline would mean to risk a reversal of the financial conditions that today favor a revival of consumption, investment and employment...Experience

shows that fiscal imbalances damage, more than they benefit, the long-term effectiveness of the state. The effectiveness of the state in reducing poverty, generating opportunities, fostering production, science, culture and citizen participation, does not depend so much on what is spent during a fiscal year, as it depends on the possibility of applying sufficiently consistent and persistent policies to effect lasting changes. (*La Tercera*, March 18, 2001)

As damaging as a struggling economy was, there was a strong case to make that the country's greatest malaise of recent years was not economic stagnation, but political stagnation. The seeming inability of the political class to give signals of consensus and understanding and the concomitant absence of legislative achievements on projects of economic importance did little to uplift the mood of investors, foreign and domestic. It was recognition of this reality that finally convinced Carlos Ominami and other reluctant socialist senators to back the Boeninger-Foxley proposal. The objective of changing agents' expectations trumped all other considerations. It was another sign of the lengths to which Chilean politicians across the political spectrum were willing to go in order to reactivate the economy. The year 2000 had been plagued by good intentions gone astray because of the excessive politicization of the economic debate. As many of its key figures made clear, the Lagos government was determined to avoid repeating this mistake.

By mid-2001, the painstaking work of senators Boeninger and Foxley to convince all political parties to back their income tax reform had succeeded, as the legislators of the *Concertación*, designated senators, and those of *Renovacion Nacional* gave their approval. On its part, the UDI gave its tentative support as long as alternative methods of fiscal compensation were found that did not involve a rise in companies' tax burden. Even some *concertacionistas* had doubts about increasing income tax on firms by three percentage points, for this would diminish their profitability at a time when it was already low. In supply-side fashion, it was argued that the greater VAT intake derived from greater economic activity would compensate the $200 million in revenues lost from the income tax reduction. As had been the case throughout the 1990s, economic authorities promptly dismissed such arguments on (self-evident) grounds that growth generates its own additional expenditure needs. RN president Sebastian Pinera warned that this compensation measure would generate a fall in investment of the order of $700 million and accompanying unemployment.

While the government was willing to consider different compensation schemes, now minister Eyzaguirre added another condition that the project's sponsors needed to fulfill: the project had to command consensus within the business community. Predictably, business associations sternly opposed the increase in corporate taxation as a way to compensate lost revenues, though some important ones were willing to take on a 1 percent increase—and argued that the rest should come from increased VAT collection. But business associations, knowing that a political accord with the RN had been reached and the reform was thus a fait accompli, chose not to exert their veto power to derail the reform.

The bill that Eyzaguirre finally sent to Congress entailed a careful compromise between business considerations and the different views within the *Concertación*. It involved a reduction of the top marginal income tax rate from 45 to 40 percent (as well as similar reductions for lower income brackets), and augmented the minimum threshold level exempted from income tax from 335,000 to 380,000 monthly pesos—thereby amplifying the base for tax-exempt Chileans by 125,000.[5] This last measure was aimed at satisfying the leftist sectors within the *Concertación* that questioned the project because it allegedly favored high-income earners, not the middle classes. Fiscal losses generated by the aforementioned reductions, about $150 million, was to be compensated with a two percentage point increase in corporate taxation, from 15 to 17 percent over a period of three years. All in all, the reform was officially said to benefit 1 million Chileans, with 750,000 seeing reductions in income tax by amounts ranging from 10 to 50 percent. The income tax reduction was approved in the senate with thirty votes in favor (*Concertación*, RN, and institutional senators), one against, and ten abstentions (UDI). However, the fiscal compensation clause that increased corporate taxation was only approved by the members of the governing coalition (*El Mercurio*, August 8, 2001).

Noted independent academics voiced doubts about the technical underpinnings of the law and its purported reactivating effects, well summed up by dean of the economics department at the Universidad de Chile, Ricardo Paredes:

> The use of fiscal policy, and in particular tax policy, as a reactivating instrument is widely dismissed by mainstream economists due to its relative ineffectiveness. More fiscal spending (economic stimulant) must be financed with more taxes, present or future (economic depressant),

and it is this balance which in great measure acts as a source of fiscal policy's ineffectiveness...The exact balance of fiscal equilibrium and investment promotion via one sole instrument is possibly very difficult to reach. (*La Tercera*, March 31, 2001)

However, there was undoubtedly a perspective from which the bill's approval was truly positive: it showed that brokering transcendental accords built on the basis of a consensus involving the government, opposition parties, and the business class was still possible in Chile.

Conclusion

Pressures to deviate from the "equity and growth" model ultimately had two sources. First, there was the lower rate of economic growth post-1997, which made the concurrent pursuit of various economic and social goals (trade openness, competitiveness, equity, poverty, etc.) much more difficult. In a slow-growing economy, policy tradeoffs, particularly those of an efficiency-versus-equality sort, become much sharper. The fiscal squeeze stemming from economic slowdown naturally reduces the government's scope of maneuver in tax and spending decision-making. Second, the cooperative, consensus-seeking political dynamic that characterized the first half of the 1990s began to show strains and fractures. The mere passage of time often has a debilitating effect upon any alliance, and the wear-and-tear of office began to take its toll on the tripartite relationship among the PS, the PPD, and the DC. More importantly, parties' incentives to cooperate regularly in all policy areas were reduced by the saturation with the political class among citizens. Tensions within the governing coalition also arose from the powerful incentives facing *Concertación* parties to manufacture differences when jockeying for electoral position, because their programmatic differences had been blurred by their membership in a long-standing coalition.

The conjunction of new political and economic conditions in the latter half of the 1990s made the reaching of an accord on global tax reform rather difficult, as the fate of Aninat's proposal showed. The Frei and especially the Lagos government also faced significant pressure from the left within the Socialist party to increase public expenditures so as to deal with manifold deficiencies in the delivery of health, housing, and education services, even if this meant a temporary letdown in fiscal discipline. Chile's techno-bureaucracy wielding economic arguments consistently won this battle against the politicos.

The effect of economic slowdown (post-1997) significantly modified the public debate on economic and tax policy. Political actors centered the debate on ways to ensure the sacred goal of reactivating economic growth, although obviously the views concerning the adequate instrumentation of such an agenda differed. This meant that tax policy objectives changed from an extractive focus (how to secure more resources for the state), to one centered on the reactivation of domestic consumption. Authorities thus enacted a number of supply-side tax reductions. These reductions always came accompanied by other tax measures that ensured the revenue-neutrality of the changes.

The tendency to generate surpluses in public finances declined in the latter half of the 1990s—a surplus of only 0.4 percent in 1998 and a deficit of 1.9 in 1999. Two factors explain this declining trend. The first is found in the many commitments made by the Frei government in modernizing education, improving physical infrastructure, and reforming the judicial system, among others. Moreover, the government was forced to attend to sectors that had been neglected throughout the years whose salaries were unreasonably low—in particular, teachers and public health workers—as well as the improvement of the low end of the scale of pensioners. A second factor that impacted upon public accounts was surely the economic crisis of 1998–1999, which had an important effect upon revenues. Moreover, the price of copper diminished to less than 70 cents in 1999, while it had been 103 only two years earlier, cutting the earnings of CODELCO and consequently government revenues.

The Lagos government came to office with a plan to combat evasion to obtain resources needed for its programmatic agenda. While it is true that evasion levels had stagnated around 24 percent for the past five or six years and a strategy to reduce it was called for, it can be said that the Socialist-led government focused on evasion by default: the political climate was still infertile for a revenue-enhancing tax reform—in spite of the many unresolved critical social problems afflicting Chile. Yet, a significant tax proposal (Foxley-Boeninger initiative) was able to gather sufficient political support by virtue of the interaction between its special characteristics (reduction of the marginal income tax rate, which everyone agreed was too high) and the economic context in which it was aired (as the proposal could be sold as a plausible reactivating measure). At the end of the day, Lagos administration resolved the increasing tension between social objectives and the need for business-friendly measures in favor of the latter. The ongoing mediocre performance of the Chilean economy spelled the continuation of supply-side tax measures aimed at reactivating the economy and the subordination of social solidarity and poverty considerations (with accompanying revenue-enhancing tax reforms) to that overarching priority.

3

Argentine Tax Policy under Menem I (1989–1994): The "Tax Revolution"

Introduction

The contrasts between Chile and Argentina in terms of state autonomy and the quality of their institutions are substantial, as explained in the introduction. Chile's legalistic culture developed from a strong centralist state, with high initial levels of legitimacy (Bergman 2009. A relatively efficient tax administration (particularly by Latin American standards) acted to reinforce this tax compliance culture. Argentina lacks a state with similar levels of social legitimacy and therefore for any given level of enforcement capabilities, worse tax compliance results. That low level of legitimacy partly stems from a well-grounded perception that the Argentine state has often promoted private interests, rather than the common good. While no one in the Pinochet government tried to obtain personal or group favors from the nation's tax agency, in Argentina "the DGI became vulnerable to the dictates of the military and later to political appointments" under the democratic Alfonsin government (608). This penetration of the state by particular social groups, coupled with Argentina's high level of politico-institutional instability (see chapter seven), has yielded a relatively inefficient (and corrupt) tax administration. Its enforcement capabilities have, not surprisingly, been much weaker than those of its Chilean counterpart. Tax noncompliance by Argentine citizens has been regularly rewarded by an absence of sanctions (including frequent tax amnesties), further consolidating a weak tax culture.

Clearly, the Menem and Aylwin governments confronted very different institutional and cultural legacies in their respective attempts to reduce evasion, enhance the efficiency of their tax administration, and, ultimately, prop up tax revenues. Therefore, it is apparent that for Argentine authorities progress in reaching these objectives would require greater commitment in terms of expending political capital and resources. The next two chapters seek to demonstrate how neglect of the mentioned legacies on the part of reformers eventually came to undermine a reform effort that was initially successful. The search for a politically painless, quick-fix solution, rather than the more protracted effort at serious institution-building, doomed any hope for success.

Antecedents of Argentine Tax Policy

Argentina has a long history of inferior tax collection, which can be attributed to a myriad of factors. The tax system has long been used for goals other than the maximization of revenue generation. Policy capture by interest groups that penetrate the organs of the state has significantly lowered tax collection. The tax structure has been traditionally molded and modified by government technocrats to favor particular economic constituencies or lobby groups. As new democratic or military governments came to power, tax exceptions and reductions, industrial promotion plans, regional development schemes, and a web of decrees, laws, and regulations with manifold rates, exemptions, and loopholes have created a labyrinth-type legal tax code of colossal complexity. Much like in the area of public expenditure, political parties or military rulers used the tax system as a tool to curry favor with numerous political allies in business and elsewhere. A good testament to this reality is that even the VAT (conceptually a broad-base tax) had at its inception in the mid-1970s a restricted base that remained restricted until the Menem administration. Another facet of "policy capture" exacerbating the limited extractive capacity of the Argentine system has been the pervasiveness of tax incentives to many sectors of the economy and geographic regions (Schvarzer 1990). Tax incentives were introduced in the early decades of the twentieth century but increased exponentially from the 1970s onward.

A second crucial factor shaping the Argentine tax system has been the policy environment in which it has been embedded. Argentina's chronic fiscal deficit has exerted constant pressure on the tax system, as economic authorities sought to alter existing rates or to create new inefficient taxes (tax handles) to fill fiscal gaps. This dynamic has prevented the consolidation of a reasonably stable tax structure—as concerns rates, bases, number, and types of taxes.

In turn, these and other factors have contributed to Argentina's exceedingly complex tax system, further complicating the task of tax administration. An unwieldy tax code requires a tax agency that is politically autonomous, highly efficient, and well endowed (in high-quality human capital and technological resources) if the tax system to be effectively administered. Yet, throughout its history, Argentina has sorely lacked anything resembling an efficient federal tax bureau. Moreover, the effective administration of taxes has been made elusive by the sheer complexity of norms and regulations that constitute the Argentine tax code (Llach 1999). In turn, such a web of exceptions and loopholes provided perverse incentives and opportunities to evade taxes. Detecting and proving fraud under such circumstances becomes a Herculean endeavor, something taxpayers have known and used to their material advantage. Even in those rare cases where the DGI was able to find its way through the labyrinth of laws and regulations to determine fraud, the Argentine tax agency often faced legislation that constrained its ability to prosecute law offenders.

In light of the aforementioned facts, it is not surprising that the Argentine state has traditionally suffered from a chronic fiscal crisis. A survey of Argentina's economic history shows that the secular rise in the nation's public spending has been financed with progressively greater difficulties (Diaz Alejandro 1970; Di Tella and Dornbush 1989). Traditional sources of taxation (i.e., income taxes and other forms of direct taxation) have historically yielded meager revenues in Argentina. Taxes on income, inherited wealth, and capital have been modest sources of revenues, whereas taxes on some consumer goods such as fuel, cigarettes, or alcohol have been unduly important. However, the state counted on two sources of fiscal revenue to compensate for this deficiency. On the one hand, export and import taxes, on the other, the surpluses yielded by the public social security system (due to the favorable imbalance between contributors and recipients). When these sources were insufficient to meet spending commitments, the state made use of the domestic capital market in order to borrow internally. It also printed money in moderate amounts. By the 1960s, the state lost much of its ability to finance itself internally, due to macroeconomic mismanagement and the consequent lack of credibility vis-à-vis currency and bond holders. But it was able to take advantage of the greater availability of foreign finance.

Eventually, all of the aforementioned wells of finance outlined earlier dried up. Export taxes became a diminishing source of revenues due to deteriorating terms of trade, while the social security surplus became a deficit by the 1970s. More traditional sources of taxation came to progressively yield less and less revenue, due to the deterioration of the "fiscal pact" between state and society: as governments desperately resorted to higher nominal tax rates (in a desperate race to cover building spending responsibilities) and offered little to Argentine taxpayers by way of adequate public services, evasion, elusion, and delays in payments became pervasive. Concurrently, a weak and discretionary administration of taxes (which favored certain economic groups, sectors, and even particular firms and individuals) steadily consolidated a tolerance for noncompliance, which, in turn, undercut tax administration efforts, perpetuating a most intractable vicious cycle. In sum, a titanic deficit of legitimacy has traditionally plagued the tax system: citizens never did perceive that the tax burden they were asked to bear was fair (in light of the low return on their "investment"), and never trusted that tax administration was equitable. Breaking out of such a mutually reinforcing and perverse state-society dynamic posed a colossal challenge for any incoming administration willing to contemplate embarking upon such task. Most changes affecting the state-society fiscal contract in the past did little to encourage voluntary tax compliance. In fact, it can be said that in tandem with exacerbating public finance shortfalls and politicizing economic policy, the tax system grew much more complex and incoherent (particularly from the 1970s onward), reinforcing the fundamental vicious dynamic at work.

Argentina's tax agency, the *Direccion General Impositiva* (General Tax Directorate or DGI in its Spanish initials), has traditionally been burdened with almost the entire spectrum of maladies that can conceivably afflict a public bureaucracy. First, it has suffered from poor or inadequate inputs, partly accounting for its high inefficiency.[1] It has historically been staffed with poorly trained personnel and burdened by protective labor regulations that make exceedingly difficult the firing of personnel known to be inept or corrupt.[2] Second, as is the case with most Argentine public institutions, the DGI has been captured by special interests. A good number of industries, via their political lobbying and influence, have traditionally been able to secure and retain tax exceptions, reductions, and privileges. Firms covered by the industrial promotion regime have also been able to maintain an inadequate legal apparatus in place that allows them to resort to outright evasion with impunity. To be sure, this proliferation of exceptions for particular regions, economic sectors, industries, and even firms has jeopardized horizontal tax equity, adding to society's perception of an unjust tax system. Another institutional failure plaguing the DGI has been blatant politicization of the personnel function (Sanchez 2011). Recruitment and remunerations have been based not on merit, but on political patronage. Finally, corruption has not eluded the DGI. In fact, it has been rampant. To this respect, current academic and former high-level DGI technocrat Oscar Oszlak affirms: "the DGI has a large professional staff, but it is an institution invaded by corruption, at all its levels, from the time of its creation" (interview). Moreover, the DGI's effectiveness has been hampered by deficiencies in other state institutions, including the legislature (which does not perform efficiently its supervisory role) and the judiciary (which lacks independence and is overburdened). The agency has had to manage with an inadequate legal framework. It has therefore lacked the legal teeth necessary to foster taxpayer compliance with the tax law. While many of the aforementioned illnesses characterize most tax agencies in Latin America, perhaps what sets the Argentine case apart is the frequency of political turnover at the top. This malaise, a reflection of the nation's chronic political instability, has plagued all Argentine public institutions, creating damaging shifts in public policy. Turnover here refers both to frequent changes in political administrations and in high-ranking government officials (including ministers), leading to high rotation rates in top managerial positions. Inevitably, political volatility has resulted in tax policy volatility. In turn, frequent change in tax laws and regulations, as in any other area of economic policy, shortens the time horizon of economic actor—and fosters noncompliance.

Another classic Argentine problem is the pervasive politicization of public institutions. The *Direccion General Impositiva* has been severely harmed by a lack of built-in institutional autonomy. For all the critical importance of the tax system and its effective administration in contributing to fiscal and macroeconomic stability, Argentine politicians have not shown the foresight to isolate this institution from political influence in order to improve its long-term performance.

On the Absence of Major Fiscal Reform during Alfonsin's Administration (1983–1989)

The onset of the Debt Crisis in the early 1980s meant that nontax sources of finance suddenly evaporated. Domestic borrowing became more and more difficult to secure, for the instability of the Argentine economy and precarious state of public finances meant that the government was forced to offer higher interest rates and shorter maturities to would-be debt-holders. Printing money carried higher costs because capital flight led to higher rates of inflation per given amount of money creation. In short, throughout the 1980s, the structural fiscal deficit became a practical day-to-day dilemma for the government to contend with. Because of a lack of reliable and stable sources of financing, the Argentine state could no longer play the role that it had traditionally assumed. This protracted process came to a head in the later half of the 1980s, a period famously conceptualized by economist Ricardo Carciofi (1990) as the "dismantling of the fiscal pact." By 1987, the fiscal deficit was a staggering 7.3 percent of GDP, even though total spending on public payrolls, public investment, and pensions was much lower than had traditionally been the case (Gerchunoff and Llach 1998).

Embroiled in such an inauspicious fiscal climate Juan Sorrouille, Raul Alfonsin's minister of the economy, was to explain publicly the nature of the titanic challenge facing the country:

> The existing multiple roles of the state, which have evolved in the past half century as a result of a social consensus, can no longer be fulfilled with efficiency or retaken without consequences for economic stability...In order to advance towards renewed economic growth it is imperative to effect changes upon that crucial pillar of our national life: the state...The crisis of the old economic model is not resolved via the false dilemma of a bigger or smaller state, but via the construction of a new state. (Quoted in Gerchunoff and Llach 1998, 412)

The great importance and urgency of the task was all too obvious. Yet, no serious, concerted, long-term governmental attempt to reorder and streamline public finance (let alone "construct a new state") took place during the 1983–1989 democratic administration. Some scholars have argued that the Alfonsin government did not count with the political capital necessary to implement such a pathbreaking reform (Smith 1989). Others contend that he was the victim of Peronist obstructionism (Torre 1993). Whatever the case, what is clear is that the main blunder of Alfonsin's tenure in office was the downplaying of economic troubles, which the Radical president felt could be attended to with short run, ad hoc measures, rather than fundamental, sustained reforms. Throughout his term in office (1983–1989),

Alfonsin's attention and political capital was largely devoted to political rather than economic issues, which he personally despised. He was persuaded that, as his famous phrase read, "with democracy you eat, you get educated, and you get cured"—implying, among other things, that democratic governance was enough to guarantee economic success. Events would prove him tragically wrong. What is more, undertaking a profound transformation of public finances in order to achieve a sustainable fiscal equilibrium may indeed have been anathema to the Alfonsinista ideological line of the Radical party, as Radical economist Adolfo Canitrot (1994, 35) has observed:

> Alfonsin's ideas on state reform were directly related to his democratic creed. Alfonsin saw himself as a reformer when he restored the Supreme Court to its former dignity and independence or...when he proposed reform of the Constitution to introduce a parliamentary system...His initiatives all demonstrate that Alfonsin's reformist intentions were limited to political and institutional arenas. Alfonsin, his political entourage, and most of the Radical party lacked the ideology needed for the economic reform of the state.

When the Alfonsin administration was cornered by a worsening economic climate, there was only a half-hearted change in priorities, which came too late to be effective. There was also a strong constraint on economic reform: a powerful and purposefully obstructionist political opposition in the Peronist party, which controlled one chamber of the legislature (Mustapic and Goretti 1992). When the government's economic team attempted to pass urgent economic measures, Peronist leaders often aborted them either in the National Congress or on the streets (via their political control of labor unions), not least to undermine governability and hasten their return to power. The Peronist party knew time was on its side as Alfonsin's failed economic performance foreshadowed the Radical party's electoral ruin. The utter failure of the various (heterodox) stabilization programs adopted to quell inflation (Austral Plan, Primavera Plan) can be attributed to their technical incoherence, and above all, to the absence of solid political support. The sustainable solution to the inflation conundrum required rather draconian measures on both fiscal fronts—increasing public revenues and decreasing public spending. Permanent tax reform was necessarily a major part of the first half of the equation, for the prevailing Argentine tax effort was patently insufficient. A last-ditch effort to put public finances into some order took place in early 1988, but in line with past attempts the fiscal adjustment attempted was half-hearted and insufficient. Inflationary expectations grew in the second half of 1988, and by the second trimester of 1989 Argentina was experiencing hyperinflation.

Only in this overall context of economic instability and rising inflationary flames, largely caused by fiscal imbalance (and attendant money creation), can the urgent economic imperative to reform the tax system be understood. Tax collection had been declining throughout the 1980s both at the national and the provincial level, and the tax system relied ever more heavily on export taxes, which made public revenue highly procyclical. This diminishing revenue performance can be blamed on three primary factors: the continued proliferation of tax promotion regimes (incentives to provinces and economic sectors); the increasing prevalence of tax evasion, which became more difficult to detect in the context of a more complex tax system; and the lower real value of tax collection due to the Tanzi-Olivera inflation effect. A telling testament to the magnitude of the revenue crisis was the fact that the inflationary tax had averaged an astounding 40 percent of total revenues in the 1982–1989 period (Ahumada et al. 1993). The 1989 hyperinflationary experience, in addition to its devastating economic and psychological effects, represented the de facto disarticulation of the fiscal pact between state and society in Argentina (Carciofi 1990).

The Preconvertibility Period (1989–1991): "Muddling Through" in Tax Policy and Other Economic Matters

What installed Carlos Menem in office six months in advance of the constitutionally mandated date was a monumental crisis of governability. Hyperinflation ate away any remaining amount of "output legitimacy" the Radical government may have once enjoyed, forcing President Raul Alfonsin out of office early. The imperative to regain a measure of control over the economy in order to avoid the political fate of his predecessor did not escape Menem—by all accounts intent on seeking reelection. Regaining control over the levers of the economic boat required bringing the state's public finances under equilibrium. Carlos Menem, the leader of a populist party with a history of economic heterodoxy, faced a credibility gap vis-à-vis domestic and external economic agents—agents with economic (and thus political) veto power over the success of his administration. His populist electoral campaign promised to enact a *salariazo* (salary hike) and a "productive revolution" did little to win the confidence of markets. As Rodrik (1989) has shown, governments that face a credibility deficit have an incentive to engage in "policy overshooting." In Menem's case, this meant an extremely aggressive program of free-market policies and economic orthodoxy to overcome such reputation. The quest to develop a new reputation by demonstrating a new, irreversible commitment to economic orthodoxy was seen in the vigorous deregulation program, the speed-of-light privatization process, aggressive trade liberalization, and others. (Incidentally, this does not mean that Menem had necessarily undergone an ideological transformation and that he was therefore intellectually committed to a new economic model.[3]) Much the same logic applied in fiscal affairs. As in most policy areas, the antecedents in tax policy and tax administration were very poor.

Within the first twenty days in office, Congress passed two laws that Menem's entourage had previously negotiated with the Radical party as a condition for taking office six months before the constitutionally stipulated date: the Law of Reform of the State (law 23.696) and the Law of Economic Emergency (law 23.697). The first declared the entire national administration under a state of emergency; the second delegated legislative economic powers in the National Executive for a period of six months. It is the enactment of these omnibus laws, conceding the executive congressional prerogatives, that explains the overabundance of economic norms between 1989 and 1992: no less than one thousand laws, decrees, and resolutions were directly or indirectly related to the reform of the state. Of these, about five hundred corresponded to executive decree laws (Blutman 1999). Such a flood of normative changes could not help but be implemented in a highly disorderly and incoherent manner, as indeed happened.

It was clear that increasing the state's fiscal extractive capacity was essential in attempting to close the fiscal deficit. A very timely 1989 World Bank report on Argentina argued that the hyperinflationary explosion of that year had been a product of the chronic crisis afflicting the tax system, and laid out how the tax system should be restructured:

> The tax reform must have two main objectives. First, it must increase overall revenues to levels compatible with the resumption of investment and growth...Second, it should lead to a reduction of economic

inefficiencies and the drawbacks induced by the progressive loss of importance of modern taxes and the proliferation of tax handles...A tax reform compatible with growth would aim to increase the tax ratio by 3 to 4 percent of GDP...The second objective will pose the greatest challenge. Restoring high revenue elasticity and reducing economic distortions will imply not only additional taxation on sectors that are now shielded in one way or the other, but also the elimination of several specific taxes that are earmarked to funds catering to special interest groups. (World Bank 1990b, xii)

The specific policies the World Bank recommended in order to increase tax collection and economic efficiency were: reducing the total number of taxes; broadening tax bases; reducing tax rates; abolishing inefficient taxes; making the income tax, a national property tax, and a generalized VAT the three pillars of the tax system (i.e., half of national revenues); levying specific taxes on tobacco, alcohol, and energy products; and eliminating the earmarking of revenues (ibid., xiii). The basic soundness of these recommendations escaped no policymaker in Buenos Aires.

It is not surprising that a government elected into office in the midst of what was Argentina's greatest fiscal crisis in its history might want to undertake a comprehensive reform of the country's tax system with a view to enhancing overall revenues. Because the option of overhauling the taxation structure curried favor with the IMF and the World Bank, whose help was needed in overcoming the crisis, the economic and political case for undertaking this most difficult of economic reforms was very strong indeed. The devil, as usual, was in the details. That is to say, which taxes would be levied on whom and at what rates? After all, tax reform would face rather different levels of political opposition according to the general contours it took. Was direct or indirect taxation to take the brunt of the revenue-seeking reform? Should industry, agriculture, or services (or all three) carry higher tax burdens? Which activities and goods were to come under new, broader tax bases? But as important as all of these questions were, they turned out to be of secondary concern for DGI and Ministry of Economy decision-making technocrats. In the context of a state starved for revenues what mattered was to undertake tax changes and innovations that would rapidly yield the greatest amount of additional resources, regardless of the sectoral or household income distribution of the burden, or the efficiency implications of the new tax structure.

A high-level panel of experts composed of past director-generals of the DGI was appointed to study tax reform in August and September of 1989, as soon as Menem entered the *Casa Rosada* (presidential mansion). Led by Raul Cuello, the panel concluded that poor tax collection was partly the result of an inadequate division of labor within the bureaucracy. The responsibility of both collecting tax revenues and monitoring expenditures on the secretary of finance was counterproductive, because in practice the all-important task of tax collection was neglected, the Commission argued. The political process of imposing annual budget limits on the various cabinet ministries overshadowed all other priorities (Eaton 1998, 309). Thus, an organizational change was needed that would endow the department in charge of tax collection higher political status.

Following the Commission's advice, Menem elevated the Subsecretariat of Public Revenues to Secretariat status. Now Raul Cuello, the chosen secretary of public revenues, would be directly accountable to president. This move, which caused the resignation of Finance Secretary Rodolfo Frigeri and a concomitant political crisis within the cabinet, signaled that Menem had a genuine interest in improving tax administration and in having direct authority over the Federal Tax Bureau. It proved that the president was ready to pay a significant political cost for the cause of added revenues (*Pagina 12*, October 27, 1989). In that spirit, Menem picked individuals publicly committed to fiercely attacking the evasion cancer. He appointed Ricardo Cossio, a lawyer known to favor limited legal protection for taxpayers suspected of evasion, as head of the DGI. Because the chief of the DGI is the only official empowered to interpret tax laws through bureaucratic resolutions, his personal views have a sizable impact on how the DGI and its agents operate in practice. As in other issue areas, the president was willing to sacrifice legality for the sake of efficacy and so he personally filled the top ranks of the DGI with people philosophically inclined to this modus operandi.[4] It must be noted that the organizational change that upgraded the status of the head of tax collection in the government's hierarchy was laudable, but this did not address the problem of the agency's politicization—within the DGI and between it and the executive. The resulting quandary was all too apparent: if the president's commitment to tax collection or antievasion efforts should ever waver (or if he unilaterally decided to change the tax tzar), that could well be enough to fatally undermine the DGI's efficacy and operating results.

To transform the tax policy proposals outlined by the expert commission into pieces of legislation, the Menem executive then faced the strategic choice of either pursuing statute changes in the legislature or issuing *Decretos de Necesidad y Urgencia* (Necessary and Urgent Decrees) (Eaton 2002). Because of pressing fiscal urgencies, the president and the economic team chose the latter, judging that the administration could afford neither delays in implementation nor the watering down of tax initiatives concomitant to the process of legislative deliberation (Sabaini, interview). Most tax policy innovations were made by decree. (In fact, the largest number of decrees issued by Menem in his first term pertained to taxation policy.) And yet, a conscious political decision was made that the most important tax policy measures, such as the broadening of the VAT base, would be passed by statute rather than by decree, as this would make the reversal of tax policy changes more difficult.

Economy minister Nestor Rapanelli was personally convinced of the imperative need to tackle evasion if the Menem administration wanted to avoid the fate of Alfonsin. Rapanelli named former DGI director Raul Cuello as secretary for public revenues and Ricardo Cossio as head of the unwieldy *Direccion General Impositiva*.

Secretary Cuello had a clear directive from his superiors: to urgently increase tax revenues by any and all necessary means. In January 1990, he announced that the VAT base would be generalized to include all products, levied at the prevailing 13 percent rate (only books, medicine, milk, and newspapers would remain exempt). According to official documents the original idea was that "with a uniform rate of 13% the regressive bias [of the VAT] is attenuated due to its relatively low level" (Ministerio de Economia 1990). Maintaining such a low level would keep a lid on inflationary pressures and thus preclude the most regressive of taxes: the inflationary tax. Yet, pressing fiscal urgencies forced economic authorities to yield to the IMF viewpoint and raise the rate to 15.6 percent. This very announcement signified a breakthrough of major proportions in tax policy intentions as only a few months before the extension of the VAT had been the subject of intense debate and disagreement among tax experts, the business sector, and even officials within the Economics Ministry. High-ranking officials of the IMF had taken part in the elaboration of this proposal. In particular, it was the opinion and intellectual capital of renowned fiscal economist Vito Tanzi (who headed the IMF's Fiscal Affairs Dept) that seemed to be the factor tilting the balance in favor of the VAT's generalization (Sabaini, interview). With this measure the DGI expected to collect an additional $2,000 million annually; the VAT would now raise about 6 percent of GDP in revenues rather than 2.5

percent (*La Prensa*, January 6, 1990). This broadening of the VAT base would be one of the most significant tax policy changes of the 1990s, and by far the most important from the point of view of revenue collection.

The next important step in the multifaceted strategy to prop up revenues was the promulgation of a law that would drastically increase the penalties for evasion: the *Ley Penal Tributaria* (Penal Tax Law). During Congressional debates Senator Eduardo Menem took the leading role in summoning support for the law on the practical grounds that if that state passively accepted evasion as a fact of life, it would end up strapped for cash. The Radical party gave its support to the measure on grounds that it was "ethical and solidarity-minded" insofar as it aimed to improve horizontal equity. Ironically, the measure met reservations on the part of some Peronist deputies and senators, while other lawmakers who supported the new Penal Law warned, reasonably enough, that this would not be a sufficient tool to combat evasion successfully: it had to be accompanied by a more efficient tax administration by the DGI. Notwithstanding these valid criticisms, the law was approved.

The third pillar of Cuello's strategy in propping up revenues was the promulgation of Presidential decree 435 in March 1990, which stripped industrial promotion regimes during the following six months. Such provincial promotion schemes entailed a cost of no less than $1,200 million a year for the National Treasury! Predictably, upon knowledge of the imminence of this decree, a coalition of affected companies placed direct pressure on President Menem and managed to elaborate a watered-down version copy of the measure, which was circulated around. In response, Cuello threatened to resign if the original version of the decree was not enacted, and Menem was forced to back his taxation tzar. Menem's unyielding attitude toward powerful lobbying groups in taxation matters attests to the fact that, at that time, stabilizing the economy and gaining a measure of governability came second to none in his ranking of priorities. The decree's promulgation allowed the administration to exclude two thousand firms from tax benefits derived from provincial promotion schemes (Santoro 1996, 77).

The question arises as to why the business community—which was being loaded with a heavier tax burden and was traditionally a political player with veto power—did not pose a more significant opposition to tax reform (Acuna 1998). Although the new tax scheme was highly regressive, it could not help but affect business interests, as the idea was to increase the total tax level in such a way as to make the alleged new fiscal solvency of the state credible vis-à-vis international investors. The aggressive elimination of exemptions and the elimination of promotional regimes certainly hurt firms that had hitherto enjoyed tax privileges. The answer is twofold. First, the business sector had been purposely brought aboard the new governing socioeconomic coalition; indeed, this was at first done explicitly with the appointment of Nestor Rapanelli (the head of Argentina's largest agro-export conglomerate) as minister of finance, signaling that business interests were being prioritized. Second, the new economic program was being implemented as an indivisible "take-it-or-leave-it" package. Because business enthusiastically approved of the general policy orientation of the new government, and the package of measures was presented as a coherent whole, its ability to pick and choose among specific measures was limited—particularly in the context of an economic crisis of such magnitude. The hyperinflationary experience had been similarly traumatic and economically costly for Argentine entrepreneurs of all sectors of the economy. Thus, they were more than ready to pay the price (i.e., higher taxes) of a program that promised to cast the economic past aside and set the foundations of better economic times. Alfonsin's economically disastrous tenure had the effect of modifying the priorities and policy preferences of business (Schvarzer 1990). Government initiatives geared toward improving horizontal equity— such as the initiative to fight evasion among small- and medium-size enterprises, in informal commerce, and in the nation's interior (all sectors and areas where evasion was known to be more rampant)— did help in soothing large economic groups' opposition to the new tax policy designs.

The new administration was, not infrequently, also forced to accommodate business concerns in tax matters. The initial focus on inefficient taxes to shore up public finances, for instance, drew stiff resistance from large economic groups. This opposition—which had its reflection in disputes between the finance minister and other portfolios within Menem's cabinet—obliged the government to comply with business exigencies and derogate (or reduce) these temporary, inefficient taxes ahead of schedule. Menem's alliance with capitalist forces was not to be undermined under any circumstances, for it held the key to governability.

All in all, the 1989–1990 period was one where Finance Ministers Rapanelli and Gonzalez showed a weak handle over the ever-turbulent Argentine economy. They were not able to stabilize the economy, as recurrent bouts of mega-inflation continued to pose a serious, unresolved problem. In such an unstable macroeconomic context any gains in refashioning the tax system (enhancing simplification, efficiency, and extractive capacity) would be partial and temporary, and the consolidation of a new taxation structure would prove elusive. It can be said that the continuing economic instability of 1989–1991 gave the president more degrees of freedom in tax policy—much in line with the literature that posits that crisis junctures tend to produce an enhanced delegation of powers in the executive office.

Cavallo's Convertibility Plan: Macroeconomic Stability and the Revenue Boom (1991–1994)

The experience of hyperinflation (in February 1989 and again in December of 1989) had as one of its consequences a collective devaluation of politics (Cavarozzi 2000). Hyperinflation modified the priorities of society: the politico-economic calculus that interest groups and political parties had traditionally engaged in did not necessarily apply in the immediate post-1989 period. Social demands that did not contribute to economic stability were weakened or were altogether placated, thereby enhancing the government's freedom of maneuver in economic policy. Only by understanding these changed rules of the game in the state-society rapport can one understand why more resistance to the tax reforms did not materialize, particularly on the part of the business community. In a mega-inflationary context, stability came first and foremost for social and economic groups across the board; rent-seeking was a distant second.

Ever more besieged politically, it was the second bout of hyperinflation in early 1991 that put the nail in the (political) coffin for Minister Erman Gonzalez and he was forced to tender his resignation. President Menem proceeded to reshuffle his cabinet and put his hitherto minister of foreign affairs in charge of economics. Domingo Felipe Cavallo was a young, liberal economist with a doctorate from Harvard University, and founder of arguably the country's most prestigious think tank (the *Fundacion Mediterránea*). His previous experience in public service had been a brief stint as Central Bank president during the *Proceso* military regime (1976–1983), but he was known to have been preparing his entire professional life for the cherished post of minister of economics. Cavallo brought to government functions a good number of trusted technocrats from his own think tank, and other like-minded and trusted economists. Collectively they conformed a quite homogeneous group of neoliberal-oriented policymakers, thus assuring a greater degree of ideological cohesion and higher technical formation than had been true under ministers Rapanelli or Gonzalez—who came to office from outside the elite economists' circles.

In spite of important changes in tax policy and tax administration during the Rapanelli/Gonzalez period, there remained a titanic job to do in terms of streamlining the tax system and improving its still deficient extractive capacity. How Cavallo would pursue these objectives was uncertain. But there were widespread expectations that the tax policy innovations the new minister was going to push through would be philosophically in line with a study he had coordinated with a fellow economist at *Fundacion Mediterranea*. That 1989 study proposed a simple Value Added Tax (at a 10 percent rate) with a large base, and an income tax with a single rate (20 percent). Social security revenues would come from contributions by employees and employers alike, equivalent to 20 percent of salaries. The proposal included the derogation of distortive taxes with low revenue yields (such as capital gains tax, wealth tax, and stamp tax), as well the replacement of *ingresos brutos* (turnover tax) at the provincial level for another more efficient substitute. In fact, the study went further, as it proposed a drastic simplification of tax administration, basing the tax system upon approximately half-dozen main taxes. The particularly innovative aspect was that banks were to be called upon to act as tax collection and control agent for certain taxes, a measure intended to lower evasion. Developments in the taxation area soon revealed that the ideas incubated at *Fundacion Mediterranea* would indeed broadly orient actual government policymaking. Upon taking office, Cavallo made public what his broad tax policy and tax administration priorities would be:

> In a few days we will modify the form in which the VAT is applied, in order to make it more transparent and to collect it in a more aggressive fashion. The VAT will be the basic pillar of [the tax system]...Because tax evasion is a form of corruption, there will be severe penalties on those who evade or try to evade taxes, which will be done via strict controls and clear rules of the game. (*El Cronista*, January 31, 1991)

He also declared his intention to lower the tax rates levied on some goods and services, "in ways that would make it practically impossible to evade," and labeled "destructive" those taxes levied on transport and services, and foreign trade (ibid.). That Cavallo had chosen to make these and other economic policy announcements before the Budget, Public Finance and Economy Commissions of the Chamber of Deputies was no coincidence. The finance minister was keenly aware that one of the main causes of the low efficacy of his predecessors in office—and more generally, one of the chief causes of Argentina's economic ungovernability—was the historical disdain the executive had shown toward the legislative branch (Corrales 1997).[5] For economic policies to be sustainable through time, these had to emanate from a carefully built consensus that included lawmakers. These ideas and principles also permeated the thinking of the team of economists Cavallo brought on board (sometimes called the "Cavallo boys"). As one close collaborator put it, "if we want to engender a serious strand of capitalism [in Argentina], we need to strengthen all of the institutions that constitute the democratic system of governance" (*El Cronista*, February 1, 1991). The political relationship with the Radical party was now considered nothing short of "very important," insofar as that would allow the government to showcase—particularly with international investors in mind—a new "institutional consensus." The stated goal was to curry favor with legislators of all parties and persuasions, abandon "government by decree" insofar as possible, and more generally, endow the legislature with enhanced prestige and respectability. Congress was an institution that had traditionally been slighted, ignored, or devalued by most Argentine executives—including the Alfonsin presidency (1983–1989) and not least, Menem's year-and-a-half-long administration. Cavallo maintained that the laws approved by Congress would conform to "the political pillars" of his program, under the premise that "it would not be tactical political accords driving economic decisions, but the overall climate of cooperation that would create consensus" (ibid.). The task of managing such intricate and delicate issues as the relationship with the provinces, the labor unions, and the business community fell upon the newly created Sub-secretariat of Institutional Relations headed by Cavallo's right-hand man Guillermo Seita, with the idea that corporatist forms of governance would be substituted by the rational pursuit of the general objectives of the economic model to be consolidated. Within this novel approach to policymaking, Cavallo wanted to, in his own words,

> reconstruct the fiscal contract that binds the state to society: the state [must forge this link] by complying with its constitutional functions

and duties, and the citizen [must forge this link] complying with his/her obligations [i.e., paying taxes], because only thereby are the citizens' rights to public goods and services and the guarantees provided by the state legitimate. (*El Cronista*, February 4, 1991)

In principle, the traumatic experience of four-digit annual inflation predisposed citizens toward the forging of a brand new fiscal contract. Argentine politicians had traditionally been able to disguise the true burden of taxation via the inflationary tax. Recourse to money creation was common whenever fiscal deficits arose. The hyperinflationary trauma brought this practice to a stop. As Mora y Araujo (1991) has documented, there was a shift in public attitudes toward public finance, with voters preferring explicit taxation over the implicit inflation tax (money creation) that was to blame for hyperinflation. Therefore, if the state played its role responsibly, Cavallo had a potentially receptive partner in the ambitious task of attempting to forge a new fiscal pact.

But medium- and long-term objectives aside, imminent fiscal fires needed fire-fighting. The Argentine Treasury found itself in a precarious temporary situation. In January, the Treasury had a number of financial obligations that had put it in the red. Overall, economic authorities calculated they needed to raise an added $200 million monthly. But this was not to be done in any way. By then it had become evident that the fiscal adjustment process could not continue to be based on the steady reduction of public expenditure, which had been carried out to levels incompatible with governmental efficiency. And although there was speculation that the government would resort to issuing money to cover owed salary increases, the Finance Ministry rejected the idea. There was now an officially stated commitment to break with the past and cover expenses with genuine resources—that is, taxes. There were other considerations in seeking to increase revenues. First, there were menacing inflation pressures. In an economy distorted by inflation and tax evasion, it was necessary to fill the fiscal gap in order to control the inflationary dragon. Moreover, there were other increasing spending pressures on the government, such as debt service payments and increases in pensions. In sum, immediate fiscal breathing space was needed, an effort that was to be spearheaded by the new secretary for public revenues, Carlos Tacchi. The government proposed a battery of tax increases, comprising what Tacchi called a "shock of distortive taxes" intended to yield an additional $200 million a month. The contemplated tax increases were: the VAT from 15.6 to 16 percent, the tax on currency trading from 0.1 to 0.6 percent, the tax on stocks from 1 to 2 percent, and taxes on bank debits (*impuesto al cheque*) from 0.3 to 1.2 percent. With the purpose of tackling tax evaders, Minister Cavallo announced that the VAT rate for unregistered taxpayers would rise to 25 percent, in efforts to induce businessmen operating in the hidden economy to be registered in the tax roll. The tax on combustibles was increased to 33 percent of the final price, while public service rates were augmented anywhere from 25 to 65 percent—purportedly in tandem with the added costs entailed by a more expensive dollar (*Ambito Financiero*, February 10, 1991). All these changes were to apply only for one year. This fiscal package sought to balance fiscal accounts until March 1992.

On his part, Tacchi (1994, 19), the technocrat behind the details, was to justify these measures as part of new working principles:

> the new worldview that I preach in fiscal matters has as its base the adhesion to reality as a starting point. What I call the "shock of distortive taxes" intends to give the economy breathing space in order to continue with the reform effort...This must be done, even if it momentarily increases some of the tax system's anomalies, in the search for indispensable revenue efficacy.

In other words, as long as there was a fiscal gap in government accounts, closing it overrode efficiency or any other type of considerations dear to *tributaristas* (tax economists). Notably, the regressive character of the emerging tax system was not a concern in the design of tax policy, as Tacchi himself was to admit: "I feel that we must prioritize the neutrality and economic efficiency of taxes and the goal redistribution is more effectively accomplished via spending" (ibid.). While the measures announced came under intense criticism from Argentine tax specialists, mainstream economists applauded them because the tax innovations gave the economy enough oxygen (in terms of revenue) to continue with the overall reform effort.

Clearly, the shock-therapy taxation ideas promulgated by the *Fundacion Mediterranea* think tank were being shelved, not only because of immediate revenue considerations, but more fundamentally because Carlos Tacchi was heretofore the mastermind behind specific tax policy proposals. Aldo Danone, the economist who headed the aforementioned tax reform study advocating a shock treatment, had not been named to any key posts within the area of public finances and Cavallo was no tax expert. Cavallo was thereupon much more careful in his statements about tax reform, for he had purposely delegated this area to a man of much wider knowledge and experience in taxation matters in the figure of Chicago-trained Carlos Tacchi. Would-be reformists often face the dilemma of tailoring the tax reform to the existing administrative capabilities or improving upon the existing administration. In post-1989 Argentina, policymakers could hardly afford to make a choice. Both tasks were crucial, and they were undertaken concurrently. However, given the fiscal urgencies that faced him, Tacchi put most emphasis on the former. More ambitious objectives were subordinated to the task of putting the burden of fiscal extraction on taxes that were relatively easy to administer. His medium- and long-term objective was to align tax policy and tax administration more closely, so as make revenue collection easier for a given level of administrative capacity.

The ambitious new fiscal package provided a crucial test case to examine Cavallo's stated intentions of building intra- and interparty political consensus and working more closely in tandem with the legislature—all in the spirit of concocting an economic model that was sustainable in time. Nothing less than the minister's novel political conduct of economic affairs (and its potential for success) would be tested. Preceding negotiations in Congress, economic authorities dealt directly with corporatist groups. The government was to face some resistance from the industrial sector, which was being asked to carry a large part of the burden, but the urgency of the fiscal situation, and the expectation that an economic recovery was around the corner, diluted industrialists' opposition. It was the agricultural sector that proved firmer in holding ground and government operatives were forced to make some concessions to this lobby group.

It was in the legislative arena where the fate and final contours of this wide-ranging tax reform would be decided. Cavallo's team had already cleared some of the ground by consulting extensively with both Peronist and Radical lawmakers. Yet, the reform proposal was to face substantial opposition among some lawmakers on grounds that the fiscal package was potentially recessionary and lacked reactivating economic measures. Leading the government's position in the Chamber of Deputies was Peronist Jorge Matzkin (La Pampa), who argued in favor of the tax hike to fellow deputies in the following terms: "Argentina can no longer have access to internal or external credit, and cannot resort to printing money, which is the main cause of inflation...This package is based on explicit taxes so that we can bury implicit taxes, the most perverse of which is inflation" (*La Nacion*, February 15, 1991). The opposition, led by the Radical Party (UCR), opposed the measures maintaining that they were regressive and that the economy was suffering from overadjustment. "The Carlos Menem government has had ten changes of clothes already, ten different economic plans, which means an economic adjustment package every 45 days" (ibid.), said Radical deputy Raul Baglini (Mendoza). Moreover, Radical deputies argued that the package represented a clear disincentive to invest, and the country needed investment urgently. In order to assure the two-thirds quorum required for the discussion of a legislative bill, the Peronists had to make a number of concessions to the main opposition party. This included the provision that future increases in the VAT rate would have to be discussed in Congress, eliminating the executive's faculty to augment them at will.

Many equity and efficiency objectives were sacrificed on the altar of fiscal adjustment. But while the purpose of the finance ministry was to eventually reduce the fiscal deficit from 8 to 2 percent of GDP, Cavallo warned that this was not to be done in any way or at any cost:

> Fiscal disequilibrium is at the heart of lack of macroeconomic stability, and without stability it is impossible to achieve growth, because in such a climate capital flows out rather than in. So the fiscal gap is the central problem. But there are other problems involving the avoidance of distortions. I believe that, in order to attack the fiscal deficit we cannot resort to measures that affect the competitiveness of Argentine productive activities vis-à-vis external competitors. Neither can we stop providing services that are essential in the preservation of Argentina's human capital, such as education or health. (*La Nacion*, February 3, 1991)

More impressive were the changes effected in tax administration. In order to revert the Federal Tax Bureau's countless institutional deficiencies, the government invested heavily in computer equipment, technology, and human capital. Following World Bank recommendations, an overhaul of design and functioning of the *Direccion General Impositiva* was effected. This Weberian bureaucratic restructuring included a drastic increase in personnel, more competitive pay, new hiring and professional advancement criteria, and the introduction of new technology systems, among other important changes. The number of employees was increased from 10,500 in 1989 to 16,000 in 1992 and 26,000 in 1994, while average wages rose from $1,100 to

$1,800 along with wage incentives associated with performance. A new wage scale introduced greater pay differentials. Personal computers rose from a meager 20 in 1989 to 1,164 in 1992. The DGI increased the taxpaying universe on which it had specific information. By 1991, the agency only controlled and had information on about 13,000 regular taxpayers, a regression from a decade earlier, when it controlled around 23,000 taxpayers. To ensure greater tax compliance, the number of staff monitoring and controlling taxpayers rose from 1,400 to 6,200 in 1992 and the number of inspections rose from 360 to 1,800. This development had an obvious effect on the detected number of tax offenders: the temporary closing down of businesses for tax infringement jumped from 751 in 1990 to 16,000 in 1993. While nominal collection costs logically increased dramatically, they decreased as a percentage of revenues collected, which is the more meaningful statistic: from 3.2 percent of total revenues in 1989 to 2.7 percent three years later (Sabaini 1993).

Other than changing tax policy and tax administration, Secretary Tacchi was convinced that improving tax collection required engendering a new "tax culture" in Argentina. To meet this challenge, he spearheaded an aggressive public campaign to inculcate the idea that evasion amounted to stealing from society. "*No deje que le roben*" (don't let yourself be robbed) said one message. But the media campaign focused more heavily on stressing the harshly punitive actions that evaders would face. For that reason, Tacchi's scheme was characterized by many experts as the "fear model of tax collection." With the aid of a new penal tax law approved in 1990, Tacchi concentrated the efforts of the DGI toward the wealthiest contributors—including industrialists. Tacchi's tenure was only moderately successful in changing attitudes toward taxation. Opinion polls conducted by Gallup Argentina showed that while in 1992 only 13 percent showed a predisposition to pay their taxes fully, by 1996 that figure had risen only to 22 percent (Llach 1997). At the end of the day, such a (moderate) change was based upon an increased "perception of risk" among taxpayers (the "stick model"), not upon an improved fiscal covenant between state and society. Is spite of the bountiful praise heaped on Carlos Tacchi at the time both in Argentina and abroad, the strategy proved short-sighted and unsustainable (Sanchez 2011).

In spite of the very significant tax reforms pushed by Secretary Cuello in streamlining the tax system, making it more efficient, improving horizontal equity, and enhancing extractive capacity, all of these tentative accomplishments ran the risk of irrelevance if macroeconomic instability returned. Mega-inflation destroys equity, because higher income strata are better equipped to avoid its devastating effects on real income than poorer segments of society; extractive capacity is also fatally undermined because of the Tanzi-Olivera effect as well lower concomitant GDP growth; finally, simplicity and efficiency are elusive goals in the context of economic instability, eliciting ad hoc, inefficient emergency taxes, and abundant tax creation to keep revenues up. Another hyperinflationary episode in late 1990 had again severely rattled the Argentine economy. Prices rose thirteen times for the year, real investment was collapsing, and economic activity remained stagnant. The government's credibility vis-à-vis the market was at an all-time low. Over twenty stabilization packages had failed in Argentina since 1980, most because of policy inconsistencies or lack of political support (Smith 1989). Without a predictable, stable economy little could be accomplished in taxation or any other economic area.

Clearly, given the context of low institutional credibility, economic authorities needed to put in place a stabilization program that was bolder and more credible than previous ones and, above all, one that had strong Congressional support. "As I have said on repeated occasions, we have to run the economy by laws, and not by decrees or resolutions or memos, as has been done before," wrote Cavallo (1993, 6) in his book *Volver a Crecer,* a guide to economic prosperity. The new finance minister took the biggest gamble of his career when he announced what has been rightly called "one of South America's most extreme financial stabilization programs ever": the Convertibility Law. The law established a fixed exchange rate, obliged the Central Bank to convert *australes* freely into dollars, and prohibited it from printing money to cover deficits unless new currency issues were backed by gold or foreign reserves. Convertibility guaranteed that which Cavallo and his collaborators thought to be an absolute political necessity, namely, *seguridad jurídica* (the rule of law). Any change in the value of the domestic currency or the printing of more money would, under the Convertibility Law, require a supermajority in Congress.

Convertibility met with quick and phenomenal success, with inflation plummeting from a 27 percent monthly rate in February 1991 to less than 1 percent a few months later. Not only did the currency board achieve unprecedented macroeconomic stability, but it also paved the way to impressive economic growth for the next four years. This was helped along by supply-side factors. In particular, a very favorable international economic context: a time of brisk worldwide growth and unbounded optimism where investors were eagerly looking for "emerging markets" in which to invest their surplus capital. Moreover, the Argentine government's extraordinarily ambitious and rapid reform efforts (though retrospectively more at the level of policies than institutions) turned the country into the darling of the IMF and Wall Street, with all its attendant benefits. By the time Cavallo took charge of the *Ministerio de Economia*, Argentina had made large strides in trade opening, privatizations, and other market-oriented reforms, which only deepened under the new liberal-minded minister. Yet, the Convertibility Law was no panacea: not only did it need attendant economic policies in order to work its magic and be sustainable in time, but it also carried costs. These costs came, first and foremost, in the form of relinquishing control over the exchange rate, which meant the state was denying itself the most important economic tool with which to absorb and respond to external shocks to the economy. Shocks would be fully borne out by the real economy—that is, they would show up as unmitigated increases in unemployment. Fixing the exchange rate also made Argentina vulnerable to currency overvaluation, which would affect the export-oriented sectors of the economy, and could contribute to imbalances in the current account of the balance of payments.[6] These associated economic (and social) problems were real, and had no first-best solutions, as time would demonstrate. But Cavallo calculated that this currency board, this form of self-binding, was the only way to recover Argentina's massive credibility deficit. Whatever criticisms were leveled against this radical measure at the time (and there were many), it could be countered that Argentina had, by virtue of the persistent mismanagement of the economy, drastically reduced the set of policy options available to it. Simply put, convertibility was a drastic measure in response to a drastic situation.

Moving toward a Supply-Side Worldview: Improving the "Argentine Cost"

The year 1992 saw important measures with respect to the income tax. The Cavallo-Tacchi team sought ways to prop up the financial pillars of the pensions system, which was in dire straits financially. Tacchi's team advanced what was the most innovative tax policy proposal of the decade: the *Impuesto sobre el Excedente Primario de las Empresas* (IEPE), a tax on the net surpluses of firms intended to replace both the traditional income tax on business and the employer's contributions to social security. Aside from resource generation, the measure sought to alter tax incentives so as to foster a better allocation of resources, while simplifying tax administration due to the close connection between the IEPE's base and that of the VAT. Again, this was another initiative in line with Tacchi's dictum of aligning tax policy and tax administration closer together. The expected revenues from the IEPE (at a rate of 18 percent) amounted to $8,000 annually. Moreover, the proposed tax was deemed by most tax experts as an excellent tool to combat inflation, because it permitted the crossing of important taxpayer information, and extended taxpayer control to areas where even the VAT could not reach. Because of its manifold virtues—solving the pensions financing hole, enhancing overall efficiency, and contributing to antievasion efforts in one stroke. Public Revenues tsar Carlos Tacchi sold the proposal by repeating an implausible mantra: "the IEPE is the tax that solves everything."

This was nothing more than a rhetorical device intended to enhance the reform's political appeal. But the proposal floundered. The Radical party opposed such a tax innovation on grounds that "it represented an additional extraction of resources to the private sector, at a time when there is fiscal balance in the public accounts, with fiscal surpluses big enough to renegotiate the external debt in good terms" (*La Nacion*, February 21, 1992). Radicals further opposed the creation of this tax because they deemed that the management and financing of the pensions system was a task to which the state could not renounce. On its part, the business community, led by the *Union Industrial Argentina* (industrial business lobby group), opposed the innovative IEPE on grounds that the actual instrumentation of the tax on the net surpluses of firms did not foster the reinvestment of profits, as the government purported (ibid.). Intensive horse-trading with *Justicialista* deputies led to a diluted bill, which included substantial modification both in terms of tax-deductible items and the distribution of resources generated by the IEPE. Predictably, disputes within the ruling party arose over the distribution of the revenues generated by the new tax, but in the end the stipulations governing the destiny of the tax intake were agreed to. The secretary of commerce tried to convince sector leaders that the new tax burden was fiscally neutral on productive activity, and moreover that the new tax did not have an antiexport, anti-investment bias (investments and stocks were tax deductible). Initial business sector opposition had been partly based on lack of information but it was ultimately unconvinced about the new tax's benefits (Sereno, interview).

In the end, Cavallo and Tacchi decided to postpone legislative deliberation of the IEPE proposal for lack of support among social forces, and wait for a more propitious time. Key government operatives agreed that they needed more time to persuade the recalcitrant business community and although President Menem had personally instructed Peronist deputies to back the reform, there was much skepticism among Peronist legislators about the measure's alleged virtues. A second powerful reason for postponement was that the Congressional modifications to the original bill had substantially diluted the revenue potential of the new tax. Cavallo's goal now was to reintroduce "a perfected" IEPE bill for treatment in Congress in no more than sixty days, concurrently with the pensions reform project. The central government was simply not ready to give up on an innovative and highly virtuous bill that promised to alleviate important problems (evasion, pensions financing) in one stroke. But the IEPE never got off the ground. This thorough governmental defeat was a sign that Cavallo's "pro-engagement" approach toward Congress was not delivering the promised fruits. As laudable as Cavallo's "consensual politics" philosophy was, it was confronted with a time-tested political reality: the honeymoon legislators and interest groups granted Menem was nearing the end by early 1991 (Palermo and Novaro 1996). Moreover, the advent of economic stability brought about by convertibility had as an inevitable consequence the return of "politics-as-usual," meaning that, in the absence of economic turmoil, political actors did no longer see the need to continue to be pliant to executive directives. The political game was again conceived as a zero-sum game. Unfortunately, the new governing approach brought on board by Cavallo was hampered by this inescapable political context. Legislators of all political persuasions posed, from here on, increased opposition to widening tax bases, restricting tax privileges, or streamlining the tax system, to name a few measures.

In April 1992, the government, using its ample majority in both houses of the legislature, pushed through Congress an increase in corporate income tax from 20 to 30 percent. In order to ensure the backing of Peronist senators (largely accountable to provincial governors), government operatives disposed that 16 percent of receipts from the tax would be destined to the provinces, with the following distribution: 10 percent would go to the *Fondo de Financiamiento de Programas Sociales* for Buenos Aires province, 2 percent would reinforce the *Aportes del Tesoro Nacional* (national treasury contributions) under the discretion of the Ministry of Interior, and 4 percent would be destined to all provinces (except Buenos Aires) according to the index of unsatisfied needs. But the bulk of the new tax (84 percent) would accrue to the nation.

In addition, measures were taken to combat evasion. Resorting to high-handed tactics, Tacchi sought to give the DGI greater power by endowing it with more legal prerogatives. The proposed piece of legislation, the *Ley de Abastecimientos*, allowed DGI inspectors to close businesses (commercial, industrial, agricultural, or service-type) without the previous intervention of the judicial branch. Such powers of closure were to be conferred upon regular DGI agents who would proceed as "administrative judges by virtue of the power delegated on them by the DGI director." No lawyer or public accountant credentials would be needed. The capacity of accused taxpayers to defend themselves was also restricted by suspending a number of legal rights, in effect leaving them unprotected from possible abuses or excesses on the part of the Federal Tax Bureau. Predictably, criticism of this rather authoritarian measure was intensive, and came from politicians and observers of all ideological persuasions. Radicals were adamant in their contention that it left "taxpayers defenseless" and that it constituted "a fragrant violation of the basic rules of legal process." Many analysts and observers openly talked of a new "DGI dictatorship," as the conservative daily *La Nacion* titled an editorial:

> No one negates that tax evasion is a malady which must be combated with maximum energy, and with systematic rigor. However, this fight cannot be undertaken via mechanisms that justify persecution-type actions against allegedly law-trespassing businessmen, and leave them without tools to defend themselves...The way towards the achievement of fiscal sufficiency does not lay in spectacular, or scandalous measures, or extraordinary authority vested upon the tax agency. (April 12, 1992)

Not only was the law contrary to the spirit of the National Constitution, but on a practical level, it clearly overlooked many of the main causes powering evasion in Argentina—namely, structural deficiencies in the workings of the DGI, a deficient application of the law, discontinuity in the administrative and technical criteria governing the functioning of the institution, abysmal efficiency of public expenditure, lack of fiscal democratic accountability, and so on. To be sure, addressing these embedded problems required a long-term and multifaceted strategy, but Tacchi, Cossio, and their collaborators were trapped in the *cortoplacismo* (short-termism) that the chronic fiscal deficiencies and the low extractive capacity of the tax system forced upon them. Convertibility brought unprecedented macroeconomic stability and thus added revenues, but it did not by itself control spending or the fiscal gap, unlike what some economists had naively predicted. In any case, notwithstanding the opposition of a sizable number of deputies and senators, the majority of the Peronist party was enough to have the bill approved. Again, it was another clear demonstration that the Cavallo-Tacchi couple was willing to travel treacherous (indeed, authoritarian) terrain in the desperate race to collect more revenues.

Tax collection at the federal level had by 1992 increased by more than 50 percent in real terms from its yearly average in 1988–1990. The boom in tax collection brought about by economic stability and concomitant economic growth meant that immediate revenue objectives were being increasingly met. Tax revenues had jumped from 12.5 percent of GDP in 1991 to 16.6 percent in 1992.

At the end of the day, however, Cavallo was compelled to engage in a high-wire act forced upon him by his own currency board: he had to balance the use of tax policy for fiscal adjustment purposes with the use of tax policy to soothe the impact of exchange-rate appreciation (a consequence of convertibility) on competitiveness and employment. Both objectives were paramount and neither could be explicitly ignored, lest the government was willing to pay a sizable economic and political cost. In a real sense, the *Ministerio de Economia* turned to a supply-side worldview, based on the principle that low tax burdens and efficient taxes (i.e., those that interfere the least with an optimal allocation of resources) generate greater economic dynamism and thus higher tax revenues.[7] Cavallo's objective in the short run was not simply the removal of relative price distortions, but the active promotion of the tradable sectors to generate more foreign exchange and alleviate the yawning trade deficit—itself a consequence of the currency board and the attendant overvaluation of the peso vis-à-vis third currencies. In short, the minister was understandably concerned about the detrimental effects of convertibility on competitiveness. Moreover, there was a widespread recognition among government and independent economists alike that the prevailing tax system displayed a significant antiexport bias. Normative economics called for the correction of such a bias.

The official presentation of this new thinking on the part of economic authorities came in October 1992, signifying an important inflexion point in tax policy. Before an audience of one thousand businessmen in the Teatro Cervantes, Cavallo advanced his idea to create a *Consejo Nacional Economico para la Produccion, la Inversion y el Crecimiento*, with the objective of fostering investment and exports, which were being damaged by the peso's overvaluation (*Clarin*, October 8, 1992). In his speech, Cavallo called for the simplification and rationalization of national taxes, and for the tax system to be primarily based on four taxes—VAT, income tax, consumption taxes, and taxes on trade. A concomitant reform was the gradual reduction or elimination of a number of taxes that brought relatively little to state coffers and were highly distortive—including the stamp tax, the taxes on portfolio investments, and the energy taxes.[8] The reformed also reduced taxes on salaries to about half the current levels (from 34 to 17 percent), beginning with export-oriented firms. Provincial taxes were also modified (via an accord with the provinces), eliminating the distortive *ingresos brutos* (turnover taxes) and taxes on gas and energy. This amalgam of reductions and eliminations, to be implemented over a three-year period, entailed a sacrifice to state coffers of the order of 1,200 million pesos annually, a considerable amount.

But the most important measure announced was the advent of so-called fiscal devaluations—that is, tax rate reductions or outright tax eliminations ameliorating the *effective* exchange rate facing Argentine exporters. Other nontax measures aimed at improving the "Argentine cost" of doing business included social security reform, a battery of proinvestment policies (including industrial promotion regimes tied to actual performance), deregulation measures affecting both internal and external commerce, and measures that facilitated credit for small and medium enterprises, among others. A call was made for business and the labor unions to work hard to "reach agreements that would increase productivity." Meanwhile, the newly created National Economic Council, presided by Cavallo, aspired to be an institutional avenue to hammer agreements between the economic authorities and the business community, so as to channel demands coming from different economic sectors and give a "rational response to those that are legitimate."

The minister's announcements met with enthusiastic support from virtually all business sectors. "With this new rhetoric Cavallo is refocusing priorities and is really placing production at the center of his economic program. This is truly positive for the Argentine economy," declared the head of the *Union Argentina de Industria* (*Clarin*, October 8, 1992). These measures were something of a conceptual breakthrough with the economic policy pursued up to that point—a modification of priorities only possible because the relatively more buoyant fiscal situation allowed for more breathing space in the setting of priorities. Yet, these measures were not simply technical in character. The initiative also had a strong political component. Indeed, its timing was not coincidental, for the government was facing a strong and growing chorus of critics about the pernicious side effects of the new economic model, both from within and outside of the *menemista* coalition. The salary claims by the pensioners and public educators, the steady rise in poverty, building pressures from labor unions about creeping unemployment rates, and the real prospect that the agro-industry (hitherto a supporter of the new economic model) could join the opposition collectively posed a potentially destabilizing political scenario. Consequently, Menem's economic team reckoned, there was an imperative need to leave the trenches and take the political offensive.

Important changes in day-to-day tax administration practice were also taking place, a consequence of the powers that had been granted to the Federal Tax Bureau. The year 1992 saw a dramatic increase in the repressive actions of the DGI. The number of *causas penales* (tax lawsuits) totaled upward of 1,050, which, due to the slow justice system, waited to be processed. Another way to measure the DGI's hyperactivity was the number of businesses forcibly closed during 1992: around 18,000—representing close to a 100 percent increase with respect to 1991 (*Clarin*, January 8, 1993). However, only three of these closures pertained to businesses of big tax contributors, reflecting a government bias in favor of this important segment of taxpayers (which was known to DGI operatives to evade just as much as the average small merchant).

Leading signs of stagnant tax revenues were present by late 1992 and early 1993, due to lower sales (meaning lower VAT receipts), the fact that the earning capacity of firms had reached its peak, and the increase of the informal economy. The *Ministerio de Economia* worried that the obligations assumed with the IMF and those derived from the debt-reduction Brady Plan ran the risk of not being met. While the government had expected to collect 2,500 million pesos a month on the VAT, January had only yielded 1,500 million. Cavallo again took to the task of designing a plan to augment tax collection

(*Ámbito Financiero*, January 19, 1993). One option was to increase the VAT by four points and share the increase with the provinces while eliminating the turnover tax (provinces' greatest single own-revenue source). But this was rejected by Carlos Tacchi on grounds that increased evasion would wipe off much of the theoretical increase in revenues. The other option entertained was to create a new tax on final sales, similar to the U.S. sales tax.

The first step taken was to aggressively step up the fight against evasion in ways that would yield short-term revenue results. "Lately, we let down in our anti-evasion efforts and many taxpayers have summoned the courage to evade again," conceded Cavallo's second in command, Carlos Sanchez (ibid.). The antievasion campaign began with the publication and dissemination in the media of names of businessmen charged with tax evasion. The strategy focused only on social security tax evasion. But DGI officials strengthened efforts to cross information between VAT, the income tax, and the payroll tax, so that detection of evasion of any of the three would lead to increased revenues in all three. Lawsuits were fostered via the creation of a central P.O. box so that particulars could come forward with names of alleged evaders—whether companies or individuals. Further, there was increased emphasis on controlling taxpayers via computerized information, increasing the number of taxpayers on which the DGI had financial information from 70,000 in 1990 to about 300,000 by July 1993. In addition, the DGI strengthened the capabilities of DGI inspectors, translating to each province a small version of The Untouchables, a specialized unit of tax inspectors endowed with superpowers to pursue large taxpayers.

In May 1993, economic authorities issued a moratorium for general tax and social security debts, which could now be paid under a standard payment regime that facilitated their payment (up to thirty monthly quotas). The objective, as clearly stated by Carlos Tacchi himself, was to "obtain a new revenue floor, particularly in social security taxes." In an attempt to palliate the moral hazard dilemma that recurrent moratoriums inevitably create, Cavallo made strenuous efforts to inform taxpayers that the government was making payment timetables shorter (at the start of convertibility, it had been sixty months) and that the tax moratorium was a "measure that would soon disappear" (*El Cronista*, May 4, 1993). Of course, such statements of intention enjoyed very low levels of credibility among Argentine citizens. Argentina's fiscal history—full of tax moratorium episodes—underpinned such skepticism. In fact, only in the most recent three years no less than four such schemes had been instrumented—whether via facilitation payment plans, tax evasion amnesty laws, postponements, and so on (decrees 1299 in 1989, 1646 and 1809 in 1990, 2920 and 2413 in 1991). Each of these was officially presented as one-off measures; each time authorities assured taxpayers that from then onward a more rigorous monitoring of outlaws and application of disciplining penalties would follow.

By mid-1993, the revenue slump was on the way to being overcome. In no small part, this was a result of the ingenious measures of Carlos Tacchi to incorporate workers in the black market into the tax system. The news was vitally important for Cavallo's strategy to eliminate some distortive taxes because the change of the tide in tax collection made the implementation of these (revenue-reducing) policy goals more fiscally feasible. It was important not least because the economic team contemplated other revenue-reducing tax reforms to be incorporated in the 1994 budget: reduction or elimination of the luxury tax on specific items, the modification of the VAT on the agricultural sector, and a subsidy of 15 percent on sales of capital goods made locally, among others.

The "Tax Revolution" Tide Waning

"We want to continue the trend we have followed since the beginning of the Menem administration: expand tax bases, define them better, restrict evasion and lower tax rates. The aim is for every Argentine to pay less in taxes" (*La Prensa,* February 8, 1994). That is how minister Cavallo justified the extension to financial assets of the controversial *impuesto a la riqueza* (luxury tax). The measure applied to any individual or firm worth over 100,000 pesos and was levied on stocks, titles, and long-term deposits. Evasion was foreclosed because banks and firms would act as retention agents, surely something Tacchi and his team had taken into consideration. Many analysts interpreted this announcement as a desperate measure on the part of the government to close the fiscal gap in light of the lack of remaining state assets to sell. Criticisms centered on the idea that this constituted double taxation as many firms were already being charged with the tax on portfolio stocks. Another line of criticism held that the measure constituted a rise in overall tax pressure that could well slow down the economy. A third line of critics worried that this could affect Argentina's financial markets and that it was dangerous to levy a tax on investment instruments at a time when the country needed capital inflows to cover its trade deficit. Independent economists generally agreed, however, that the rate was too low to have much of an effect in financial markets. The extension of the so-called tax on riches could be justified on horizontal equity grounds, as financial activities were now no longer favored vis-à-vis productive activities as regards their tax treatment.

Simmering tensions between Cavallo and the DGI became public when the tax agency filed a lawsuit against the car companies Sevel and Opalsen. The minister maintained that the DGI lawsuit contained a number of errors while openly defending the purported evaders and criticizing the DGI, which fell under his command. The high-handed fashion in which the tax bureau proceeded in its persecution of potential evaders was causing uneasiness among key government figures, including the president. A number of powerful firms were exerting direct lobbying on key government figures to change its modus operandi. These firms were growing increasingly hostile to the DGI and were, moreover, being impacted by the negative publicity (Santoro 1996; Sereno, interview).[9] With the benefit of hindsight, it can be said that this episode signified a turning-point in antievasion efforts. That the DGI was being openly unauthorized clearly showed that the agency had not gained as much political independence as advertised. Clearly, political considerations were trumping the imperative need to uphold revenue efforts.

In September of 1994, Tacchi and Cossio were able to push through Congress a law that allowed the DGI to undertake the preventive closure of businesses (small and big) as a way to hurry along tax collection in times of fiscal shortages. To be sure, these closures had to be the result of proven infractions.[10] However, by tightly constraining the right of the accused to seek legal defense, the law was severely criticized on constitutional grounds, and was even labeled "totalitarian." The sanction by Congress constituted the de facto maintenance of a previous law (20.680 or *Ley de Abastecimientos*) to the same effect (*Clarin*, September 30, 1994).

Although not readily discernible to all, the move to restrict the DGI's freedom of maneuver signaled a lessened political commitment to fight evasion. It was a harbinger of things to come with respect to the future of tax administration in Argentina. The antievasion tide was changing. To complicate matters for an already troubled and constrained DGI, 1994 saw a number of fiscal rebellions in the interior—including Santa Fe, Rioja, La Pampa, Cordoba, and Corrientes—in which DGI officials were physically attacked when trying to undertake tax inspections or business closures (*La Prensa*, September 20, 1994). The so-called *rastrillajes del fisco* (sudden and massive inspection efforts) on the rural areas of the country began in earnest in 1993 and were accentuated in 1994. These operations were specially geared to tackle VAT evasion, a tax with higher evasion levels in peripheral than in metropolitan provinces. In many cases, DGI inspectors (deridingly called *sabuesos*) had to make use of police forces in order to check the fiscal books of those inspected. In many provincial towns, human shields were formed and radios warned merchants of the imminent arrival of DGI operatives to allow them to close in advance. Some DGI regional offices even suffered material damage. These highly visible and recurrent events could not help but have political repercussions. In a surprise move, the Chamber of Deputies voted to derogate the *Ley de Abastecimientos*, which allowed the DGI officials room to maneuver in closing businesses; however, the Ministry of Economy operatives acted in time to make sure this legislative initiative was aborted in the Senate. For good or bad, these violent acts did influence the actual working methods of the DGI in the peripheral provinces: the agency no longer carried out closures. What these signs of fiscal rebellion showed was that, as many observers pointed at the time, almost four years onto Tacchi's tenure, his widely purported success in engendering a new "tax culture" among Argentines was more fiction than fact. Whatever reductions in evasion levels were achieved, the contribution of the DGI stemmed largely from wielding the stick rather than the carrot, from deterrence rather than persuasion based on an improved fiscal pact.

It is clear that revenue collection experimented sensational growth under the watch of the Tacchi-Cossio couple and their "Untochables" team of inspectors. This success in revenue collection came to be popularly known as the "Tacchi effect." While the revenue growth was due both to the new aggressive tax administration apparatus and to high economic growth, it is clear that the second effect was overwhelmingly the most powerful.[11] Furthermore, the reverse Tanzi-Olivera effect meant that the real value of tax intake automatically rose as an effect of the economic stability brought about by the convertibility scheme.

But notwithstanding undeniable success in increasing tax revenues, government policymakers obviated an all-important long-run *problematique*: the quality of the state-society fiscal pact. There is no evidence that the state's fiscal contract with society was improved in fundamental ways during this period. There was no palpable improvement in the quality of public services, whether in education, health, transportation, or virtually any other budget expenditure item. Moreover, from December 1989 onward the Ministry of Economics was not publishing information on National Treasury public expenditure, leaving citizens stranded as to where their taxes were going. If the government wanted to increase voluntary tax compliance and to enhance the moral force of its purported "war against evasion," it was imperative to inform the public about what spending items were being financed by their taxes and above all, to supply taxpayers with better and improved services through time. The only government measure undertaken with the potential impact to improve the state-society fiscal contract was the DGI's public commitment to battle evasion among all economic sectors and every income strata, in an effort to demonstrate equality before the law (i.e., horizontal equity). Yet, the special treatment some individuals and firms received undermined this mantra. The attempt to build a new tax culture via a propaganda campaign—showing evasion by any one citizen to be theft vis-à-vis society as a whole ("*no dejen que le roben*" said one slogan)—was laudable, although in hindsight, largely unsuccessful precisely because it was not part of a larger global project to enhance the quality of the fiscal contract.

These and other measures were not part of a conscious plan to improve the state-society fiscal pact, but simply part of the plan to rapidly raise revenue by ad hoc means. To do this, both the carrot and the stick were used, with a much heavier emphasis on the latter. It is a truism that improving the state-society fiscal contract, in all of its manifold dimensions, leads to improvements in the tax system's extractive capacity. Why then was it not part of the government's overall agenda? The answer has multiple (nonexclusive) interpretations. First, the history of Argentine public policymaking has been beset by *cortoplacismo* (short-termism). Menem's administration was no exception. The president inherited a chaotic economic scene, and entered a race to balance public accounts so as to defeat inflation. Once convertibility was in place, fiscal equilibrium became all-important. The relative inability to control ever-increasing national and provincial public expenditure put constant pressure on tax policy. In effect, as this chapter shows, tax policy and tax administration were managed on a month-by-month basis, and hardly ever with a time horizon longer than a year. Tax policy was, on the whole, reactive rather than proactive. Figures on tax collection and the advent of new or rising expenditure items were the main determinants of new tax measures. To be sure, building a contract with society requires that tax policy and tax administration be informed by an overarching agenda other than that of constantly searching for new sources of revenue. On the expenditure side (a second reason why there was no improvement in fiscal contract), one must note two country characteristics: Argentina's high level of decentralization and pervasive political clientelism. The nation only controls less than half of all spending. Argentina's federal constitution ensures that provincial legislatures allocate their expenditure in any way they please, independent of the wishes of Ministry of Economy technocrats. In particular, fiscal resources are used by governors largely as a way to exert political control and "buy" votes, particularly in peripheral regions, where public employment accounts for a disproportionate share of total expenditure. Therefore, even if the national executive sincerely intended to improve public services and thus the fiscal covenant with society provincial patronage spending would dilute its efforts.

As of mid-1994 it was tempting to think that, for all practical purposes, the Argentine fiscal deficit problem had been solved. Indeed, widespread journalistic commentary in the foreign press and even within Argentina spoke of the fiscal issue as a closed chapter; they put the onus on the government's need to focus on alleviating the employment quandary and more generally, on second-generation reforms. Yet, closer scrutiny revealed something very different: that the country's fiscal stance was, in truth, delicate. This was due to several reasons. First, the prominent role played by privatizations in closing the fiscal gap spelled trouble: cash proceeds had averaged over 1 percent of GPD annually over 1991–1993 (Rozenwurcel 1994). It is obvious that a finite source of finance has to be replaced by permanent sources in order for fiscal equilibrium to be sustainable. Second, trends in international financial markets signaled the advent of higher interest rates and lower levels of capital inflows in the near future for the entire Latin American region. Higher interest rates would mean higher interest payments, whereas lower foreign finance availability would translate into lower overall GDP growth and thus lower tax revenues. Expecting the external economic environment to be as favorable in the future as in the 1991–1993 period was unrealistic. On the expenditure front, there were serious challenges ahead for economic authorities. Strong fiscal expansionary pressures loomed on the horizon. First, age-old political dynamics (pork barrel spending) and economic difficulties at the provincial level meant provinces had not followed the federal government's actions on the fiscal front. Second, public investment had reached historically low levels and would need to be raised if a collapse in economic and social infrastructure was to be prevented (ibid.). Third, presidential elections in 1995 and legislative ones in 1997 were sure to generate uncontainable spending pressures. This amalgam of factors, depicting a fragile fiscal situation, inevitably affected future tax policy and tax administration. In order not to let fiscal disequilibria get out of hand (a key principle to uphold the currency board's credibility), future governments would inevitably need to create genuine public resources. Everything pointed to busy times ahead for the Ministry of Economics, the Secretariat of Public Revenues, and the *Direccion General Impositiva*. Argentine policymakers needed to make use of their complete reservoir of patience, creativity, and stamina for fiscal urgencies reoccured throughout the second half of the decade with distressing frequency.

Conclusion

The implementation of Cavallo's currency board in March 1991 (Convertibility Plan) signified an inflexion point for Argentine tax policy and tax administration. The strategy of the economic authorities thereafter was to keep elevating permanently the overall tax burden and to restructure the tax system. Such main priorities were pursued via the following measures: the increase in tax bases and the elimination of exemptions and preferential treatments; the decrease of nominal tax rates considered to be excessive (and thus fostering evasion); the focusing of the tax system on a few taxes of proven revenue effectiveness, in particular the VAT; and the overall simplification of the tax system via the elimination of minor and distortive taxes. To be sure, these tax policy changes did not follow any given order. They were not part of a coherent plan. Although Undersecretary of Public Revenues Carlos Tacchi had a clear idea of what tax system he wanted to bestow upon his successor, actual policy innovations and modifications were dictated by time-specific macroeconomic and fiscal circumstances. Tax policy and tax administration changes and innovations were, more often than not, reactive rather than proactive. Although economic growth was brisk during much of this period, tax stability proved elusive: spending urgencies, the need to stay within the bounds of IMF fiscal conditions, unexpected shocks slowing the inflow of revenues, or sudden bouts in evasion, all contributed to create a climate of permanent fiscal urgency. In that unstable context, the objective of revenue creation cast a long shadow over other important potential priorities of tax policy (efficiency, simplicity, equity, etc.). Economic authorities were constantly on the defensive in the race to keep revenues in line with new (and often unexpected) expenditure burdens.

Nevertheless, reformers were able to reshape the tax system in important ways toward greater overall simplification and in particular, endow the system with more extractive capacity in comparison with the past. By 1993, tax revenues as a share of GDP had reached 20 percent and stabilized around that level in subsequent years. The reverse Olivera-Tanzi effect and the amplification of tax bases allowed the government—if in an abrupt, disordered fashion—to restructure and endow the tax system with more rationality. One of Carlos Tacchi's guidelines was to align tax policy to tax administration. This meant centering the system on taxes that could be more easily administered and evasion could be more easily kept in check—given the manifold historical capability constraints plaguing Argentina's Federal Tax Bureau. Much headway was made in that regard.

Yet, the phenomenal success achieved in increasing tax pressure, based on indirect taxation as it was, came at price: a highly regressive tax system, whose burden was paid by the popular classes. This reflected the historical, structural difficulties found in taxing income directly, as well as the need to engineer an increase in tax revenues rapidly. It is not coincidental that the emphasis on the VAT reached dizzying heights: its rate was raised from 13 to 15.6 percent in November 1990, then to 16 percent in February 1991, then to 18 percent in March 1992, and finally to a sky-high 21 percent in 1995. Vertical equity was explicitly discarded by Argentine policymakers as an objective of tax policy, much in line with prevailing public finance orthodoxy, which held that redistribution efforts saw meaningful results only when done via (focused and efficient) public expenditure.

In spite of the epochal transformation of the economy and the advent of macroeconomic stability, Argentina's traditional "spend-and-tax" model was still at work, as tax policy continuously reacted to changes in spending patterns and obligations. Economic policy remained embedded in a populist political environment and a deeply flawed institutional setting. Economic stability and high growth proved short-lived. These factors boded ill for tax stability and tax reform consolidation during the latter half of the 1990s, as the next chapter will illustrate.

4

Argentine Tax Policy under Menem II and De La Rua (1995–2001): Politicization, Firefighting, and Decay

All Good Things Come to an End: Taxation after the Tequila Shock

While not exempt from difficult political and institutional legacies, Argentine reformers had been able to enjoy conditions of relative economic stability and growth since mid-1991. That would suddenly change with developments in one of the region's largest economies—what IMF chief Michel Candessus labeled "the first financial crisis of the twenty-first century." While economic globalization had clearly bestowed benefits upon Argentina during the first half of the 1990s (not least by way of large inflows of foreign investment), now that same phenomenon revealed its darker face. The Mexican financial crisis of December 20, 1994, produced contagion effects throughout Latin America (known as the Tequila effects), and officially ended investors' romance with emerging markets in the region. While Chile weathered the crisis rather well due to its flexible exchange rate and its record of superior management of the macroeconomy (and in particular its well-earned reputation for fiscal prudence), for most other regional neighbors the Mexican crisis carried much more serious reverberations. But few countries were more affected than Argentina: its fixed exchange rate seriously handicapped its ability to weather the crisis. Countries with flexible exchange rate regimes could make use of monetary policy to assuage the costs of the crisis on the real economy, an avenue foreclosed to Argentine authorities. The currency board confronted its major challenge to date as the state faced growing illiquidity and solvency problems because of massive capital flight and bank runs. For treasury coffers, the sudden increase in the interest on the foreign debt meant an additional $500 million in expenditures. In addition, tax revenues took a tumble because of the incipient recession, putting further pressure on public finances. As Cavallo put it, "after examining the effects of the crisis, particularly the tax intake in January and February, the impact upon credit, the run on deposits, and rising debt service, we have had to restructure our fiscal objectives" (*La Prensa*, March 15, 1995).

In response to this worsening international financial environment, Cavallo was convinced that fresh funds from the IMF were imperative in order to weather the storm in a politically sustainable way. Other potential avenues of capital were fresh credit from other international financial institutions and the issuing of a sovereign bond. These measures would presumably allow Argentina to attend to its menacing foreign debt problem and recuperate credibility vis-à-vis investors. The financial system had taken a hard tumble and Central Bank reserves could no longer be used up, as they were at dangerously low levels (Sabaini, interview). The Cavallo team's main objective was to secure a $2,000 million credit line from the IMF. Attached conditions demanded a more solvent short-term fiscal stance. In the rush to find new sources of finance, the tax system could not help but be affected. There was agreement on the idea that the "exit strategy" from the Mexican shock had to be based on the generation of genuine resources (*La Prensa*, March 11, 1995).

In response, a number of tax-exemption provisions on income taxes and the VAT were eliminated, serving the dual purpose of producing additional revenues and greater horizontal equity. The income tax base was also amplified. Second, in what was the pillar of the proposal, the VAT was increased by a substantial 3 percentage points (from 18 to 21 percent)—to be applicable for twelve months and not shared with the provinces. Moreover, the VAT base was amplified. Third, taxes on trade were augmented while previous reductions of payroll taxes were scaled back (*Ámbito Financiero*, March 1995). Finally, a luxury tax, levied on real estate and automobiles, as well as deposits, public bonds, and stocks, among other items, was created. The entire new tax package stood to generate an additional $3,500 million in revenues. Cavallo argued before members of Congress that without these measures the government was facing an expected deficit of $4,500 million in 1995 and that the proposed tax package along with fresh external credit would translate into a sizable fiscal surplus, in line with IMF conditions. From an economic viewpoint, the main challenge associated with this *impuestazo* (tax hike) was to face up to one very probable side effect: an increase in evasion. Tax evasion and elusion increased significantly, as companies and individuals resorted to this practice as an additional source of income in a context of lack of credit availability and increased obligations.

The decline in public revenues during the first four months of the year showed that, contrary to the government's assurances, lagging tax collection was not a circumstantial event, but the consequence of a reduction in economic activity and an increase in evasion. The rise in evasion was due to the fact that economic agents were suffering from the fallout of the financial crisis and the rupture in the chain of payments. The government hoped that the new VAT rate, (which would operate starting May 1995) would make up lost revenue ground. However, there was a real possibility that the VAT increase would fuel yet more evasion.

As part of the government's concerted efforts to prop up revenues, the *Direccion General Impositiva* (DGI) declared a new moratorium. It took to sending 3 million delinquent, noncompliant taxpayers letters "inviting" them to regularize their tax situation via a battery of payment facilitating measures. The language used was coercive, and it was not much of an invitation; rather, in line with Cossio-Tacchi working methods, it was a highly threatening device that urged taxpayers to pay up or face dire consequences. Again, this was further proof that any and every tool available to the economic team would be used if required by the fiscal circumstances. Moreover, the timing of this measure underscored once more that the DGI was much less autonomous from the executive branch than advertised. The moratorium met with resounding success, as the Treasury obtained an additional 3,100 million pesos (*La Prensa*, April 26, 1995).

The Closure of the Antievasion Campaign

In addition to mounting economic troubles, Minister Cavallo's hold on the economy was complicated by the increasing political adversity he was facing on various fronts. First, the minister was on a collision course with the political wing of the cabinet, including personal feuds with two political heavyweights, Interior Minister Carlos Corach and Secretary of the Presidency Eduardo Bauza. These feuds stemmed from Cavallo's public denunciations of allegations about institutionalized corruption within the government (in his words, "*mafias enquistadas en el poder*"), generating rising tension and acrimony among fellow ministers. Second, Cavallo was facing mounting political confrontation with Peronist deputies and senators, who were increasingly rejecting his economic policy bills, measures the minister deemed vital for the sustainability of the convertibility model. Third, there emerged opposition among Peronist governors, who felt cornered by Cavallo's continuous calls and actions for further provincial fiscal adjustment, which curtailed their ability to engage in patronage spending. Finally, the once solid Cavallo-Menem political tandem was increasingly being eroded by mounting personal clash about an array of issues. These clashes had become public for months and were generating unease among domestic and foreign economic agents, fueling speculation about Cavallo's departure from government, and generally eroding governability. Ultimately, the minister and the president had conflicting political projects and a distinct vision for the country—not to speak of attitudes toward corruption. Inexorably, all of these conflicts diminished Cavallo's once-formidable political clout and severely damaged the cause of economic and tax policy reform.

If there was any doubt about Cavallo's allegations of institutionalized corruption in Argentina reaching the highest pinnacles of power, the Macri case, which came to light in mid-1994, dispelled it. Its relevance lies in that it signified an inflexion point in the executive's support for the antievasion campaign. Francisco Macri is one of the most powerful entrepreneurs in Argentina, heading a holding of more than fifty companies. He was known to have been the first big businessman that supported Menem's reelection when the economic establishment as a whole opposed a second term. In early 1994 the DGI uncovered a scheme in which 15,000 vehicles had been imported without due payment of 8 percent in VAT and 3 percent in income taxes, for a total fiscal fraud amounting to around $36 million. The fraudulent scheme involved a complex web of employees from the customs office and numerous automobile agencies, with Macri at the heart of the operation. As soon as it became public, the president ordered Domingo Cavallo to lower the political profile of the case, and the minister duly complied with the request (Santoro 1996). In what constituted the first-ever disavowal of the actions of *Los Intocables*, Cavallo publicly reprimanded the procedures of Luis Maria Pena and the fiscal audit team he headed and claimed that this was not a case of contraband. The minister, who had a history of bitter private disputes with the headstrong and incorruptible Tacchi, seems to have calculated that siding with the DGI in this case would have put his job in peril. (This must be placed in context. It was only one more instance in a string of cases that were straining Cavallo's alliance with big business.) The Macri case opened a rift that was never bridged between the Tacchi-Cossio-Pena team on the one hand, and the Menem-Cavallo duo on the other. The publicity given to the embarrassing findings of *Los Intocables* were damaging to Menem's alliance with big business as well as to close political cronies and collaborators of the president (Sereno, interview). As soon as the perceived political costs entailed by the creation of this special unit were perceived by the executive to surpass its benefits—measured substantially in terms of the government's internal and external image—the campaign against corruption sank for lack of political support.

As the freedom of maneuver of the DGI and its special unit was curtailed, its bosses isolated politically, and its findings disavowed by Menem's cabinet with increasing regularity, it was only a matter of time before the main anticorruption tsars left the scene. In August 1995, Carlos Tacchi resigned from his post as secretary for public revenues, along with his subordinate Ricardo Cossio, director of the DGI. The symbolic and substantial significance of these resignations cannot be overstated. This event sounded the death knell of an era in tax policy and tax administration. The proximate cause of the resignations was the executive's unwillingness to follow Tacchi's desire to veto a law that granted exceptions in payroll taxes to wine and tobacco producers for a few months, a seemingly innocuous affair. Although the sums involved were rather paltry, for the secretary of public revenues this was a matter of principle.[1] But this small scuffle was only part of a larger war. Indeed, since the start of Menem's second tenure in office political forces had been pushing for a change in taxation and economic policy. The Tacchi and Cossio departures can be interpreted within the broader behind-the-scenes political conflict between the economic and the political wings of the Menem government. Menem's political ministers—led by the influential secretary of the presidency Eduardo Bauza—were coming to exert increasing clout over economic policy; in particular, they were effectively vetoing a number of Tacchi-Cossio initiatives that sought to extend tax bases onto more sectors of the economy and terminate their many tax privileges. In turn, this was ultimately a political tug-of-war for power, to define "who ruled over what" during Menem's second administration. Tacchi, a man known for his unwavering frankness and pristine credibility, declared upon his exit that he had been a "victim of a political offensive orchestrated by Eduardo Bauza, whose final objective was the downfall of Domingo Cavallo himself" (*Clarín*, August 3, 1995). Future developments proved him right. But Cavallo himself had not come to the rescue of his secretary this time—as he had done countless times before when Tacchi sought the minister's help in vetoing laws that perpetuated tax privileges, kept tax bases restricted, or withered the DGI's power in the antievasion campaign.

Cavallo opted to preserve his own permanence in government. President Menem, in a not-so-subtle sign that his political commitment to push for further tax reform and tackle evasion had wavered by now, declared "The government keeps on working normally, and no one, absolutely no one, is indispensable...it is not the first time that a member of the government resigns, least of all within the economic team" (*Clarín*, August 4, 1995). Markets became somewhat unsettled due to the possibility of Cavallo's departure. Menem sought to dispel such fears, as he had done a number of times during the past months: "Dr. Tacchi and Dr. Cossio left, that is all, but no one wants to remove Cavallo...I have no problem with Cavallo. The minister has the support of the President, and that of the entire cabinet; there is absolutely no one within the government that wants to throw Cavallo out" (ibid.). There was little doubt that these resignations came at high political cost to the government. First, they raised serious questions about the commitment, nature, and goals underlying the battle against evasion. Second, they confirmed suspicions about the excessive politicization of economic policy and Cavallo's diminishing decision-making authority within the cabinet. (In fact, there were widening incursions of the political wing of the cabinet into other economic areas, including industry and agriculture.) Third, they undermined the administration's political capital, insofar as Carlos Tacchi's reputation for probity, efficiency, and determination to fight evasion was beyond dispute. From a technical viewpoint, his departure signified an irreplaceable loss simply because Tacchi was among the country's foremost tax administration experts. Moreover, taxation was an area in which Cavallo lacked high technical competency.

The increasingly politicized nature of tax policy, accentuated after Tacchi's departure, was starkly revealed in a law approved by the Chamber of Deputies and personally engineered and piloted by Secretary of the Presidency Eduardo Bauza. This piece of legislation reformed the distribution of the income tax by giving provinces an additional percentage point of collected revenues for 1996 and four more percentage points for 1997, meaning the National Treasury was stripped of $72 million and $210 million, respectively, in each of those fiscal years. While this maneuver provoked Secretary Gutierrez's public disapproval and his avowed intention to derail the reform at the Senate stage, both Corach and Bauza assured governors and lawmakers that the executive would not veto the legislative initiative. The turf battles within the government concerning tax (and spending) policy were becoming more intense and increasingly public. Menem's political operatives had the upper hand in this struggle. The difference this time was that the president was not coming to the aid of his economy minister. It was yet another clear sign that Cavallo's clout had waned. With his second term now assured, Menem had now more room for political maneuver and felt less politically dependent on Cavallo.[2] Further, the increasing social costs of the convertibility program (in particular, the steady increase in the ranks of the unemployed) detracted from the minister's political capital, as an increasing chorus of critics as well as organized political opposition questioned his policies and lobbied for a change in overall economic orientation (although within the confines of convertibility). As a newspaper editorial put it: "Cavallo's word on the economy is no longer God-sent" (*La Nación*, November 18, 1995).

Meanwhile, evasion was becoming a problem of preconvertibility dimensions and posed an additional burden for economic authorities. By 1996, the levels of tax evasion had almost risen to the level of early 1991. The government was confronted with a basic economic "law": when economic growth falters, tax compliance falls more than proportionally, for many individuals and firms resort to outright evasion as a means of self-finance in a context of low profits and low credit availability. The DGI had also failed to fully update its methods of counteracting the new evasion techniques taxpayers constantly perfected to elude the government's enhanced administrative and technological capacities of the federal tax bureau—another time-honored "law" in the cat-and-mouse game between tax authorities and taxpayers.

A New Era for Convertibility (1996): Roque Fernandez's Chicago Team and Fiscal Ultraorthodoxy

The Menem-Cavallo political bifurcation intensified in late 1995 as a consequence of deeply rooted political differences as well as Cavallo's own presidential ambitions. Moreover, the convertibility model had seen better days. A poll conducted by the *Centro de Estudios Nueva Mayoria* showed that by March 1996 only 18.6 percent of Argentines had a positive opinion about economic policy, while 50.2 percent had a negative image; only two years earlier (March 1994), convertibility had enjoyed the approval of 47 percent of Argentines (*La Prensa*, March 17, 1996).

The changed economic landscape coupled with Cavallo's public attack on governmental corruption and personal clashes with the president proved his undoing. He was forced to tender his resignation. Cavallo's replacement, Roque Fernandez, brought to the upper echelons of the Finance Ministry a team of economists from the *Centro de Estudios Macroeconómicos* (CEMA), a reputed institute of economic studies of the highest academic caliber. Like the minister himself, many of these economists had pursued graduate training at the University of Chicago, a school of economic thought characterized by monetary orthodoxy and resolute faith in free markets. If there were ever Chicago boys piloting the Argentine economy, it was now. The technical credentials of academic luminaries such as Guillermo Calvo, Humberto Petrei, Carlos Rodriguez, or Carola Pessino, to name a few, were beyond any shadow of a doubt. To understand the nature of their economic program it is important to note that they espoused a *vision fiscalista* (fiscal-centered view) of the economy, in line with their Chicago worldview; that is, they believed strongly that, as Fernandez confided, "there is no worse impact on aggregate demand than that caused by macroeconomic uncertainty over the fiscal solvency of the state..., in a country with a history of hyperinflation we must assure the solvency of the state" (*La Nación*, September 1, 1996). For these technocrats, then, solving the fiscal problem was a sine qua non and a prerequisite for economic reactivation. What was in doubt was whether these academics, not entirely experienced in the rough art of Argentine politics, would be able to withstand political pressures to achieve their objectives, as Argentine journalist and intellectual Mariano Grondona perceptively noted:

> Only by dint of an enormous and draining effort had Cavallo's team been able to keep in check the unlimited thirst [for public spending] of the political wing of the government as well as the unrelenting pressure from corporatist groups. Will Fernandez and this group of professors that accompanies him be able to follow on those footsteps? Will they not be politically naïve and therefore prone to manipulation? Or will

they show a hand of iron behind the academic shyness? (*La Nación*, August 3, 1996)

These queries were entirely legitimate and of obvious relevance. There were many signs that economic policy would become much more politicized in a post-Cavallo world. When Menem was asked why he had chosen Roque Fernandez he claimed that his decision was simply based on the fact "that he was part of the existing economic team and had had a successful stint as head of the Central Bank," and that he was "the most adequate individual to continue with the economic model instrumented in 1989" (*La Nación*, August 6, 1996). What the president was not revealing publicly was that he had purposely chosen a more malleable and politically accountable minister of economy as part of a wider, deliberate strategy to secure a greater grip on power. In fact, Menem made sure that no member of his new cabinet had presidential ambitions, and that all were individuals of strong personal and political loyalty toward him. From here onward, no one would question the president's domains of power or his ownership of the economic model. With the constitutional impossibility of seeking a third term in office, Menem knew he risked being increasingly seen as a lame duck and, by all accounts, he wanted to retain control over his own succession in 1999.

Fernandez and his team faced a conundrum in the form of three main challenges: the growing fiscal deficit, the unending economic recession (by then eighteen months in the making), and the rising "social debt" vis-à-vis the unemployed and the pensioners. There were inevitable tradeoffs between these goals. For example, increasing taxes to reduce the deficit would risk deepening the recession, while potentially reactivating measures threatened to exacerbate the fiscal deficit. Tending to the unemployed and to pensioners also entailed fiscal costs. In short, economic authorities would have to perform a high-wire act in order to avoid major decision-making errors. Roque Fernandez, upon taking office, guaranteed the continuation of convertibility and pledged there would be no new tax hikes. Fully conscious that one of the biggest obstacles Cavallo had faced in managing the economy was a mediocre tax revenue performance, he assured that this issue would be primordial during his tenure and that he would pursue fiscal balance in public finances. Moreover, he criticized hyperactivity in tax policy: "it is not good that a country be constantly modifying its taxes" (*La Nación*, July 29, 1996). This was a statement of the obvious, but the new minister could not then visualize the extent to which his predecessors in the job had been peons of the instability of the Argentine economy, or the extent to which their economic measures had been reactive. In addition to a chronic fiscal deficit, the minister had to face political pressures from the political wing of the cabinet, which consisted of figures who in the absence of Cavallo felt even more empowered to voice and push their views on a range of economic issues. Menem himself declared: "We will not accept pressure [from the IMF], least of all pressure to augment rates in the tax area...If we raise taxes all we are going to achieve is greater tax evasion" (*La Nación*, August 7, 1996). This was now seemingly an area within the president's direct domain of responsibility and expertise.

Menem's newly acquired command over economic matters was manifested when the Ministry of Economy presented the president with three fiscal adjustment packages of different degrees of austerity in order for him to choose. All of the options included the increase in the price of combustibles, the generalization of the VAT, the elimination of subsidies, the reduction of reimbursements for exports, and the reduction of public salaries. What differentiated them was the magnitude of the changes. In the case of gasoil, for instance, the possibilities ranged from an increase of 6 percent to one of 36 percent. Menem chose the harshest economic medicine. The ideological tenet that economic reactivation required fiscal adjustment met with strong criticism from some of the country's foremost economists, including Daniel Artana, Jose Maria Fanelli, and Eduardo Curia, to name a few.[3] Many reputed economists considered that the new minister and his advisers were being more rigid and orthodox than the IMF itself (Fanelli, interview).

Roque Fernandez announced the new measures his team had settled on: to modify the income tax so as to reach sectors below the existing nontaxable minimum salary; to increase the price of gasoline by 13 percent and that of gas by 38 percent; to apply a 5 percent VAT rate to transportation and 10.5 percent to cable TV, publicity, private schools, show business, and medicine; to increase the retirement age for women from sixty to sixty-five years; and to eliminate or reduce export reimbursements, among others. This was the most drastic fiscal adjustment since Menem had assumed office in 1989. It raised well-founded questions about the adequacy of the adjustment in the midst of a recessionary economy. Fernandez reassured skeptics by asserting that these changes would not deepen the ongoing recession and that "the lack of resolve over public finances could have a greater effect on markets than these measures" (*La Nación*, Agosto 13, 1996). What was clear was that, by virtue of the strict economic orthodoxy that informed the new economic authorities, there was no place for (heterodox) supply-side policies, terminating the practices Cavallo had first put in place in 1992. In a sign of the newly politicized times, the president asked his economy minister to do away with three of his measures: the application of the VAT to private schools and books, and the rise in payroll taxes. Menem was effectively exercising direct veto power over economic policy, marking a sharp departure with the modus operandi during Cavallo's tenure.

The predictably strong reaction against the drastic adjustment from business and other corporatist groups forced Fernandez to drop the VAT extensions on education and public transportation before the formal introduction of the package in Congress. The executive had also asked that the increase in energy taxes not be shared with the provinces (as the law stipulated). This added $1,600 million to National Treasury coffers, which was to be directly channeled to the national pension system, whose precise deficit figure was a source of contention between the current and previous economy ministers. After substantial give-and-take between Ministry of Economy officials and both legislative chambers, Congress turned into law an increase in income taxes from 30 to 33 percent, a hike in the tax on gasoline by 0.10 pesos a liter and a new tax on natural gas. As to the reduction of public salaries, the Chamber of Deputies elevated the cutoff point to those employees earning over 1,500 monthly pesos, while the Senate elevated that to 1,800 for some regions of the Patagonia, and some departments in Salta, Jujuy, Catamarca, and Mendoza. In short, the lobby game produced a marked watering-down of the initial adjustment project, but the fiscal belt-tightening on course was still substantive.

A New Figure at the Tax Bureau: Carlos Silvani and His New Tax Policy Priorities

In November 1996, there was a changing of the guard at the DGI. The new tax tzar, Carlos Silvani, was part of the team of tax experts within the IMF's Fiscal Affairs Department headed by Italian Vito Tanzi. Silvani was someone with intimate first-hand knowledge of the workings of the DGI, not least because he had participated in many IMF missions to audit Argentina's fiscal accounts. The new chief of the DGI came to Buenos Aires with a strategic plan that, in his words, "would be justified in the medium and long term" (*La Nación*, November 7, 1996). His vision for the federal tax bureau included: augmenting the efficiency in the enforcement of unpaid taxes (*deuda morosa*); improving tax administration; and facilitating tax payment procedures. He pledged "to do a few things but do them efficiently, and without spectacular actions" (ibid.) in what amounted to a clear dismissal of the working ways of Tacchi's *Los Intocables*. In short, the aim was to build an environment in which the tax contributor was treated as a client, rather than a potential evader. It was the "carrot" approach to eliciting tax compliance. Silvani also pledged to simplify the tax system, give special attention to big taxpayers, and focus upon the largest debts owed the DGI. In Silvani's judgment there had been two negative factors affecting the taxation area in recent times: the greater weakness of the tax administration due to the reduction of personnel devoted to that task, and the political nonviability of tax simplification, notwithstanding social demands to make paying taxes a simpler and less costly exercise.

Silvani's team wanted to maintain tax policy unchanged for 1997, but start working on a tax reform plan to submit to Congress so that the changes to the tax code would be operative in 1998. The undersecretary of tax policy Guillermo Rodriguez proposed that the twin objectives of the reform would be the simplification of tax structure and the gradual reduction of the tax burden on labor "up until its elimination, whose natural replacement will be income tax" (ibid.). The rationale behind this was clear: unemployment, which stubbornly continued to creep up (standing at a staggering 17 percent), had become a political time-bomb of utmost importance (Pastor and Wise 1999). In fact, orders to improve the employment panorama came from the highest echelons of power. Other issues the reform tackled were tax administration and tax avoidance, the latter by eliminating loopholes in the tax code that allowed plenty of room for well-paid advisors to legally reduce tax burdens for their well-off clients. One of the chief weapons in Silvani's arsenal of measures against evasion was the *Ley de Clausuras* (Law of Closures), endowing the DGI with police powers to close commercial businesses or any other type of activity in the agricultural, industrial, or service sector that violated manufacturing and registration statutory norms.[4] It also punished customers who did not ask for tax payment receipts, a measure that was said to have worked in other latitudes. Yet, this law, unlike Cossio's *Ley De Abastecimientos*, allowed defendants to appeal for justice; it established sentences of anywhere from two to nine years of prison for evaders.[5] Congress approved this law in December 1996. Silvani's avowed intention was to follow the tax tracks of the "big fish" of the economy. It was not intended as a measure against the small merchant. The new tax tzar maintained that fighting VAT and income tax evasion would constitute the pillars of his tenure, and thus reincorporated some of the figures that had played an important role under Tacchi, including the chief of *Los Intocables*, Luis Maria Pena. In an unusual act, President Menem purposely made a public appearance with Silvani at the headquarters of the DGI, intended to show presidential support for the policies advanced by Silvani in his fight against evasion. It was the first time a president had publicly scheduled a meeting at the DGI. What it truly illustrated was that the government had lost credibility in its willingness to attack tax evasion.

Long-term goals aside, Silvani would be soon awakened to the fact that in Argentina policymakers need to be adept firefighters. A scandal involving tax evasion in the *Administracion General de Aduanas* (National Customs Office) again thrust into the public light the pervasive malaise of institutionalized corruption in Argentina. This massive, well-organized, contraband-type scheme involved mafias in various sectors that used an *aduana paralela* (parallel customs) that faked documentation and stamps, robbing the Treasury of hundreds of millions of pesos in tax evasion. It permitted the entry into the country of goods in transit destined for other markets, without paying VAT, income tax, or import tariffs. Obviously, such a well-functioning fraudulent machine had many accomplices within the state structure, including high-ranking government officials. Judging that such scandals were beginning to seriously tarnish his government and thus affect the already flagging economy, the president sought to fashion a new public image for his government:

> I will take personal charge of this crusade against remaining corruption enclaves... There are three problems that affect economic growth and conspire against the existence of our peoples: corruption, fraud and tax evasion... From the start of my [first] government we began a take-no-prisoners war against corruption, evasion and contraband. We began with public enterprises, veritable centers of corruption. We conquered a corrupt state system that no other government had been able to confront. (*La Nación*, October 9, 1996; my translation)

While this self-styled conversion to the anticorruption cause was devoid of any credibility, it signified a symbolically important inflexion point, as Menem had always publicly denied the presence of institutionalized, widespread corruption within his government. The president declared the intervention of the Aduana and its fusion with the DGI. It was reckoned that if all tax administration was in the hands of one institution rather than two, tax evasion could be better controlled.

For 1997 the Ministry of Economy predicted GDP growth of 5 percent and an unemployment rate two points below the prevailing 17.3 percent figure. In the tax arena, the objectives of the economic authorities, as announced by Fernandez, were the extension of the VAT and income tax to the greater part of hitherto exempted sectors of the economy, but to effect this generalization "at a lower rate." Such goals, laudable insofar as they increased horizontal equality and introduce a measure of social justice into the tax system, would only be possible insofar as Menem's technocrats were able to reactivate the economy (thus increasing tax collection). In the light of what had transpired in its first few months in office, there was understandable skepticism about the economic team's degree of political power and institutional autonomy. This was compounded by a politically malleable minister of the economy, who in response to such criticisms repeatedly defended the right of Argentine politicians to opine and intervene freely in the design of economic policy (something unthinkable under Cavallo). A standard public comment from Fernandez reads thus:

> There is a great level of political maturity in Argentina. It would be naïve to think that politicians do not have influence [in economic policy], and it is all right that they have it, because they have been elected by the people and carry the democratic responsibility of making wrong decisions... We [the economic team] cannot pretend that they [politicians] will come to always accept technical decisions. (*La Nación*, December 19, 1996; my translation)

In fact, the integral reform of the tax system was the main pillar (along with reforms in the labor code) around which an Extended Facilities accord with the International Monetary Fund revolved. The technical groups created to design the new tax reform were assisted by the IMF's Fiscal Affairs Department. This potential accord involved a number of structural reforms, had a duration of three years (up until the end of Menem's tenure), and substituted the stand-by agreement that Argentina had with the financial institution, set to expire in December 1997.

The goal was for income tax to have a place within the Argentine tax structure more akin to the one it has in OECD countries. The state was collecting around 6,000 million pesos in income taxes, or about 2 percent of GDP; the official intention was to situate it around 10 percent of GDP or at about 30,000 million pesos. This was criticized by some economists who argued that the most efficient tax structure was one centered upon the VAT, contradicting the official discourse. Changes to the income tax also aimed to reach a broader base of taxpayers. One of the arguments Fernandez, Pessino, Rodriguez, and other officials often made was that in countries such as the United States those with incomes over $1,000 a month were levied with this tax. Such views were clearly influenced by Vito Tanzi, who was an external advisor to Silvani (as well as his former boss). Tanzi lamented that the income tax in Argentina only collected 2.3 percent of GDP, "whereas the average for countries outside of the OECD is more than double, and for OECD countries it is six times that figure." He reckoned the income level at which the tax started to apply in Argentina was "too high" and this "provokes a significant erosion of its collection potential" (*La Nación*, August 15, 1997). Finally, economic authorities intended to use the income tax as a tool for vertical redistribution. Rodriguez considered that "this is a tax with plenty of redistributive potential that is not being used."

The official promise that taxes would not be altered in 1997 had everything to do with the fact that legislative elections were scheduled for October 1997. This was indeed a thinly veiled imposition Menem made on the economic wing of the cabinet. In fact, a stir was created when the Secretary for Economic Policy Carlos Rodriguez launched a public debate about the merits of applying a national-level real estate tax to substitute the existing luxury tax. The very mention of this idea caused strong opposition among governors, since that was a tax that belonged to provinces and they were understandably concerned about losing revenues. President Menem himself, who was again stepping onto the taxation domain with complete freedom, forcefully reprimanded the economic team: "tax legislation will not be modified. If there is to be a study about tax changes in the future it will be something that will be publicized once it is analyzed in depth" (*La Nación*, May 9, 1997). It was a stark reminder to his subordinates that in this second administration, economic policy had to get the approval of the president—and more broadly, the Peronist party at large.

The Year of the IMF-Inspired Tax Reform (1998)

In order to clear some of the political obstacles to the tax reform, the economic authorities began to sell their tax project in early 1998 as one that was redistributive in nature (i.e., it would improve the secondary incomes of the poor). Secretary Rodriguez, somewhat distorting reality, claimed that since the new economic team took office, it had wanted to engender "an equitable tax system, in which the poor pay less." This was meant to deflect criticism about the regressive effects of extending the VAT to hitherto exempted sectors of the economy. In truth, Roque Fernandez designed a reform that was revenue-neutral—contravening the preferences of Tanzi's IMF team, who argued that a revenue-increasing reform was needed to both cool the economy and secure the medium-term fiscal horizon in the face of international instability. Indeed, Roque Fernandez peddled it as a "popular tax reform," in reference to its alleged redistributionist characteristics. Predictably, the planned VAT generalization soon became less comprehensive than originally designed, as consultations with *Justicialista* lawmakers forced the exclusion from the tax base politically sensitive areas such as education and basic consumption items. While the extension of the VAT was correct from the viewpoint of orthodox tax doctrine (i.e., it would introduce horizontal equity and reduce evasion opportunities), many objected that it would inevitably raise domestic prices, including that of basic consumption products. Unlike many other arguments based on corporatist self-interest, this argument was substantive and important.

The economic authorities also denied that the tax package as a whole signified a rise in the overall tax burden shouldered by society, and labeled it as neutral. Menem was deeply concerned about the political repercussions of a rise in taxes upon a much debilitated government and Peronist party, which had been handed important electoral defeats in 1997 and faced a real political challenge in the increased popularity of both the FREPASO and Radical parties. Indeed, the post-1997 political context further contributed to the politicization of economic policy, and few economic issues (if any) were as politically sensitive and touched more citizens than taxes. In an outstanding exercise of political contortionism,

Menem publicly denied the existence of an imminent project to alter taxes:

> There is absolutely nothing [planned to extend the VAT to virtually all sectors of the economy], any project about taxes has to pass through the desk of the president, who is the one who must introduce it to Parliament...I am thinking about lowering taxes not raising them...[Any news about the extension of the VAT to almost all products] is a despicable maneuver by some media organizations. (*La Nación*, February 12, 1998)

Economic authorities intended to introduce a *monotributo*, an all-purpose tax to be paid by small commerce and industrial businesses with sales of less than 144,000 pesos a year, in replacement of VAT, income, and labor taxes. The measure was part of the attempt to build a new simplified tax structure and expand the universe of taxpayers. This would purportedly allow the DGI to incorporate into the legal economy hundreds of thousands of would-be taxpayers that operated in the informal economy.

In direct negotiations between Peronist lawmakers and Ministry of Economy officials, an accord was reached to apply a reduced 10.5 percent VAT rate to most goods of the basic family basket, while the nontaxable minimum at which the income tax applied was not be reduced, contravening the advice of the IMF on this matter. This obviously forced policymakers back to the fiscal drawing board, as they had expected to collect an additional $2,000 million with this measure. The gist of negotiations centered on how to fill the vacuum left by the virtual elimination of labor taxes, which would create a fiscal hole of anywhere from 2,600 to 4,500 million pesos a year.

The tax reform project had been sitting on the desk of the minister of economy since entering office in mid-1996, but it now acquired preeminent political relevance, second only to the 1999 elections. Its newfound critical importance lay in the fact that the economic dangers associated with its legislative rejection were increasingly palpable (as the IMF had warned), prompting Menem to take a personal, proactive role in the matter. The political opposition, smelling the sweet scent of upcoming electoral victory (in 1999), simply played an obstructionist game in the legislature. It thus opposed the tax reform as well. The argument used by Frepaso and Radical party lawmakers (and including party leaders "Chacho" Alvarez and Fernando de la Rua) was simply that the executive had to either spend less or make public expenditure more efficient, rather than reforming the tax structure. To be sure, this general, all-purpose critique did not address the dire economic contextual circumstances the country was facing. It was yet one more reminder of the lack of political maturity and responsibility of Argentina's entire political class. Their intransigent position finally drew the ire of the normally cold-blooded minister Fernandez who accused them of putting a political price on everything. In truth, of course, no Argentine politician was free of fault on such matters.

What were the merits of the tax proposal? After many years of regressive tax reforms and innovations mainly motivated by the revenue motif, the executive was coming forward with a revenue-neutral proposal that promised to introduce a measure of progressiveness. But its centerpiece lay in the presumed increase in the overall competitiveness of Argentina's economy via the reduction of labor taxes.

Once the tax reform entered Congress formally, Menem worked full steam for its approval, for which he needed to cajole around twenty-five–thirty deputies of his own party (given that opposition parties had already made clear their resistance to the idea). Backing his enfeebled economy minister, the president publicly referred to the tax project as a preventive measure needed to face the Asian crisis with fortitude, whose length and severity had been underestimated. A fierce intraparty battle was set between the executive and *justicialista* deputies. Lawmakers rhetorically opposed the reduction of payroll taxes on grounds that when Cavallo undertook a similar measure employment did not only fail to decrease, it actually increased.[6] But the genuine sticking point was the generalization of the VAT to cable TV, magazines, information agencies, and the publicity industry (TV and radio), and medicine.[7] Needless to say, these lobbies enjoyed much political clout because of their direct influence upon electoral outcomes. The roadblocks the executive was facing were daunting, not least because the president of the Chamber of Deputies, Alberto Pierri, was himself an owner of both cable TV and radio enterprises. Roque Fernandez singled him out as "the greatest obstacle for the reform's passage." Economics vice minister Carlos Rodriguez tendered his resignation when the lower chamber excluded the generalization of the VAT. It was a testament to the large political capital that Menem's executive and his economic team were staking upon this reform.

While the reduction of labor taxes could benefit the industrial sector, the overall tax package provoked the strong opposition of this sector's foremost business associations, including the *Grupo de*

Ocho and the *Union Industrial Argentina* (UIA), in addition to more than seventy business chambers and federations. In addition, many questioned the timing of the reform. "It is very inconvenient to be introducing two reforms (labor and taxes) as important as these in a protectoral context" said UIA chief Claudio Sebastiani echoing the sentiment of Argentine business (*Ámbito Financiero*, April 15, 1998). Their logic was simple enough: the reduction in payroll taxes did not compensate the increases in income taxes, and above all, the recreation of the tax on financial instruments and the application of a 15 percent tax on foreign loans. More vociferous were the specific corporatist groups affected by the rise in domestic taxes (beer, wine, tobacco) as well as specific taxes on publicity, cable TV, and magazines. Even the U.S. Chamber of Commerce drafted a strongly worded eleven-page statement that it handed to the Argentine Congress saying that "the tax reform negatively affects the judicial security, the image of the state vis-à-vis foreign investors, and includes new taxes of clear constitutional breach" (*Ámbito Financiero*, April 11, 1998). With such a powerful amalgam of opponents, Argentine deputies harbored strong reservations about the contents of this reform—in particular the generalization of the VAT, and the rise in income tax and domestic taxes—and wanted the executive to effect drastic modifications.

To compound the DGI's lackluster performance in its fight against evasion, legal troubles ensued. Revenues tsar Carlos Silvani was dealt a big blow when the Supreme Court ruled the *Ley de Clausuras* was unconstitutional and openly criticized the "repressive character" of articles 10 and 11 of Law 24.765 in place. From now on, the DGI was seriously limited in its ability to close a business, as it was only authorized to do so with a judicial resolution. Silvani's men had closed 10,000 businesses up to that point, most of them small enterprises.

By late 1998, in the aftermath of the Brazilian and Russian financial crises and the concomitant slowdown in Argentine economic activity, Fernandez's tax reform remained of the first order of importance for the executive, but its purpose had changed: it was now seen more as a warranty to maintain fiscal health in view of a recessive economic horizon in 1999. Fiscal accords with the IMF were in peril. In fact, continuing low tax collection forced Silvani to adopt some extraordinary measures at this juncture, such as bringing forward due payments of income tax levied on individuals and firms alike, as well as fiddling with minor taxes—all in order to collect an additional $180 million (*Ámbito Financiero*, November 17, 1998). "What we are saying with these tax changes is that we are respecting our commitment to Convertibility and fiscal balance. We are saying that, in face of the unpredictable, we are ready to take drastic measures" (ibid.), pointed out Secretary Silvani. Again, the lack of the monetary policy instrument to navigate and soothe the impact of external shocks left the economic authorities vulnerable. This shock had a greater impact upon economic activity than it would have had under a different exchange rate regime, thus provoking ad hoc changes in the tax system to keep revenues up. Such a situation, along with forecasts of a feeble economy in the forthcoming year, reinforced the need to pass Fernandez's tax project. Silvani also reminded Argentines that this was an opportunity to somewhat improve the fairness (horizontal equity) of the tax system:

> Congress must approve the tax reform the government wants and eliminate all of the possible exceptions that turn the system into something deeply unjust. There are things [in the tax system] that are inexplicable. Little by little we are turning the tax system into a gruyere cheese. Judges do not pay taxes because they are judges; actors don't pay taxes because they are actors, etc.... Neither do show business, cable TV, football games, industrial promotions, and thousands of examples like that. (*Ámbito Financiero*, November 17, 1998)

The reform was approved by the Senate in December 1998, a full nine months after it had first been introduced to the legislature by minister Fernandez. Throughout months of negotiations with lawmakers and lobby groups, the executive had to accept a watered-down version of their intended reform. First, the executive's generalization of the VAT was less general than sought: cable TV and medicine was levied at a rate of 10.5 percent, while mass media publicity at 21 percent. In Argentina, crisis junctures seemingly did not generate enough political impetus to put a halt to the tax privileges of some sectors. As Radical senator Antonio Berhongaray shrewdly remarked: "what we have left is an unwieldy generalization of the VAT where what has been finally approved is more the result of pressure from different sectors than what is best for the country." And added, "the weakness our political system showed vis-à-vis lobby pressures is evident in the disappearance of domestic taxes from the reform" (*Ámbito Financiero*, December 7, 1998). The elimination of the proposal to levy taxes on beer and wine erased $700 million in revenues. Moreover, the original raison d'etre of the reform had now seemingly vanished. That is, the proposal to reduce labor taxes in order to improve the competitiveness of Argentine businesses was now entirely contingent upon the vagaries of tax collection. In the context of Latin American financial instability and a weakening Argentine economy, the government's need to demonstrate fiscal rectitude simply became more important than improving competitiveness.

Profound changes were effected in the income tax, consisting in the introduction of the concept of *renta mundial* (tax on global sales). With an extensive legal architecture based on over ninety articles, the *Administracion Federal de Impuestos Publicos* (Federal Tax Bureau; AFIP) could not collect tax on income that Argentines earned via investments in foreign countries. It was a project that policymakers had previously tried to incorporate into the tax code without success. Another change in the income tax that the economic authorities hoped would bring added revenues was the introduction of control mechanisms over transfer pricing, so that firms would have to justify the setting of goods prices traded within the firm and between it and its branches abroad.

Another component of the reform that was approved was the re-creation of the taxes on portfolio investment at a rate of 1 percent, a tax that had been eliminated by Domingo Cavallo during the first months of his tenure. Another ad hoc tax innovation was that levied on entrepreneurial indebtedness, at a rate of 15 percent. Resort to tax handles told much about the increasing desperation of the economic authorities. These latter two creations were severely criticized by many, including Cavallo, who warned that these measures could aggravate unemployment and discourage domestic investment. Cavallo estimated that the added tax collection coming from these changes would be "insufficient to [cover the reduction] of labor taxes," so that "we are left with a higher tax burden on business without the benefit of lower labor taxes" (*Ámbito Financiero*, December 8, 1998). While many economists praised various aspects of the reform—particularly the generalization of the VAT (if uneven)—a good number shared the former minister's concerns.

The Law of Fiscal Responsibility: An Exercise in Futility

Economic data for the first quarter of 1999 showed that the Argentine recession was only deepening. Expectations for a quick recovery were dashed by the weakness in both internal and external demand. The

Brazilian crisis had a greater impact on Argentina than first thought. This obliged economic authorities to enact new adjustments that only worsened the struggling economy. In addition, the deceleration of growth in the European Union and the United States only complicated the local economic panorama. By the second quarter, it became clear that economic recovery would be postponed until late 1999, if at all, and the Finance Ministry admitted that GDP could contract by 2 percent for the year (*La Nación*, April 4, 1999). Unlike the Tequila-induced recession of 1995, this one was developing alongside price deflation, which negatively affected firms' profits, banks' portfolios, the level of employment, and surely, tax collection.

As a way to shore up its declining credibility in fiscal matters vis-à-vis international investors, the executive worked on a project that would theoretically bind the government to fiscal discipline. The more specific goal was to reduce the ever-larger country-risk component in interest rate payments, which were proving a serious burden on public finances. The bill introduced in Congress was the *Ley de Responsabilidad Fiscal* (Fiscal Responsibility Law). This measure, also known as Fiscal Convertibility, drew a timetable to achieve fiscal balance by 2003 via the incremental reduction of the fiscal gap every year. The law stipulated a number of measures: the real rate of public spending growth could not supersede the real rate of GDP growth; 2 percent of National Treasury resources was to be destined to a Fund of Fiscal Stabilization; funds or institutions that implied extra-budgetary spending were forbidden; and finally, all decentralized institutions whose financing by the national treasury exceeded 90 percent of current expenditure was to be eliminated by 2000, with the exception of national universities. A number of contextual factors accelerated negotiations in the legislature, including jittery markets, rumors about the devaluation of the Argentine peso, scathing declarations by George Soros about Argentine economic policy, and talk of Roque Fernandez's exit from government. According to PJ deputy Oscar Lamberto, one of the law's chief defenders, "[the law] will be a strong signal that there is not only currency convertibility but also a guarantee of fiscal stability fixed by law" (*Ámbito Financiero*, May 25, 1999). This widely shared view was rather naïve. As Radical politician and intellectual Rodolfo Terragno rightly warned, "fiscal discipline is not something obtained by dint of laws" (ibid.). The Law of Fiscal Responsibility drew strong support from Radical presidential candidate Fernando de la Rua, who instructed Alianza legislators to approve the measure on the grounds that it was "a necessary tool for fiscal balance and also disciplines public spending" (ibid.). The two main Alianza economists, Jose Luis Machinea and Aldalberto Rodriguez Giavarani, had pressured de la Rua to publicly back the measure. Rightly or wrongly, de la Rua's economic team reasoned that not only would such a declaration help to bolster the public image of the Alianza but it would also be a useful instrument to prop up economic governance in an eventual Alianza government. The approval of the Fiscal Law was repeatedly postponed, as Peronist and opposition parties could not agree on the specifics, with the latter desiring a more strict timetable as well as measures to reduce the highly political and wasteful *Gastos Reservados* and the *Aportes Nacionales del Tesoro* (ATNs). Although the Fiscal Law was cynically sold as part of a new set of *políticas de estado* (crucial policies that command widespread political consensus are generally "above politics," and remain unchangeable throughout different administrations), the reality was more mundane: it was one of those measures the Argentine political class dare not reject in public, but hardly a measure commanding consensus. Any talk of *políticas de estado* was belied by continuing political bickering over the approval of Fiscal Responsibility, which steadily lost its signaling objective vis-à-vis the markets each week the government delayed the project.

Notwithstanding its good intentions, the law was an act of political voluntarism: it was impracticable and did not have any enforcement mechanism—a well-known Argentine malaise. Predictably, markets were unimpressed and the measure did not have any positive effect on the sovereign country-risk. The law's lack of credibility was due in good measure to the fact that it was enacted in a recessionary context, making continued fiscal retrenchment politically unsustainable. Had fiscal retrenchment been applied in previous years, the reaction might have been different. Moreover, the measure could backfire: if the belt-tightening was enforced as stipulated, the economic recession could well be aggravated. In sum, markets interpreted the *Ley de Responsabilidad Fiscal* as a case of a government doing "too much, too late."

The Alianza Government: Firefighting as Tax Policy

With the Alianza's victory in the October 1999 presidential elections, there was widespread nervousness about how the incoming government, not known for having taken a strong stand in favor of fiscal discipline while in the opposition, would handle the disarray in Argentina's public finances (Curia 2002). Radical party economist Jose Luis Machinea, the shadow finance minister, sought to dispel such doubts and made it clear that his foremost objective was to

> put public finances in order. Otherwise, it will be impossible to think of sustained growth and the reduction of unemployment...More than rhetoric, we have to think hard about the crude fiscal reality that the coming government will face. The effort to reduce the deficit will have to be bigger than the one undertaken during the past three years. (*La Nación*, November 5, 1999)

Indeed, the main economic task facing the de la Rua government was of how to reach the $4,500-million deficit (1.5 percent of GDP) established by the Law of Fiscal Convertibility for the upcoming year, when the deficit stood at around $10,000 million for 1999. Machinea publicly stated that given the way the outgoing government had negotiated and settled upon a budget for 2000, the fiscal deficit objective of 1.5 percent would not be reached. It became clear that, in order to rearrange the fiscal panorama, the upcoming government needed to act on a threefold strategy: first, seal a fiscal pact with the provinces; second, plan further cuts in public expenditure; and third, complement it with a comprehensive tax reform.

While the government was forced to make more concessions than expected to get governors to sign a new fiscal pact, it was able to ratify the agreement relatively quickly (Sanchez 2011a). The Alianza sought spending cuts in the order of $1,400 million for the 2000 budget, but only after a revenue-enhancing tax reform was negotiated. Negotiations promised to be anything but easy. The tax project included: the elimination of VAT exemptions; the amplification of the income tax base from 1.5 to 2.5 million taxpayers; the creation of an inheritance tax for goods exceeding 100,000 pesos; a rise in the tax rates on income, luxury, and domestic taxes; a tax rate of up to 20 percent on privileged pension schemes. De la Rua's economic team planned to collect an additional 2,900 million in the year 2000 with this tax package. From late July, figures showed that industrial and economic activity was improving, thus signaling a timid economic recuperation. The economic authorities were hoping to capitalize on this potential recovery.

The Senate approved with significant changes the tax reform bill that had been passed by the lower chamber, by putting the accent of the added tax burden on the financial rather than the productive sector. At the end of the day, however, Alianza deputies imposed their majority in the lower chamber to approve the tax reform essentially in the form that the executive had originally sent it in. To be sure, the law was severely criticized by the Peronists, but more worryingly, it was also questioned by more independent-minded analysts on similar grounds. Former minister Domingo Cavallo summed up the thinking of many when he maintained, "with this law the rate of economic growth will diminish, evasion will augment and we will not be able to reach the goal of a $4,500 million deficit agreed for 2000" (*La Nación*, December 30, 1999). On a similar vein, Carlos Rodriguez, a key member in Roque Fernandez's team, wrote in the CEMA's newsletter: "the discretion, bad timing, and awful design of these new taxes affects the credibility of the rules of the game which will reduce national savings, foreign investment and augment the incentives to evade" (ibid.). While the tax reform also included some measures to fight evasion as another avenue to close the deficit, the planned administrative effort was modest: the government expected it to yield an additional $450 million in 2000—a meager 2 percent of revenues lost to evasion. By this time, the initial gains made in the battle against evasion had been lost (Sanchez 2011b).

This can be interpreted as an implicit recognition of failure on the evasion front. It signaled deeply rooted skepticism about the state's ability to effectively tackle this Argentine malaise in the context of economic stagnation. In short, notwithstanding its rhetoric and high-profile anticorruption platform, the Alianza government was effectively giving up the fight against evasion from the very start of its tenure in office. In a book paying tribute to Carlos Tacchi, Professor Vito Tanzi warned, "a tax reform of great scope has to include the revision of incentives that push taxpayers to comply with their tax obligations." The Alianza was contemplating nothing of the sort. In effect, the government was simply increasing the tax burden on those who already complied, which in a recessionary context could be rightly deemed counterproductive for tax collection purposes. Machinea's team was toeing the *fiscalista* view of Roque Fernandez, much in line with the thinking of Secretary of the Treasury Lawrence Summers who, referring to Argentina, had asserted: "the key to achieve sustainable growth is the return of investor confidence. The road is only one: to lower the deficit, so that interest rates can fall and growth can resume" (*La Nación*, January 5, 2000). Imprudently, the means by which fiscal equilibrium was achieved did not seem to worry the new government. Only the end result mattered.

President de la Rua had put enormous political capital on a fiscal adjustment package of measures that had effectively cut short his "honeymoon" period. Raising taxes is always unpopular, but it was all the more so given the increasingly dire economic conditions affecting Argentines. (To add insult to injury, the president had promised to lower taxes during the electoral campaign.) More than a few *aliancistas* worried that these stringent economic sacrifices would come at too high a political price for the governing coalition's own good. By the end of the first trimester some private think tanks were reporting a fall in domestic consumption. Consumers had predictably undertaken even more frugal consumption patterns in light of the tax hike—amid Machinea's promises that economic reactivation was around the corner.

Following an unhealthy Argentine tradition, Minister Machinea decreed a fiscal moratorium in May 2000, with which the government hoped to add $400 million to state coffers. It was the twenty-seventh such measure since 1955, this time offering taxpayers seven different ways to facilitate their overdue tax payment obligations. As usual, the moratorium was presented as the last of de la Rua's government—once more offending the intelligence of Argentine taxpayers. Many experts feared that the complicated economic situation would not bode well for the moratorium's success. Furthermore, de la Rua's fierce antievasion rhetoric was being thoroughly contradicted by both a fiscal adjustment whose brunt was borne by those who already paid their taxes and by the fiscal moratorium (which effectively rewards those taxpayers who do not regularly comply with the law). In short, the new government lacked just as much credibility on tax matters as the previous Peronist government.

Political squabbles further destabilized shake the federal tax agency. In mid-2000 a long in-the-shadows fight within the government ended with Carlos Silvani's resignation from the helm of the Federal Tax Bureau. Vice President Chacho Alvarez, along with chief of staff Rodolfo Terragno and associated sectors of the cabinet's political wing, had long worked to have Silvani removed—a man in whom they never had full political trust given that he was inherited from Menem's government. (Moreover, he was accused of representing the IMF.) The resignation manifested the indiscipline and lack of homogeneity of views within the governing cabinet, reflecting the latent political tensions between de la Rua and Alvarez, and between the Radicals and the Frepasistas (Morales Sola 2001). "Although the President asked me to stay, there came a point at which I sensed

I was being toyed with [by the political wing of the government]" (*La Nación*, June 3, 2000), said Silvani justifying his decision. This conflict-ridden political climate evidently boded ill for Silvani's successor, whoever would be chosen. It was not coincidental that more than twelve candidates who were approached for the job instinctively refused! Not only would the eventual tax tzar have to deal with the amalgam of economic factors conspiring against effective tax collection and evasion-fighting historically present in Argentina (in addition to a stagnant economy), but he or she would also have to work without a solid, cohesive political patron endorsing this titanic endeavor. Building on the political inertia derived from the ousting of Silvani, Rodolfo Terragno and other government political heavyweights considered the renewed institutional separation of the DGI from the customs office, effectively returning to the pre-1997 situation. But what worried many economic agents was the seriously entertained idea of reducing the powers of the AFIP. Among the features of this project was the creation of a separate, independent institution that would control the principal 200,000 taxpayers of the country, which would have delegates from the Ministry of Labor and Justice and would be under the command of the chief of staff Rodolfo Terragno. It also included the creation of an institution, the *Sistema de Identificación Nacional Tributario y Social* (SINTyS), in order to cross data from various government registrars. In truth, plans to cut the powers of the Federal Tax Buerau (AFIP) had been circulated since de la Rua's government entered office, contradicting Alianza's promises of a "strengthened tax agency" during the electoral campaign. Clearly, the new government did not exhibit any more political maturity than their *menemista* predecessors in envisioning a professionalized, independent tax bureau, making a mockery of Silvani's aspiration, which he spelled out as follows: "I hope that the AFIP will be gradually transformed into something similar to the Central Bank" (*La Nación*, June 3, 2000).

Labor union leader Hugo Moyano, condemning the continuing tax increases imposed on the working masses as an affront on social justice, urged Argentine taxpayers to renege on their tax obligations by publicly calling for a widespread "fiscal rebellion." It was not the first time that tax evasion was publicly legitimized in Argentine political discourse.

Wishing to avoid the confrontations that had characterized the Silvani tenure and aiming to conquer another parcel of power, both the economic and political wings of the government were actively searching for a low-profile substitute that would be subservient to cabinet members and to the minister of economy. The desired profile was found in the person of Hector Rodriguez. Rodriguez delineated his priorities thus: "We will try to strengthen the AFIP, to give it a lower public profile and better results. My job is to improve tax administration in line with the public compromise the President has expressed." And paying lip service to the tired antievasion rhetoric, he added, "this will not be the Rodriguez administration but that of a government that is ready to fight endlessly against evasion. Our objective is to increase taxpayers' perception of risk in order so that those who evade taxes stop their practices" (*Ámbito Financiero*, June 8, 2000). Although Rodriguez declaredthat the AFIP needed stability and autonomy in order to ensure effective operational and intellectual independence (*independencia de criterio*), he knew that this was little more than a normative statement, not applicable in Argentina. Minister Machinea made clear that the head of the tax agency was simply "one more figure within the economic team," foreclosing any measure of meaningful institutional independence for the Federal Tax Bureau.

To add to brewing political and economic troubles, a political scandal of major proportions erupted onto the public scene in September of 2000: some lawmakers had been allegedly accepting bribes by government operatives to favor legislative approval of labor reform. The executive pushed through antievasion laws and the Law of Economic Emergency with the same strong-arm tactics *Radicales* and *Frepasistas* had criticized as "authoritarian" when President Menem resorted to them: in this case, the threat to use presidential decrees if Congress did not approve or delayed the bills.

In a surprising change of strategy, the government announced in September 2000 that it was devising an "integral and definitive" tax reform to reduce taxes, a bill to be introduced in the legislature in the medium term. The proposal centered on the reduction of tax rates levied on consumption and income, while concurrently amplifying their respective bases. Chief of Staff Rodolfo Terragno announced that until the contours of the project were finalized and it was sent to Congress the operating philosophy was to not raise taxes again, so as to avoid policy uncertainty. Such declared intentions represented an implicit official admission that the Alianza's tax policy measures since taking office had been a failure—and a monumental one at that. Terragno stated that "the entire tax system needs to be reformulated. There needs to be an integral and definitive reform, and we will push for it" (*Ámbito Financiero*, September 2000). Leaving aside its previous *fiscalista* ideas (i.e., balanced fiscal accounts would prop up investor confidence and reignite growth), the government was now engaging in a remarkable about-face by resorting to an intellectual framework last employed by minister Cavallo: supply-side tax policy. It was yet another sign of the utter lack of policy direction in taxation matters.

The worst fears voiced by the tax reform's critics had come to pass: the reform acted as a fiscal time bomb that annihilated the timid economic recovery witnessed in the second half of 1999. Not only was economic recovery (however tentative) halted in its tracks, but the national treasury was now collecting less in tax revenue. It became painfully clear that, burdened by continued economic stagnation, the government's *impuestazo* of December 1999 had not accomplished its revenue-enhancing aims—by some estimations only 43 percent of the expected revenue gains had been collected. Now, the finance minister sought to alter the anti-investment bias in the country's tax structure. Again, much as in Cavallo's tenure, an inadequate instrument (tax policy) was used to accomplish an overambitious goal (the reactivation of the economy, pulled by the external sector).

Argentina's political economy map changed with the resignation of Vice President Carlos Alvarez in October 2000, taking the Frepaso party with him and leaving the Radicals alone at the helm of government. Needless to say, the event raised serious questions about governability in the minds of domestic and external economic agents—not least because it increased the number of veto points in economic policymaking. Although Alvarez exited government in protest at the president's lackadaisical attitude concerning the well-founded accusations of government bribes to senators to help approval of labor reform, the tensions between both coalition partners had been bubbling since they took office. (There were also serious personal clashes between de la Rua and Alvarez.) The reaction of the markets to this political earthquake was reflected in the increase in country-risk. Argentine public bonds now stood at a rate eight percentage points over and above U.S. Treasury bonds, leaving Argentina outside international capital markets. In his three-pronged response to this financial crisis, Machinea asked the IMF for help and enacted more cuts in public expenditure, but he also made use of tax policy, resorting to fiscal devaluations. In particular, Machinea planed the progressive reduction in a number of taxes considered distortive for domestic producers, thereby intending to improve competitiveness.

Cognizant of the fact that the fiscal crisis could well unravel his presidency, Fernando de la Rua took the unusual step of appearing on national television to demand a fiscal sacrifice from Argentine society, prodding citizens to pay their taxes and to make use of the moratorium in place. (Incidentally, the government had extended the life of the moratorium and made its terms yet more generous.) Between the lines, many analysts understandably read a rather desperate attempt to help reverse the trend of diminishing tax revenues in any way possible. In utmost secrecy, a so-called *reforma tributaria total* (total tax reform) was being debated within the government. This scheme implied the radical simplification of the country's tax system into only four or five taxes that are easy to pay, and above all, easy to collect (*La Nación*, May 4, 2000). Such a simplification was, to be sure, be based upon indirect taxes. Many government technocrats reckoned that economic conditions urgently demanded such a simplification, while opponents worried about the regressive nature of the scheme.

Cavallo as Minister of Last Resort

Minister Machinea was already performing a high-wire act to retain the confidence of markets. Three blows to his management of the financial crisis provoked his resignation: the absence of improvements in tax collection, the rise in the fiscal deficit, and the political offensive against the president of the Central Bank, Pedro Pou. Machinea, seeking to take the economic initiative to calm jittery markets, proposed Domingo Cavallo as Pou's substitute, but when de la Rua rejected the proposal, Machinea tendered his resignation. President de la Rua, in his never-ending battle to attain (elusive) credibility vis-à-vis the markets, needed a substitute with impeccably orthodox economic credentials with recognized prestige among financiers. He thus chose the Chicago-trained, ultraorthodox economist Ricardo Lopez Murphy as director of the *Fundación de Investigaciones Económicas Latinoamericanas* (FIEL). Murphy had reasoned on previous occasions when rejecting offers to take over the *Ministerio de Economía* that his designation would not make sense because he would face insurmountable political problems in implementing ambitious (liberal-oriented) economic reforms. His prediction proved remarkably prescient. The new minister promptly elaborated a severe fiscal adjustment that faced down the "structural sources" of the public deficit, including: the health and education budgets; subsidies on the consumption of gas in the Patagonia; subsidies on the production of tobacco in the north; fiscal transfers to provinces; and tax exemptions, among others. Lopez Murphy and his orthodox team contended that Argentina's financial crisis was not a crisis of liquidity but one of solvency, and that this permanent insolvency lay in the deficient structure of the national budget. After seeking in vain legislative support for his adjustment package, the government decided to implement the measures by decree. This prompted the resignation of two Radical ministers and several high-ranking Frepaso officials, leaving de la Rua with no choice but to change economic policy direction. Lopez Murphy was forced to resign immediately after attempting an overhaul of public accounts. It was a clear reminder, if any was needed, of the towering political transaction costs involved in conducting serious fiscal reform in Argentina. The country's desperate financial situation (amid widespread talk of an "inevitable debt default"), proved insufficient to convince the Argentine political class to streamline public accounts. This reflects the fact that there are structural political factors that keep public finances in disarray. In fact, it can well be maintained that fiscal profligacy is functional to Peronism and the clientelistic practices that endow the party with political power.

Disregarding calls to rebuild the Alianza, the president reorganized his cabinet with people he trusted. In so doing, he inevitably accentuated his government's political isolation and increased the number of veto points to economic reform. In what was clearly his last political card, he named the father of convertibility to head the economy. Naming Cavallo as minister of economy was the ultimate manifestation of the fact that the Radical government had abandoned its campaign promises (or any coherent direction in policymaking): it was simply in the business of economic firefighting and political survival. Cavallo had been an unremitting critic of the policies pursued by Machinea. Cavallo made clear that he considered the Argentine financial crisis to be a liquidity problem, rather than a solvency quandary, turning on its head Lopez Murphy's assessment. The Harvard economist's answer was to put all of the policy eggs in the basket of economic growth. The fiscal deficit would disappear quickly, he reckoned, "if Argentina can grow at a rate of six or seven percent annually" (Cavallo 2001). Cavallo maintained that investment opportunities had been reduced with the rises in taxes and regulatory confusions enacted in the 1997–2000 period. Deregulation, the derogation of norms that artificially set prices or limit competitiveness, would unleash an investment boom comparable to that of the early 1990s. Cognizant that there was nothing approximating a political consensus on economic policy and that time was of the essence, the new minister sought to implement this deregulation plan entirely by decree.

Trying to take the economic offensive, Cavallo ambitiously aimed to reignite growth and bring solvency to public accounts via his grand *Plan de Competitividad* (Competitiveness Plan). There were two instruments to stimulate economic activity. The first was the Law of Competitiveness, which was aimed at diminishing the cost of production via reductions in labor taxes and tariffs on the imports of capital goods, the creation of some tax exemptions, and a tariff increase on the imports of consumption goods. The second measure entailed tampering with the currency board by incorporating the euro into a two-currency basket that backed up the peso (operative only when the euro reached exchange-rate parity with the dollar), otherwise called amplified convertibility. While these measures were nominally aimed at changing the incentive system of the Argentine economy, their chief intention was to inject optimism and change the mood and expectations of market operators. As a matter of fact, the Euro was not expected to reach parity with the dollar in the coming months, which meant that the de facto devaluation of the peso would not materialize in the short- to medium-term horizon. Without changing market expectations, as officials at the *Ministerio de Economia* knew, little could be accomplished: Argentina was depending entirely on external sources of private finance to remain afloat.

The amplified convertibility backfired, as economic agents understandably interpreted it as a "devaluation-in-waiting" of the peso: Cavallo was taking a visible step that tampered with the foundational, basic pillar of the Argentine economy. In addition, the first trimester of 2001 had registered a substantial fall in revenues. (March alone had recorded a 12.9 percent fall with respect to the previous year.) Most worryingly, in those three months Argentina's deficit was $1,000 million over and above the deficit figure accorded with the IMF. To restore fiscal solvency, Cavallo created a Tax on Financial Transactions, meant to levy all financial movements. This implied that simplification of tax collection methods were at the helm of efforts to prop up revenues, as banks were in charge of collecting this new tax.

Although the new economy minister had created a new tax that would yield $220 million a month, modified convertibility, and announced a $700 million-expenditure cut during his first month in office, this seemingly did not amount to a complete economic package in the eyes of Wall Street or the IMF. IMF chief Horst Kohler publicly stated that Cavallo needed to "clarify with greater detail what are the policy components of his [economic] program. The financial markets and all of us are waiting to see what happens" (*La Nación*, April 25, 2001). It was no mystery that the IMF and market participants favored an adjustment of the dimensions Lopez Murphy had (unsuccessfully) pushed for. While Kohler spoke well of the competitiveness orientation of the new measures, he shared many of the doubts of market operators and did not refrain from stating, "Argentina is a perturbing element in the world economy." After all, the eventual growth of the Argentine economy (presumably spurred by the new competitiveness plan) was entirely hypothetical, while the growing fiscal deficit was a palpable reality.

Urged to move fast on the competitiveness front, the government announced it would immediately implement the elimination of a number of taxes in order to foster the competitiveness of the productive sectors of the economy. Carlos Sanchez, the Secretary of Industry, summoned provincial representatives to study the feasibility of eliminating the turnover and stamp taxes and substituting it with a provincial-level VAT. This, however, was not a short-run project, for substituting the most important source of provincial own-revenue was no easy task. More tax changes ensued. In addition, tax evasion remained exceedingly high and had augmented during the first four months of 2001. More worryingly, Cavallo announced that the fiscal gap was larger than he had initially thought. "Lopez Murphy talked of $2000 million, I thought of $3000 million when entering office, but we found out that the deficit is really of the order of $4000 million," said Cavallo (*La Nación*, April 27, 2001). To compensate increasing deviations from IMF targets, the tax on financial transactions was increased from 0.025 to 0.040 percent. The rate of this tax was being almost doubled after less than a month of existence, not least prompted by the fact that the initial revenue projections for this tax were off the mark. In addition, the tax code exemptions on the VAT and income taxes were eliminated (in the case of VAT, with the exception of education, books, and transportation). Cavallo's team reckoned that generalizing the VAT would bring added revenues not only by expanding the base but also by way of simplifying tax collection. To foster competitiveness, the VAT on capital goods was lowered from 21 to 10.5 percent. Notwithstanding this last reduction, the tax measures clearly amounted to an *impuestazo* (abrupt tax hike). This tax hike was yet another act of desperation, not least because it contradicted the broad supply-side orientation in taxation Cavallo had brought to office only a few weeks before. To be sure, it worked against his overarching gamble to reactivate economic growth. The application of the VAT to new sectors necessarily affected their competitiveness. The generalization of tax bases could well further accentuate the economic recession as well as lead to inflationary pressures. When asked about the counterproductive effects of the tax hikes Cavallo offered implausible denials:

> No, the [tax hike] will not affect the middle classes. That has been a totally false interpretation. It does not affect the middle classes because none of those sectors that will now have to pay the VAT will be able to raise prices…In truth, [this measure] is about eliminating privileges, because the fact that some sectors do not pay the VAT is a privilege…If any sector has a problem of competitiveness [due to these measures], it must design a solution…The problems of lack of profitability are solved with a competitiveness plan, not backtracking on the generalization of the VAT. (Ibid.; my translation)

Economic authorities were faced with an inescapable dilemma: improving the (economic) humor of Argentine citizens on the one hand, and sending signals of fiscal solvency to international markets, on the other, were objectives at cross-purposes. Cavallo's pursuit of both was a virtually impossible mission.

At the end of the day, all of the tax handles enacted throughout 2001 were to no avail in keeping revenues up. The government was swimming against an uncontainable economic tide, which swept away the Alianza government in December 2001. A transition government led by San Luis governor Adolfo Rodriguez Saa officially declared a default on Argentina's sovereign debt later that month—the largest sovereign default ever recorded.

Conclusion

The second Menem administration was characterized by a marked politicization of tax policy—and indeed, other economic arenas—largely due to Menem's ambition to accumulate more personal power. There was in this period an increasing divorce between tax policy and tax administration, as they were no longer conscientiously brought together by Carlos Tacchi and Domingo Cavallo and legislators and cabinet members encroached upon tax policy with relative ease. Tax tzar Carlos Silvani and finance minister Roque Fernandez were unable to put their own stamp on revenue-increasing strategies.

During the second half of the 1990s, the external economic environment became more perilous. The Tequila shock of 1995 and later the contagion effects of the Asian financial crisis of 1997 and the Brazilian crisis of 1998 caused successive economic slumps in Argentina and induced investors to take a closer look at the nation's public finances. There was therefore an added cost to fiscal indiscipline via the increase in country-risk levels. The "spend-and-tax" Argentine fiscal model remained in place: tax policy and tax administration measures reacted to unpredictable and ad hoc changes in spending patterns, which boded ill for the coherence of the tax system, its simplicity or its efficiency.

The extremely regressive nature of the Argentine tax system (by the mid-1990s, the IMF ranked Argentina as having the third most regressive system out of 177 countries), generated a perverse self-sustaining dynamic: because of tax collection's very intimate link with the economic cycle, periods of economic recession yielded very low revenues, enticing the economic authorities to either raise nominal rates on existing indirect taxes or to create (distortive) tax handles, accentuating the regressive nature of the system (and also evasion). The internal coherence and the relative simplicity of the tax system bequeathed by Tacchi steadily worsened, erasing many of the gains of the first half of the 1990s. Meanwhile, the cancer of evasion had come full circle: the post-1995 return of evasion levels to those prevalent in the preconvertibility era persuaded economic authorities to steadily raise nominal tax rates on those Argentines who did comply with their obligations to prop up moribund revenues, further undermining the legitimacy of an extremely feeble fiscal pact and enticing many law-abiding citizens to evade—often in order to survive economically. In short, the government's inability and unwillingness to make serious inroads into the evasion malaise enticed economic authorities to put the onus of revenue collection on nominal tax rates, in turn fueling tax noncompliance.

The Alianza had vowed to be the government of postadjustment policies, promising to fine-tune the economy and implement a social agenda that would soothe the sizable social costs of convertibility. Part of this package included a more progressive tax system to further fiscal justice. None of this came to pass. Not only did de la Rua's government inherit public finances in disarray but also a recessionary economy. Tax policy during the Alianza administration was marked by a desperate attempt to prop up declining tax revenues in the context of a worsening economy. Growing economic instability and fiscal insolvency proved a poisonous cocktail in which the fiscal achievements of the early 1990s years drowned.

5

Institutional Correlates of Tax Reform Consolidation: Success in Chile and Failure in Argentina

Introduction

Chapters one through four have provided an empirical account of tax policy and administration reform efforts in Argentina and Chile, embedding them in the evolving politico-economic environment of the 1990s. This chapter seeks to present a more conceptual analysis that will clarify the reasons for the very different reform patterns and outcomes documented in the preceding chapters. A number of key variables have shaped prospects for the consolidation of tax reform—defined as the consensual acceptance of tax policy changes so that a new pattern of interaction comes to define the state-society fiscal rapport. Four overarching factors that have fostered tax reform consolidation in Chile are emphasized in this chapter: a strong institutional setting (including a capable state and an institutionalized party system), institutions that foster fiscal discipline and macroeconomic stability, the prevalence of encompassing organizations that facilitate collective action, and informal institutions that promote policy reform consolidation (a pattern of inclusive pact makings, called *democracia de los acuerdos*; and the enshrinement of policy stances that garner consensus, called *politicas de estado*). In Argentina, by contrast, a weak and politicized state, an underinstitutionalized party system, the absence of encompassing civil society organizations, and the presence of injurious informal institutions (particularly clientelism) have all conspired against state-building in the taxation arena.

Tax Reform Consolidation in Chile

Strong Institutional Environment

History and Institutional Path Dependency

The origins of Chilean democracy and Chilean institutional strength can be traced back to the mid-nineteenth century. The "political-crisis" literature developed by political scientists posits that all countries face three main overarching challenges in developing democratic institutions and that their success in attaining democratic stability lies in the timing and sequence of those challenges. These challenges consist in establishing national identity (creating a sense of national community), authority (creating viable state structures), and participation (incorporating the masses into the political system). The chances of a political system developing in a nonauthoritarian, democratically viable manner are maximized when these hurdles are overcome successfully and in the order just outlined (Nordlinger 1968). The Chilean case conforms neatly with the democratic outcome pattern. Chile's military victory in the war against the Peru-Bolivia Confederation and the subsequent victory in the War of the Pacific are widely credited with giving the small republic a new sense of national identity, confidence, and purpose. Political authority in Chile was consolidated as a result of a number of factors. General Manuel Bulnes set the tone for future political presidents by insisting on working within the framework of established political institutions. While in office, Bulnes willingly accepted the role of Congress in policymaking, the autonomy of the judicial system, and allowed ministerial cabinets to formulate the government's agenda. He could have used his popularity and command of the most powerful armed forces in the country to establish personal rule much like Rosas in Argentina or Santa Ana in Mexico, to name simply two of many Latin American *caudillos* of the time. He thus contributed greatly to establishing the legitimacy of democratic institutions. Second, state autonomy in Chile emerged early in its independent history (Cleaves 1974; Valenzuela 1984). It is estimated that by 1860 there were already 2,500 people working for the state, not including local officials or members of the armed forces (Loveman 2001). The respect presidents Manuel Bulnes (1841–1851) and Manuel Montt (1851–1861) granted to constitutionally mandated institutions made a crucial contribution to the strength of legal norms and democratic procedures evident throughout Chile's political history (Collier and Sater 2003). After 1830, all presidents (with the exception of several chief executives during the turbulent years of 1924–1930) were elected to office and finished their constitutional mandates.

Another factor that contributed to establishing political authority was the control of the armed forces by civilian figures. A number of deliberate political actions established a tradition of civilian supremacy over the military. (In particular, a professional military establishment was not created until after the War of the Pacific.) A couple of military challenges to civilian rule in the 1850s were defeated, setting the tone for future civil-military relations. In turn, state autonomy and civilian monopoly over the use of force contributed to conservative support for democratic governance. In the absence of obvious avenues of exercising influence available to other elites in Latin America, Chilean conservative elites (including large landowners) turned to the democratic rules in place as the most reasonable option to advance their political and material interests. As one noted scholar of Chilean politics puts it: "Chilean elites, initially hostile to democracy, came to embrace democratic rules as a conscious choice for political survival, in the process contributing to the strengthening of those institutions over the years" (Valenzuela 1999, 214). This deliberate and discrete political choice led to the creation of the Conservative Party. Since then, the political views and interests of the Chilean right have been well channeled and well represented (Garreton and Espinosa 2000). Democracy became "the only game in town" in Chile, and the institutions underlying democratic governance were respected and accorded legitimacy by the main political actors. (The 1973 coup stands as an aberration in the context of Chilean political history and that partly explains the fascination it has exerted among historians and political scientists.)

Historically, the Chilean state was one of the most extensively structured in Latin America. By the end of the 1960s, direct public investment constituted 50 percent of all gross investment. Alongside the growth of the state, a far-flung bureaucracy developed with its own dynamic and considerable independence from executive power. State expansion involved the creation of an ever larger array of decentralized and semiautonomous agencies, which depended only nominally on particular ministries for control. The relative efficiency and probity of the Chilean state has often been considered to be the result of a long history of competitive party politics, in which opposition parties and Congress kept a close watch on the conduct of public affairs. A career in public service has historically been valued, and the

Chilean state counted on many dedicated and well-educated officers from Chile's middle classes (Valenzuela 1984).

Institutionalized Party System
Political parties have been so decisive in Chile's political development that they have been called the backbone of the country's political process. Along with Uruguay, Chile has the highest levels of party system political institutionalization in Latin America (Mainwaring and Scully 1995). The implication is that agreements reached in Congress among political parties on tax policy can be effectively considered as a fiscal pact in which the major socioeconomic groups have had a voice. Tax policy output throughout the 1990s can be conceptualized as a function of the equilibrium attained in the interaction of parties' economic ideologies, political strategies, and political clout. Understanding where the political left and right stand on the taxation issue is important in a country with a highly institutionalized party system such as Chile because in such political settings policy is significantly shaped by ideas—unlike in clientelistic, nonprogrammatic party environments.

Let us therefore delve into the precise ideological views and economic policy stances espoused by Chilean parties, centering our attention on the relevant parties situated on the extremes of the political spectrum—the Socialist Party and the *Union Democratica Independiente*. The Socialist party has not renounced the tax instrument. Throughout the 1990s, the socialists opposed tax projects that they deemed regressive, such as the Foxley-Boeininger proposal to lower the income tax (affecting only the upper 30 percent of Chileans) under the Lagos tenure. Socialists generally advocated and lobbied in favor of a tax system that relied more on the income tax and less on consumption taxes (essentially regressive). (Roughly 70 percent of Chilean tax revenues come from indirect taxation and 30 percent from direct taxes, in line with many developing countries of a comparable level of development.) In this endeavor they faced powerful political and intellectual obstacles. As concerns the first, the business community was reasonably successful in keeping in place a low level of corporate income taxation (at 17 percent) by international standards. Regarding intellectual obstacles, mainstream and right-wing Chilean economists vigorously defended consumption-based taxation on the incontestable grounds that they are less distortive of economic activity. The standard conviction among non-Socialist *concertacionista* technocrats and legislators was that income redistribution should be effected via public expenditure. According to this logic, if fiscal policy is to redistribute income effectively, the tax system must simply aim at increasing its extractive capacity in order to then use the proceeds toward well-targeted social programs.

Whatever differences of opinion about economic policy may exist between Socialists and their *concertacionista* allies, the Socialist-led Lagos administration did not stray from the path laid down by Christian Democrat-led governments. A former government minister from the ranks of the Socialist party explains why:

> The government led by the Socialist Party is obliged to be particularly orthodox in economics. It is the syndrome of the alcoholic. You cannot get close to a glass of wine or they [the opposition, foreign investors] will hammer you. The past [i.e., the Allende experience] leaves a lasting imprint, a lasting reputation.

The pursuit of economic orthodoxy under Lagos offered at least two lessons. First, within the Socialist party liberal *tecnicos* had more clout than old-style *politicos*. Whenever a conflict over fiscal policy arose between these two sectors, President Lagos consistently backed the views and policy orientation of his (liberal) minister of finance Nicolas Eyzaguirre, a technocrat. Second, the Socialist party was constrained in its policy direction by having to weigh the opinions of their coalition partners, particularly the Christian Democrats, their most senior associate. Adherence to "consensus politics," the disciplining modus operandi that allowed the *Concertación* to hold power for two decades, precluded any significant deviation in public policy from that of past post-Pinochet governments. In fact, the *Concertación* alliance has been conceptualized as a single political party (Navia 2001). In short, the dissenting economic views of a powerful sector within the Socialist party simply did not pose a threat to tax reform consolidation or more generally, to the institutionalization of orthodox fiscal policy.

Let us now turn our attention to the political Right. *Renovacion Nacional* and *Union Democratica Independiente* both combine a conservative social agenda and a doctrinaire belief in liberal, free-market economics.[1] They are both defenders of a smaller state so as to allow market forces more scope to operate: thus their penchant for a lower tax level. In particular, they have adamantly defended lower tax burdens on business, regarded as the engine of growth and employment. Yet, notwithstanding their affinities in economic matters, they took a very different approach in their negotiating stances and their political interaction with the center-left ruling alliance. The UDI, more closely linked to the military regime, showed throughout the 1990s an ambivalent adherence toward democratic governance and the political compromises that it entails. UDI leaders' conception of politics was zero-sum, much in line with "old-style" Chilean politics, according to which principles and ideology are non-negotiable. As a consequence, they consistently eschewed cooperation with the government in changing the tax structure, even when reform projects were substantively in line with their economic ideas. The RN, by contrast, under the young and dynamic leadership of Andres Allamand, sought to reevaluate the right's historic distrust of the party system and refashion itself as a modern, Western-style, mass political party. In that quest, it sought to move closer to the center of the political spectrum and win over floating voters. The party leadership saw its own political future success as tightly linked to a successful transition to democracy. This explains its cooperative stance vis-à-vis the *Concertación* in undertaking political and economic reforms that would "democratize" economic policy, enhance democracy's mass appeal, and forge the RN as a modern party, concerned with social equity. In comparison with the UDI, Renovacion Nacional was more willing to compromise on its economic thinking in order to be able to influence policy.

The Chilean right proudly embraced the economic legacy of the Pinochet regime and, all in all, its views on the economy have largely prevailed during the postauthoritarian period. However, the issue-area where the "Chicago model" of development has been most frequently and ferociously criticized is its neglect of equity considerations. Chile, after all, displays one of the most unequal income distribution patterns in Latin America and the world. On this issue, right-wing *tecnicos* and *politicos* alike have been on the defensive. From the perspective of the Chilean right,

> inequality per se cannot be attributed to a given economic model, but to individuals' capacities and to the incentives and opportunities with which they are endowed in order to progress materially...Improving the distribution of income means shortening the socioeconomic distances among social groups, something that can only be achieved in the long run and once individuals have overcome conditioning factors of poverty perpetuation. (Camhi et al. 1999, 13–16)

Technical arguments aside, the Right did not focus on inequality as a specific objective of policy when it was in power. Rather, the Right put the accent on "trickle-down" economics: simply put, the idea that brisk economic growth alone eventually reduces poverty and lowers inequality.—and may well improve income distribution.

On balance, there was a fair degree of consensus among Chile's main parties about what the primordial objectives and principles governing the tax system should be. These are chiefly: the pursuit of efficiency (neutrality) in the design of tax policy so as not to interfere with an optimal, market-guided allocation of resources; and the pursuit of horizontal equity (ideally a unified tax rate) so as not to grant artificial benefits to particular taxpayers (whether individuals or corporations), which again interferes with the market mechanism— and promotes tax evasion. There was also, with the exception of the Socialist *autoflagelantes,* consensus on eschewing the tax system as a tool for redistributing income, considered to be best achieved via public expenditure. Vertical equity was thus not an objective that informed tax policy in Chile. All of these operating principles were in line with prevailing economic orthodoxy in the taxation realm.

Institutional Configurations

Interest Aggregation: Encompassing Organizations

Collective action problems arise when (beneficiary) agents have no incentives to cooperate in the provision of a good or service because the cost of organization is larger than the potential benefits to be reaped. In such a context there is a great incentive to free ride on the efforts of others. As Mancur Olson (1982) famously argued, encompassing organizations facilitate collective action. That is, the existence of broad organizations that encompass a significant number of diverse interest groups (in contrast to a multiplicity of narrowly based ones) makes agreements between the national government and civil society on public policy more feasible. There are two main reasons for this. First, encompassing organizations receive a large share of national collective goods. Because they are affected by general problems, they pay a large cost for narrowly self-interested behavior. Second, transaction costs (costs of negotiation, enforcement, and monitoring) are lower when the main societal actors have encompassing organizations to represent them (North 1990). Encompassing organizations foster the generation of moderate demands and promote win-win approaches to political negotiation. Narrow or maximalist-type demands are eschewed. Encompassing organizations also make it easier to reach binding accords and help consolidate reforms because they make the monitoring of compliance easier. Consequently, when there are fewer significant actors, the cost of deviating from previous political agreements becomes greater. In short, those actors have a greater stake in keeping their end of the bargain, not least because a consensual political environment fosters political and economic stability, collective goods of great value to any organization pursuing broad interests.

Both labor and business have peak organizations in postauthoritarian Chile. Most sectors of labor are represented by the *Central Unitaria de Trabajadores* (CUT), while most sectors of business have their interests defended by the *Confederacion de la Produccion y del Comercio* (CPC). Although both labor and business are represented by other organizations,[2] these two have de facto been treated as the official interlocutors by the government.[3] This recognition has, in turn, provided these associations with greater incentives to defend the common interests of their entire classes and seek national goals, so as to keep their privileged positions as "official negotiators" intact. As concerns the party system, the formation of a broad-based party coalition has played a similar role to that of encompassing organizations (Weyland 1997). Insofar as the *Concertación* was accountable to left and center-right constituencies while in power, it faced strong electoral incentives to promote national-level goals rather than cater to specific sectors, classes, or regions. The governing alliance was loath to make any promises or introduce any biases into policymaking that would compromise its overarching objective of combining economic *and* social development. The pursuit of growth alongside enhanced social justice surely involved short-term policy tradeoffs, but *Concertación* governments were careful not to sacrifice too much efficiency for the sake of equity and vice-versa.

In sum, most major social and political actors (the governing coalition, the RN, the CPC, and the CUT) perceived that contributing to the success of the "growth with equity" agenda fostered their interests. This moderated the policy positions of business, labor, the left, and the moderate right, while contributing to incremental (rather than abrupt) change. In turn, the fact that sectoral and group interests were framed in such an encompassing fashion goes a long way toward explaining the ability of the party system to build and deliver consensual policies. Only the UDI remained outside this cooperative game in the 1990s, partly on the basis of party principle and partly on the basis of pragmatism—as it reckoned that being a maverick, nonconformist actor increasingly paid off in electoral terms.

Institutions to Promote Macroeconomic Stability and Fiscal Discipline

A first factor that contributed to the sustainability of tax innovations was the dogged maintenance of macroeconomic stability by economic authorities throughout the 1990s. An unstable macroenvironment often "obliges" economic authorities to modify the tax code at regular intervals because of short-term revenue urgencies. Needless to say, many of these changes often act to either unravel previous ones, or otherwise accentuate the incoherence of the tax system as a whole. Economic instability per force acts to shorten economic horizons in policymaking, which precludes a vision of tax system objectives for the long haul. In such environment, objectives today (say, tax efficiency) are liable to be overtaken by different objectives tomorrow (say, tax sufficiency). A stable economic milieu is therefore a necessary condition (but not sufficient) for tax reform consolidation.

The reasons for the obsession with fostering a stable environment must be found in Chile's traumatic past of economic instability. As a result, economic stability and predictability have acquired paramount value, absolute priority. (Some have made the analogy to Germany's obsession with price stability as a result of past hyperinflation.) Within the *Concertación*, ensuring stability was partly born out of a desire to avoid a populist cycle so typical of Latin American countries, and out of a concern with establishing a reputation for economic orthodoxy vis-à-vis Chilean entrepreneurs and international investors, as explained in chapter one. It also stemmed from the recognition that an unstable economic environment hurts the lower socioeconomic strata the most. For all of these reasons, Chilean policymakers developed instruments and institutions that promote macroeconomic stability. As regards monetary policy, in 1994, the Central Bank was granted formal autonomy, allowing the institution to carry out its duties largely free from political interference. Because of its high reputation for economic prudence and high technical capacities, the Central Bank acted de facto as a check on any expansionary fiscal impulses by the Finance Ministry.[4] It also used its institutional powers to foster economic stability any way it saw fit. For instance, against the advice of the IMF, Chilean monetary authorities instituted capital controls in the early 1990s, obliging foreign investors to retain their funds in Chile for at least a year before they could withdraw them. There is widespread consensus that capital controls had a stabilizing effect upon the economy and allowed Chile to weather international financial crises relatively well.

Fiscal discipline also served as a privileged framework within which to effect changes in the tax system because it reduced discretion and arbitrariness in the formulation of tax policy. Chilean technocracy has installed a "tax and spend" model, meaning that every increase in permanent public spending must be fully financed with domestic tax resources and no spending is allowed without an explicit source of tax-derived financing. Tax policy is not made to serve sudden, unpredictable expenditure items. Rather, revenue-enhancing tax reforms have been shaped to meet specific spending needs.

The institution inherited from the military government that has played a key role in fostering fiscal rectitude is the set of budgetary rules (constitutional laws) dating from the *Ley de Administracion Fiscal* enacted in 1975. This law responded to Pinochet's economists' wish to attain a high degree of economic governability and thereby avoid the fiscal indiscipline of times past. These rules bestow strong prerogatives on the Chilean finance minister to overrule "political" ministers (always inclined to increase their budgets) within cabinet negotiations on the formulation of the budget (Marcel 1998). These rules also limit the capacity of the legislature to amend the budget proposed by the executive in September of every fiscal year. Congress cannot augment spending or decrease taxes, only reduce overall expenditure. There is, moreover, an unwritten institution: the discussion concerning the allocation of expenditure is not one between the president and his cabinet, but one between the president and the minister of finance. This means the minister of finance does not have to formally face the rest of the ministers, facilitating the reining in of total expenditure. To be sure, the technical strength of Chilean institutions, in particular that of the *Direccion General de Presupuestos* (Budget Office) contributes to fiscal discipline. This is a major difference between Chile and most other Latin American countries.

Fiscal discipline had a reinforcing logic. As Chile achieved consecutive years of fiscal surpluses that fostered economic stability and allowed it to weather economic crises relatively unscathed, fiscal discipline came to be widely recognized by Chilean economists as one of the principal assets distinguishing Chile from its Latin American competitors. This recognition extended to the international financial community resulting, among other benefits, in lower country-risk ratings and thus lower borrowing rates. In light of these tangible benefits, it is not surprising that Chilean technocrats developed a number of formal instruments to further promote discipline in public finances. Noteworthy are the Copper Stabilization Fund, which acted to smooth the economic and revenue volatility resulting from year-to-year fluctuations in the price of copper, and the Oil Stabilization Fund, which aimed to avoid transferring the full cost of drastic oil price increases to consumers. Following in the footsteps of some developed countries, Chilean authorities developed fiscal policy indicators in order to avoid a pro-cyclical bias in the management of public finances, evaluate better the macroeconomic impact of fiscal policy, and reinforce fiscal discipline. Finally, the introduction of the structural surplus budget rule by Lagos's technocrats was yet another institution created to foster fiscal rectitude. As former director of the budget Pablo Arellano explains, fiscal discipline has turned into a "political weapon" for Chilean politicians. Many projects and proposals fall by the wayside politically when they carry with them some fiscal risk or they damage that principle (Arellano, interview).

Informal Institutions

Politicas de Estado

An important informal institution contributing to tax reform consolidation has been the enshrinement of *politicas de estado* as regards economic policy. *Politicas de estado* are policy stances on which there is widespread consensus among the political class such that they remain invariant through time, regardless of which party comes to power. Two such policy stances in Chile concern the maintenance of macroeconomic stability and fiscal balance. The second is, of course, an important component of the first, but they are analytically distinct. These two *politicas de estado* were crucial—almost sine qua non— environmental conditions that have allowed for high levels of stability in tax policymaking and contributed to tax reform consolidation. Because of such underlying economic stability, tax policy was generally not used to shore up public finances in the short term or fulfill other urgent objectives thrust upon policymakers due to economic instability. This begs the question of what allowed macroeconomic stability and fiscal balance to coagulate into sacred tenets of Chilean economic policymaking. The answer lies in the convergence between the Left and the Right in economic viewpoints.

The convergence in the economic worldviews of the military regime's economists and opposition economists began during the

1980s (Puryear 1994). During Pinochet's first decade in power, the Chicago boys maintained that they were guided by economic "science" in the formulation of policy and thus impervious to mistakes, while the opposition was doggedly critical of the regime's economic policies. After 1983, largely as a result of the 1982 bank crisis debacle, the dictatorship's economic team gradually came to adopt a more pragmatic stance, less informed by rigid liberal economics axioms (marking the onset of what is sometimes called "pragmatic neoliberalism"). The opposition also came to recognize and praise many of the regime's policies and their impact on growth, coming to accept a more market-friendly version of economic policymaking. This ideational convergence translated into a higher level of trust when the RN was brought to the negotiating table to support tax reforms at the outset of Aylwin's term.

The excellent economic performance of the Chilean economy since 1985, when the benefits of reform started to be felt, forced opposition economists to come to terms with the virtuous aspects of liberal economic policy. As former finance minister Alejandro Foxley (1987, 180) has written: "We, opposition economists, who were very critical of the management of the economy by the military regime, especially during the first ten years of this experience, have also learnt the positive lessons offered by such experience, in particular during its most recent phase." Oscar Munoz, another prominent figure of CIEPLAN, makes a similar observation:

> Perhaps we had been very convinced of certain approaches and had developed at great length the arguments to defend them. When we saw that in fact things functioned well under a different approach, we began to pay more attention to those other arguments, to look at them more and find ultimately that there was no one truth. (Quoted in Puryear 1994, 115)

A perusal of articles written in the principal academic journals (such as *Cuadernos de Economia, Estudios Publicos, Coleccion Estudios CIEPLAN*) in the late 1980s shows that the areas of coincidence between the Chicago boys and Christian Democrat and even left-wing economists was quite large (Hojman 1993). Leftist economists, on their part, were forced to come to terms with the failure, both economic and political, of the Unidad Popular government (1970–1973). The momentous fall of the Berlin Wall in 1989 brought Chilean leftist politicians closer to the fold of free-market economics. Perhaps more significantly, the experience of exile altered the politico-economic worldviews of leftist intellectuals and economists (including the likes of Carlos Ominami, Ricardo Lagos, Jorge Arrate, Manuel Marfan, or Sergio Bitar), who came to adopt less provincial perspectives. Many of the figures that came to dominate the left had pursued graduate studies in economics in the United States and Europe. The views of these *tecnicos* came to exert an even stronger influence on the official policy platforms of the *Partido Socialista* or the *Partido por la Democracia* than was the case of the Christian Democrats. This does not mean that free-market economics reigns unchallenged within left party cadres, however.

The preponderance of economists, or at least their disproportionate influence within Chilean political parties, means that traditional *politicos* themselves underwent a process of ideational convergence in economic policy as well. In fact, the most accentuated policy differences across the major political parties in post-Pinochet Chile belong not to the realm of economics, but to that of social and political policy. Sectarianism among Chilean political parties was drastically reduced, and antagonistic, highly ideological models of development of yesteryear eventually converged in a new (neoclassical) synthesis. Moreover, there was a powerful political rationale behind the ideological and policy rapprochement of opposition *tecnicos*: the need to foster political harmony to prepare Chilean society for the transition to democracy. In a country burdened with bitter ideological confrontations—accentuated by the traumatic experiences of the Unidad Popular and Pinochet governments—most would-be democrats agreed that the country needed to put away the recent past, heal its deep wounds, and install a game of cooperation.

What are the practical consequences of the two informal institutions mentioned here? The most obvious one is that these informal institutions spawned formal ones to ensure macro and fiscal stability, which have been detailed earlier. Another is that the tenet of fiscal stability has shaped a "tax and spend" model of economic conduct: any political proposal to increase spending in one public policy area must be fully paid for by either a change in the tax code that increases revenues or a proportionate cut in spending in other areas of the national budget. Proposals that deviate from this norm are dead on arrival, as they potentially jeopardize fiscal balance.

Democracia de los Acuerdos: *Consultative, Multilateral Decision-Making*

When the *Concertación* coalition first came to power, its members were fully aware that the main perception they needed to dispel was the notion that this new government would return the country to the Allende era of economic instability and social chaos. Many voices in the right had also doubted the *Concertación*'s commitment to protecting property rights. It was in order to advance its legislative agenda, while assuaging the Right and the private sector, that the *Concertación* engaged early on in a pattern of negotiations known as *democracia de los acuerdos* (democracy of pacts) (Siavelis 2006). This informal institution has guided the behavior of all governments in post-Pinochet Chile. Major executive policy proposals have become law only after a process involving extensive discussion, negotiation, and input from the business community, organized labor and all major political parties, including the opposition. The Chilean Congress approved no significant tax reform project in the 1990s exactly in the original form intended by government policymakers. Rather, economic authorities were forced to make concessions to business, opposition parties, and even *Concertación* member parties. In a real sense, then, the final contours of tax reform represented the resulting vector in the distributional and political battle among the relevant social and political players. This is important in understanding the lasting strength of the nation's policy near-consensus: it has been forged by including all relevant players.

What is important to note is that the *democracia de los acuerdos* has been spearheaded by the *Concertación* governments, but it has informed the actions of most of the relevant actors with a stake in economic policy. That is, this regularized pattern of informal pact-making has been promoted and nurtured by political and social actors that are not natural allies of the Center-Left coalition. This includes organized Chilean business. Although it often exerted virtual veto power over proposals it strongly opposed, it generally sought to reach a compromise. Perhaps only with the active participation of business at the negotiating table could the income tax rate on companies have been raised from 10 percent in 1990 to 17 in 2001, as its concerns were met in other policy areas. All in all, the Chilean entrepreneurial community contributed greatly to the task of building societal consensus on the overall economic policy orientation of the country, and reaching agreements on tax policy was an important part of that task. The myriad technical tax proposals that business associations elaborated show that business' contribution was not only political, but also technical. What Chilean entrepreneurs consistently favored and actively advocated was tax stability to afford economic agents the benefit of stable, long-term economic horizons. By and large, Chilean technocrats and politicians alike showed themselves to be in tune with the imperative of nurturing economic policy predictability. They deemed this to be an indispensable requirement for fostering investment, and promoting capital formation became a healthy obsession in Chile. The overlap of interests between government and its political and social interlocutors in engendering high economic growth rates permeated tax policy negotiations throughout the 1990s. Agreement on basic underlying objectives certainly made the reaching of accords on taxation easier. The heated and nonstop debate since 1998 among business associations and political parties of all ideological persuasions on how to reignite the economy is a testament to the overwhelming priority accorded to economic growth, over and above sector-specific or short-term electoral interests. It is well to note that the prioritization of national economic growth, which may seem self-evident, is simply not nearly as characteristic of state-society interactions in most other Latin American countries. Much the same can be said about the *democracia de los acuerdos* as an informal institution that guides political behavior.

The Absence of Reform Consolidation in Argentina

The institutional factors conspiring against the consolidation of tax reform in Argentina comprise a historically feeble institutional environment, including a rather underinstitutionalized party system), an economically irrational federal fiscal system, and a pattern of exclusionary decision-making that eschews dialogue and compromise.

Feeble Institutional Environment

History and Institutional Path Dependency

Argentine history shows that political actors have been generally unwilling to adjust to existing institutions; to the contrary, they have adjusted institutions to fit their (short-term) objectives, plans, and ambitions. On the issue of institutional fragility, renowned Argentine historian Tulio Halperin-Dongui has remarked: "Argentina is one of the most foolish countries that I know in creating institutions: it has no respect whatsoever for them; it does not show any attachment to them" (*Clarin*, December 12, 1997). Donghi's statement raises the obvious question of why Argentina is so "foolish" about its institutions. In other words: why has Argentina been unable to forge efficient institutions that yield rational and durable public policies? Any attempt to answer this intricate question can profit from the analytical tools provided by institutional economics and the concept of transaction costs. Path dependency centers on the idea that history matters: past institutional arrangements decisively influence and narrow the choice of new ones, so that change takes place in an incremental way. Moreover, the nature of past institutional arrangements shapes the likelihood of future efficiency-promoting institutional change. A country's governance structure refers to the basic mechanisms of decision-making in a political system. The nature of that governance structure determines political transaction costs. When we consider political governance structures, these are more likely to embody inefficient transactional outcomes than economic ones, not least because collective action problems are more common in purely political arenas (North 1990; Dixit 1996).

Argentina's political and economic trajectory, like that of any other country, is crucially shaped by two factors: its initial, basic institutional characteristics and its level of institutional stability. The basic characteristics of Argentina's constitutional arrangement are presidentialism, bicameralism, federalism, and a largely majoritarian electoral system. These overarching rules of the game have through time resulted in high political fragmentation, bureaucratic and parliamentarian short-termism, and an ineffective and politicized Judicial Power (Tomassi and Spiller 2003). This governance structure, coupled with harmful politico-historical legacies, has been a major impediment to the construction of "technologies" that could have induced other political players to invest in the creation of more efficient and value-laden institutions.

Endogenously created institutional instability has, in no small measure, stemmed from the discretion afforded to and abused by the national executive. Historically, Argentine executives have enjoyed ample discretion, as they have been relatively unconstrained in its actions by Congress, the judiciary, or the public administration (Corrales 2001, 2003). Notwithstanding nominal rules, effective checks and balances have been weak. Executives have found few incentives to compromise with other political actors in building neutral and more effective institutions. Argentine presidents have tended to undermine stability by the frequent use of Decrees of Urgency and Necessity, the constant renovation of the Supreme Court, the thorough turnover of public service personnel, the recourse to partial vetoes, and similar practices. In other words, Argentine presidents have repeatedly undermined political property rights. The rules of the game have not adequately constrained the range of possible outcomes (North 1981).

Therefore, political and economic actors have been deprived of a reasonable horizon of stable expectations. If excessive presidential discretion and abuse of power have undermined political property rights, so has political instability. A weak government whose rule is in question because it may be shortly replaced by an authoritarian government cannot possibly ensure political or economic property rights. In particular, this instability has had a number of deleterious effects: it has increased the rotation of members of Congress, reducing its check-and-balance function; it has increased the rotation of public servants, politicized public administration and reduced its professionalism; and it has decreased drastically the average tenure of judges, including those in the Supreme Court. This institutional environment has fostered short-term and opportunistic behavior on the part of all political actors. It has also rendered intertemporal agreements elusive.

Important exogenous sources of instability have also plagued contemporary Argentine history. They stemmed from frequent coup d'etats, a result of "the impossible game" that characterized Argentine politics (O'Donnell 1976). Democracy became an "impossible game" because Peronism was the political movement with a natural majority whenever elections were held, but that political outcome was utterly unacceptable to the nation's business elite and military top brass. Whenever a winner emerged from restricted elections (i.e., excluding the Peronist movement), the country became ungovernable. The result was an inherently unstable equilibrium, in that either one of the two dominant political forces was unsatisfied with the status quo at any given point in time. Peronism, as a movement representing the working classes and seeking political hegemony, was anathema to dominant class interests. The crystallization of a highly polarized Peronist/anti-Peronist political dynamic conspired against any semblance of political, economic, and institutional stability (Romero 2002). Each antagonist rejected the legitimacy of the opponent and conceived politics as a zero-sum game. In such sociopolitical context, constructing democratic governance and building independent, value-laden democratic institutions that were stable through time proved elusive. Scholars have long observed that Argentineans historically never seemed to have developed a strong belief in the legitimacy of the institutions of democracy. Some have pinned responsibility more narrowly on the economic elites. Writes academic Atilio Boron (2003, 150):

> The ruling classes...never came to accept the democratic rules of the game as the only valid mechanism for the constitution of public

authority. The rich in Argentina never believed that the dominant classes should ratify their political supremacy in the electoral arena or pay taxes. Thus, when the threats of communism, "subversion," or populism were perceived to be imminent, the upper classes asked the military to intervene to protect their interests and prerogatives, sacrificing without major scruples public freedoms and democratic institutions.

Yet, putting blame for the failure to build democracy on one of the two protagonist political coalitions would be myopic. There can be little doubt that Domingo Peron himself and Peronists generally conceived of democracy instrumentally (as a means to power) rather than substantively (Sebreli 2002). Halperin-Dongui (1994) has analyzed how Peron failed to seize the opportunity to relegitimize Argentinean politics on the basis of the universal right to vote. Peron's influence was nefarious insofar as he did little to institutionalize political procedures, relying instead of plebiscitary personalism. (That legacy remains well entrenched in the Peronist ruling class.) Upon gaining power through means fair or foul, Peronists and anti-Peronists (with the Radical party at the center of this coalition) both took actions to systematically revamp the institutions (conceived both as organizations and rules of the game) put in place by their predecessors, in an attempt to "remake" Argentina in their image. In short, the Argentine political class misdirected political capital and lost almost every opportunity it had to improve governance and the quality of institutions.

Political instability is a fruitful starting point to uncover the riddle of Argentina's low taxation level (Andre Melo 2007) as well as other ills plaguing its public finances. In her landmark study on state reform in Latin America, Barbara Geddes (1994) persuasively argues that both democracies and dictatorships face obstacles in building state capacity. In a democratic setting, presidents have strong incentives for wanting to initiate institutional reform, as their future careers may depend on accomplishing programmatic goals. However, they also often face incentives to discard such reform initiatives, either because they need to preserve patronage resources or because they need to cater to certain clienteles in order to survive threats of overthrow. The upshot is that presidents who are more secure in their hold on power are more likely to initiate reform. This intuitive insight sheds much light on the Argentine case. In post–World War II Argentina, democratically elected presidents have headed "threatened" administrations (including Juan Peron, Arturo Frondizi, Arturo Illia, and Isabel

Peron). The military took direct control of government in 1955, 1962, 1966, and 1976. Presidents who see their survival threatened use the resources and political capital at their disposal to sustain their position in the political struggle with antidemocratic foes, rather than to build administrative competence. Even for reform-minded executives, institution-building comes second to political survival. Freed from the electoral and democratic constraints or the need to elicit the cooperation of other political actors, one may well predict that authoritarian Argentine governments may have had a better track record in the initiation of institution-building reforms. However, obstacles for the provision of collective goods in authoritarian settings are different but no less formidable than those that obtain under democratic rule. Argentine military governments achieved no better record in this area than democratic ones, not least due to state penetration by private interests, the low level of professionalism of public administration, high corruption, and incompetence. Yet, the worst of all worlds for building competent and effective state institutions obtains when there are frequent transitions between democracy and authoritarianism, as Geddes (1994) documents. That is the fate that befell Argentina from 1945 to 1983. Rules and institutions initiated by military rulers were seen as illegitimate and tended to be abandoned during (brief) transitions to democracy. Feeble democratic interludes, in turn, were infertile ground for building state institutions. Whenever newly elected governments face a context of high political polarization, social instability and the threat of ouster, institutional reform is bound to be demoted on the list of executive political priorities. These analytical observations lead to an inexorable conclusion: Argentina's historical political environment has rendered the country an optimal candidate for institutional inefficiency and state decay.

Weakness of the Argentine State
The Argentine state has historically been rather weak (Smith 1989; Sikkink 1991, 1993; Canitrot 1994; Oszlak 1997a,b; Berensztein and Spector 2003), as measured by standard indicators of state capacity and autonomy (Evans, Reschemeyer, and Skocpol 1985; Huber 2000). In comparison to its Chilean counterpart, it has not been a cohesive unitary actor and has lacked a dominant state bureaucratic class (Teichman 1997). Societal groups have heavily penetrated the Argentine state. The private sector, in particular the most powerful business interests, had a privileged say in decision-making. Although under Peronism the state gained a high level of autonomy from the

traditional dominant classes, this was perceived by the latter as a case of "inverted instrumentalism," whereby the state was serving the interests of the working classes (Sikkink 1993, 173). In short, the Argentine state has never been perceived as a neutral arbiter in pursuit of the general interest.

Frequent changes in economic policy have reflected shifting coalitions of state elites and societal allies. Historically, then, the Argentine state has not performed in a predictable, calculable, and rational manner. As a corollary, public institutions have lost validity and legitimacy vis-à-vis society, spurring the multiplication of illegal behaviors and weakening the social fabric. The state in Argentina took on an interventionist stance since the early 1930s, increasingly enlarging its sphere of action in the regulation of economic and social life. The period from 1955 to 1976, characterized by chronic economic and political instability, "witnessed state actions that were not based on stable governmental projects, but on demands for intervention that were contradictory, meaning that a growth of bureaucracy went hand in hand with a weakening of state capacities" (Sidicaro 2001, 33). According to the different political and economic interests of the governing teams, the demands of different players and sectors of the economy were accepted or denied, whether in regard to public subsidies, transfers of income, or tax policy. The military dictatorship of 1976–1983 engineered a qualitative jump in furthering the "crisis of the state" that led to a virtual collapse of public institutions in their ability to ensure the rule of law (ibid.).

Tax reform consolidation has been undermined by low state capacity to enforce compliance with the law, including the tax code. Changes in tax policy do not often map into expected outcomes (in terms of revenue, or increase in economic efficiency, etc.) because of inadequate implementation and enforcement by the state, which often prompts economic authorities to enact new changes. The Argentine federal tax bureau, the biggest of all state institutions, resembles that of other Latin American nations (but differs from the Chilean) in its inability to elicit the allegiance of citizens due to its lack of transparency, equanimity, and efficiency. A clear symptom of this malaise is the salience of tax evasion, which reaches a dazzling 50 percent of theoretical revenues. Much the same can be said with respect to tax avoidance. Both reveal that the fiscal pact between state and society in Argentina has been fractured for a long time.

Another sign of state weakness is given by the large size of the informal economy, which constitutes a formidable obstacle for enhancing tax revenues and tax compliance (Tanzi 1992; FIEL 2000). Because a sizable part of economic activity lies beyond the legal framework, the state is deprived of taxable revenues. Overcoming this obstacle requires changing the incentive structure in ways that create powerful motivations for workers in the black market to come out of the shadows into the legal, formal economy. The tools required to effect such changes often do not fall within the taxation arena (though a few do, such as reducing the costs of tax compliance, or altering the perception of risk).

Party System: Medium Level of Institutionalization
Unlike Chile, Argentina's political parties do not structure the debate and outlines of economic policy, including taxation. Social actors have not generally pushed their demands via the party system. Interest representation has been traditionally structured through corporatist arrangements. Political life participation in Argentina still suffers from factional tendencies. Personality-based factions, rather than political parties per se, continue to define much of the political arena. Unlike Chile, political parties are not the backbone of the political system. In fact, both the nature and the very existence of the Argentine party system have been called into question in the past (Cavarozzi 1984; De Riz 1986). The Peronist Party (or Partido Justicialista, PJ) and the Radical party (Union Civica Radical or UCR) have dominated Argentine politics since World War II, establishing a presence throughout the national territory backed by a dense network of provincial political machines based on clientelism and patronage (Calvo and Murillo 2003; Levitsky 2003a).

The return of democracy in 1983 thrust political parties into a more prominent role and by the mid-1990s the Argentine party system was classified as moderately institutionalized (Mainwaring and Scully 1995). (What does lend some degree of institutionalization to the party system are the longevity of the PJ and the UCR and their deep roots in Argentine society.) It can be maintained, however, that this assessment has been proven transient in light of political developments since the mid-1990s, as witnessed by the rise and fall of new parties (Accion por la Republica, FREPASO), the sky-high abstention rates of the congressional 2001 elections, the recognized decline in levels of party identity, and the virtual electoral disappearance of the Radical party at the national level, among other developments. More than twenty years after the transition to democracy, Argentina's party system displayed medium to low levels of institutionalization (Abal

Medina and Suarez Cao 2002; Levitsky 2003b). Menem, known for his preference for personalism in the exercise of power, undertook actions that weakened the party system.

The lack of a party system that is programmatically structured makes intra- and interparty discussions and negotiations revolve around interests rather than ideas. This renders the consolidation of economic reforms (let alone *politicas de estado*) more difficult than otherwise. Neither the Peronist nor the Radical party (UCR) showcases a defined economic agenda (Cavarozzi 1995; Sebreli 2002). Throughout their history, successive leaders of these political formations have shown a wide array of viewpoints in regard to economic and fiscal affairs (Manzetti 1993; McGuire 1997), and given leaders have held contradictory ideological tenets—including, of course, Domingo Peron himself. In practice, the quest for power has consistently trumped adherence to ideological doctrines. Moreover, the prevalent logic of clientelism has further eroded the influence of ideas.

To be sure, the UCR was founded upon certain political principles, including the defense of a liberal democracy and the rule of law. In practice, it has behaved in a pragmatic, opportunistic fashion. Not unlike Peronists, the Radicals have also deferred their internal party structure mechanisms to strong, charismatic leaders, such as Hipolito Yrigoyen or Raul Alfonsin. In the realm of economics, the party's ideas and policy have changed substantially.[5] The UCR cannot be said to be a party with a defined economic program, with an ideological vision on how to govern the economy. The PJ also lacks a defined economic agenda. Peronism, in fact, approximates more a movement than a modern political party. It has traditionally been a "catch-all" political formation, encompassing an assortment of ideological persuasions. It has surely undergone a process of institutionalization since the death of its founder and the transition to democracy, but even today it can be argued that its level of institutionalization is low (Mustapic 2002; Levitsky 2003a). In a real sense, the party has always been fluid and mutable, making it very adaptable. Built around the figure of an army colonel, rather than a programmatic agenda, it is a populist party of easy slogans of little substantive content. When in power, the PJ has introduced an array of economic policies that could not neatly be associated with any given overarching ideology. Moreover, the economic agenda of different Peronist administrations has differed radically—from Peron to Menem to Kirschner. While Peron favored heavy intervention in the economy, Menem adopted a fairly radical free-market agenda. Contrary to what is commonly argued, the turn toward liberal economics starting in 1989 reflected political expediency rather than ideological conversion to a given "faith." Whenever political considerations required deviation from liberal economics, policy deviated from liberal tenets. It is political pragmatism and the logic of clientelism that have largely driven the PJ's economic policies. A corollary of these facts is that electoral campaigns in Argentina lack substantive economic content, allowing presidents a greater degree of discretion once in power. Incidentally, the increase in programmatic flexibility witnessed in both parties has lowered party identity levels, further accentuating the country's deficit of representation (Torre 2002).

What the aforementioned lack of economic compass means for tax policy is straightforward: interests have overwhelmingly ruled over ideas in the configuration of the tax system. Whatever ideas have informed the tax system have been the lone voices of some finance ministers and high-raking technocrats operating in an environment hostile to ideas. Thus, the solidification of a tax system via the slow building of a minimum-denominator accord has proved elusive. Perhaps even more importantly, political party apparatuses have had little say over economic policy, as the executive power has usually bypassed Congress as a pertinent agent of policymaking (Mustapic 2000).

Institutional Configurations

Atomized Interest Aggregation

The structure of interest aggregation can alter the amount of polarization that the political process projects into policymaking. Where the representation of business and labor is fragmented in an already conflict-ridden society, policymaking may well be unstable and unpredictable. The weakness of the Argentine party system has inevitably distorted the adequate representation of business and labor interests. Peronism and Radicalism were characterized by their loose organization and institutionalization. Movementism has historically trumped the logic of structured modern political party dynamics. Interest mediation within groups making up the movement (Yrigoyenismo, Peronismo, Menemismo), and between the latter and groups outside was unstructured. Rather, the task fell on the initiative of the leader. The restriction or banning of parties during intermittent authoritarian interludes from 1945 to 1983 meant that power resided increasingly in the executive, the state bureaucracy, and specialized agencies (Snow and Manzetti 1993). Indeed, as political parties proved incapable of promoting stability and interest mediation, organized groups resorted to lobbying the executive and administrative branches of government directly. This practice carried on to the post-1983 democratic period.

To be sure, interest representation in Argentina has been hampered by the institutional weakness of the parties themselves. Interest groups have therefore concluded that their needs and demands are better served by ad hoc, temporary, nonbinding agreements. Historically, rural and industrial groups have had a very adversarial relationship. Agricultural interests are represented mainly by the *Sociedad Rural Argentina* (SRA) and the *Confederaciones Rurales Argentinas* (CRA). These associations have enjoyed long leadership continuity and relatively low internal dissent (Manzetti 1993, chapter 7), especially in comparison to the fragmented and unstable business and labor coalitions. Entrepreneurial interests have been led by the *Union Industrial Argentina* (UIA), the *Confederacion General Economica* (CGE), and the *Confederacion General de Industria* (CGI), and a plethora of other smaller groups focused on more specialized interests—such as the *Asociacion de Bancos Argentinos* (ADEBA), representing the financial sector (ibid., chapter 8). Unity of purpose among industrial associations has been hampered by its multiplicity and heterogeneity of interests. The cleavages promoting overt discord and cacophony include those between domestic corporations against multinationals, big business against small and medium-sized companies, and industries in Buenos Aires against those of the "interior." Intra-association dissent has been common over trade opening, subsidies, and state intervention. These factors have conspired against the creation of an umbrella organization representing industry. They also help explain why the industrial sector has suffered from weak, divisive leadership. Consequently, the business community has often been unable to present a unified front as regards tax policy.

Like the entrepreneurial sector, labor also presents a fragmented organizational structure and divided, unstable leadership. Although Argentine unionism is considered by far the strongest in Latin America, since the 1980s its power and coherence has been undermined by divisions. On paper, the umbrella organization is the Peronist-dominated *Confederacion General de Trabajo* (CGT), but it is ridden with factions that deal separately with business and government. Historically, the CGT has not represented a united front. Moreover, during the

1980s Peronist unions (the most powerful and politically influential) broke into four rival factions, with different ideological stances: the Group of 25 (left), Ubaldini-led faction, the Group of 15 (right), and "62" (traditional Peronist unionism). Personal, ideological, and party issues have divided the leaders of these and other unions, and deprived the body politic of a unified labor interlocutor. In addition, because the manufacturing sector declined as a share of the economy and the service sector gained prominence, sector-based cleavages further accentuated divisions within labor unionism.

In short, it can be concluded that both governability and economic policy coherence in Argentina have been hampered by absence of coherent, encompassing interest groups.

The Kafkaesque Federal Fiscal System
Argentina's federal fiscal regime greatly hinders the articulation of national goals with respect to fiscal and tax policy. The regime's enormous deficiencies not only make macroeconomic management difficult but also undermine democratic accountability and the fiscal system's overall legitimacy in the eyes of Argentine taxpayers (Jones, Sanguinetti, and Tommasi 2000; Sanchez 2011a).

The most important problem afflicting the coparticipation regime is the lack of fiscal correspondence between taxation and spending powers at all levels of government—also called "vertical fiscal imbalance" (FIEL 1993). At the beginning of the 1990s, no less than 47 percent of total public spending in Argentina was undertaken by provinces and municipalities while these levels of government together only collected about 24 percent of total tax resources (ibid.). Another way to gauge vertical imbalance is this: provinces only collected 31 percent of the resources they spent, while the federal government collected the remaining 69 percent (ibid.). Such disequilibrium carries a number of economic problems. First, it fosters what economists have called "fiscal illusion" at the provincial level—that is, taxpayers enjoy the benefits of spending while its associated costs are made invisible to them. From the point of view of democratic governance, the inexorable result is the lack of accountability and transparency, obscuring the taxpayer's ability to assess the fiscal behavior of their politicians or more generally, the nature of the social contract between state and taxpayer. From an economic viewpoint, vertical imbalance produces a number of perverse behavioral incentives—affecting public spending, tax policy, and tax administration (Saiegh and Tommasi 1999). First, provinces, which are largely relieved from the task of tax collection and guaranteed monthly transfers of funds from the center, can act as though they face no hard budget constraint (Porto and Sanguinetti 1998). Each subnational government has an incentive to engage in chronic deficit spending. Second, the fact that provinces do not pay the political cost of tax collection means that local administrators do not have an incentive to engage in efficient public spending or an incentive to tackle evasion, so that large sums of taxpayers' money are effectively wasted. Third, the system fosters pervasive tax avoidance and tax evasion, as taxpayers perceive low benefits from the level of government to which their tax payments are destined. In sum, not only does vertical imbalance distort the efficient allocation of resources but it also limits the autonomy of provinces and restricts the exercise of democracy (insofar as voters' choices have little impact on spending and taxation policies).

From the point of view of resource allocation, taxes excluded from the revenue-sharing pool (or taxes that are shared to an unequal extent between the nation and the provinces) constitute an acute problem. Each of these specific taxes has a tailor-made and complex revenue-sharing formula. This feature of the system means that the federal government has an incentive to focus its efforts on those taxes that accrue solely or disproportionately to the federal level, which may be among the least efficient.

By contrast, Chile's highly centralized fiscal system facilitates the articulation of national economic policy goals. Attempts at fiscal decentralization have been systematically opposed and aborted by authorities in Santiago. Fear of instability in public finances is the main reason fiscal decentralization measures have been aborted, as a former director of the budget explains. There is consensus that fiscal policy as a macroeconomic tool only exists as long as there is centralized control of it.

Informal Institutions

The Scourge of Clientelism

Citizen-politician linkages in Argentina are substantially pervaded by clientelism (also called patrimonialism). Clientelism represents a transaction, the direct exchange of votes (or general political support) for direct payments or access to employment, goods, and services (Kitschelt and Wilkinson 2007). Clientelism constitutes an informal institution insofar as it guides the behavior and expectations of political actors and sanctions are meted out for behavior that deviates from the understandings implied in this type of exchange. It is well established that clientelism is correlated with underdevelopment: the poorer the country, the more extensive the practice. Argentina constitutes somewhat of an outlier in this regard, as its levels of clientelism are similar to those observed in significantly less developed countries. The Peronist party is well known for its extensive clientelistic networks reaching even the smallest village in rural Argentina (Ayuero 2000; Levitsky 2003a, 2007). To be sure, in some countries, parties pursue diversified portfolios, concurrently mixing programmatic and clientelistic strategies—that is, using one or the other according to where electorates are geographically located or their income level. This is certainly the strategy the Peronist party pursues in Argentina. In any case, the pervasiveness of clientelism is higher than observed in other countries of similar GDP per capita. Moreover, the theoretical expectation that economic liberalization would dampen clientelism was not borne out in Argentina or elsewhere in Latin America. Menem's free-market reforms proved compatible with clientelism. What drives clientelism in Argentina? One important variable is its politicized economy and public administration. Argentina's politicized economic government structure allows elected politicians who appoint administrators in the executive branch and state-owned enterprises large leeway to target resources to particular supporters. The degrees of freedom to engage in clientelism are particularly high in the areas of business and market regulation, the award of specific market advantages (subsidies, loans, export/import subsidies) and procurement contracts for government infrastructure. Argentine politicians use that freedom to full clientelistic effect, particularly Peronist ones. As labor unions weakened in the 1980s and 1990s, so did the class-based identities inherent to Peronism. By default, the party's clientelistic networks became "the most important webs of relations in which the remains of a strong Peronist identity are kept alive" (Ayuero 2000, 204). The low professionalization of public administration and the prevalence of clientelism are two sides of the same Argentine coin. Argentina's politicized economy dates back decades, long before the country transited to democracy as part of the Third Wave of democratization. That economic governance structure has not been muted by democratic rule.

Programmatic party-citizen linkages are based on parties' supply of collective goods such as economic growth, jobs, monetary stability, or improving *overall* distributive outcomes as desired by a majority of citizens. Income redistribution via taxation is an example of the latter. By contrast, clientelistic relationships are not based on demands for such collective goods. It stands to reason, therefore, that the more pervasive the presence of this informal institution, the lower the level of collective goods supplied. Clientelism has important implications for economic reform because, ceteris paribus, politicians have powerful incentives to subvert reforms that threaten their patronage leeway, and thus their ability to win votes and remain in power. The impact of patronage politics on tax administration reform, including the fight against tax evasion, is direct and obvious. Tax administration reform can undermine the ability of politicians to use the federal tax bureau to reward political friends, not least with jobs or with preferential treatment in the application of the tax code. In fact, the fight against evasion spearheaded in Menem's first administration was called off as soon as powerful economic groups with links to the president were affected (Santoro 1996; Sanchez 2011). The effect of patronage politics on tax policy is quite direct as well. The logic of patrimonialism drives politicians to target spending toward specific constituents, but also to increase the overall level of public expenditure. Ostensibly, the president as well as governors and mayors have similar incentives to oil their patronage machines. The president's constituency is national, however, so theoretically the incentive of the federal government to provide public goods and avoid the costs of fiscal imbalances is greater. Yet, empirically speaking, the fiscal behavior of the federal government was not much more responsible than that of provinces during the 1990s. Political systems where the logic of patrimonialism regularly trumps the technocratic objective of economic orthodoxy produce "chronic fiscal stress" (Whitehead 1996). A collective action problem inevitably arises insofar as careless spending by all actors spawns fiscal and economic crises in which all players lose. This is a repeated occurrence in Argentina due to the entrenched logic of patrimonial dynamics, the relative absence of institutions capable of checking the spendthrift tendencies of politicians, and the politicized nature of economic policymaking, among other factors. In the interior provinces (those other than Buenos Aires), in particular, the logic of patrimonialism continues to dominate citizen-party relations. The fiscal gaps resulting from patrimonial political dynamics repeatedly drove Argentine policymakers to make frequent and abrupt changes to the tax code, further straining the state-society fiscal pact.

6
Conclusion

Why have Chile and Argentina arrived at such different outcomes in their efforts to build a more solid fiscal foundation by consolidating tax policy reforms? This concluding chapter aims to draw conclusions from the thirteen-year period (1989–2001) under examination in both countries. A key lesson that emerges is that consolidating a better tax system (of higher extractive capacity, greater efficiency, and enhanced acceptance) depends not on the technical merits of the proposed reforms, but on the broader institutional context in which they are undertaken. This broader institutional environment has resolutely shaped Chilean success and Argentine failure in the pursuit of fiscal state-building. Even more than differences in *formal* institutional configuration, what shapes outcomes most are marked disparities in institutional strength (conceived as stability and enforcement) and distinctions in informal institutions.

The quality of their institutional environments sets these two countries apart. Chile's strong institutional setting has served as a privileged framework for conducting economic policy. When the rule of law prevails in a country the difference between the official tax code and the tax system that exists de facto is narrower than otherwise. This makes it easier to map policy into outcomes. Chilean authorities have been able to know with a reasonable degree of certitude what the economic consequences of changes in tax policy would be. Consequently, they have been able to devise economic policy with the long run in mind. Argentine technocrats, by contrast, have had to devise tax changes highly uncertain of their economic consequences. For example, many tax moratoria in Argentina have yielded meager revenues because taxpayers have not perceived the need to put their legal obligations in order, in the knowledge that the state's enforcement capabilities are low and that tax amnesties are commonplace.

Argentina's feeble institutions, unable to enforce contracts, have acted as a poor framework within which to conduct tax policy. This institutional environment has fueled *cortoplacismo* (short-termism) among tax policymakers and taxpayers alike—including fiscal opportunism. To an extent hardly seen in Chile, tax policy and administration in Argentina resemble a daily "trial and error" experiment, where each player adjusts its "strategy" in reaction to the moves of other players. The perverse consequences of actors' short-term horizons for the coherence and quality of the tax system (in terms of extractive capacity, horizontal and vertical equity, efficiency, etc.) cannot be overstated.

The historical development of the Chilean and Argentine states differ in crucial ways. Inescapably, the contrasting outcomes in Chile and Argentina were significantly shaped by institutional path dependency. As Gerardo della Paolera and Ezequiel Gallo illustrate in *A New Economic History of Argentina,* macroeconomic and microeconomic institutional failures permeate Argentine history in a recurring way. The quandary of institutional weakness is indeed one with long-standing roots. During its famed period of economic prosperity (roughly from 1880 to World War II), Argentina "missed the opportunity to design adequate institutions that would secure sustainable growth and insulate society from the venality of politicians and rent-seekers" (ibid.). The 1990s can be considered another lost opportunity. Absent actions to change an incentive structure that promotes disastrous collective outcomes, the country fell into old, familiar traps. It was a decade in which crucial institutional reforms were postponed in the mistaken belief that a new economic age had dawned, not unlike what transpired during previous interludes of economic well-being. Cavallo's currency board and the aggressive pursuit of first-generation reforms (privatization, deregulation, trade opening), whatever their merits and pitfalls, were no substitute for second-generation institutional reforms (administrative and political). Their absence ultimately doomed efforts to enhance extractive capacity, rationalize tax policy, and solidify tax reform.

Institutional Framework to Resolve Collective Action Problems

On a broader level, public policy is affected by how a polity manages collective action problems. Otherwise stated, this is the quandary of governability. In Argentina and Chile, the evolution of economic policy and tax policy in the 1990s was surely shaped by the capacity of the body politic to manage and mediate among the complex array of competing interest groups inside and outside the state. In post-Pinochet Chile, political parties and interest groups have, in no small measure, worked toward broad goals that go beyond the defense of partisan or corporatist interests. This consensual political environment has been reinforced by certain institutional features of the Chilean landscape—chiefly the presence of encompassing organizations to represent business and labor interests, easing the way to broad societal agreements. By the early 1990s, political and economic stability had acquired absolute value in Chile, the quality of a public good desirable for its own sake. Although different actors surely have a different views on what constitutes "the general interest" and what policies need to be put in place to reach it, there is a bona fide national dialogue on most relevant public issues. Politics is not necessarily defined in zero-sum terms. In the realm of taxation Chilean political parties have narrowed their differences as a result of an ideational convergence in economic outlooks and their joint determination to maintain the "social peace" has bridged many differences at the negotiation table. Similarly, the business sector has also come to define its interests in broader terms than material gain, and become more conscious of its broader societal responsibilities as an important interlocutor of the government. Finally, Chile's unitary territorial structure has surely helped the articulation of national goals (by reducing collective action problems) in ways that elude Argentina.

Political power has traditionally been highly dispersed in Argentina. This characteristic, coupled with an institutional framework that discourages cooperation, has led to a recurrent collective action dilemma, rendering it extremely difficult for presidents to govern effectively. Since the return of democracy 1983, this dilemma was attenuated in some ways, but became more acute in others. In particular, Argentina has witnessed since then a federalization of power, whereby provinces have been able to steadily wrest political authority away from the center. Their power in the legislature grew in tandem. Faced with this political map, President Menem actively sought and managed to concentrate power in his office, thanks to both shrewd agency (the building of alliances with governors via pork barrel spending, a de facto coalition with the business community, etc.) and a set of time-specific circumstances (a mammoth economic crisis, the opposition's loss of credibility, atomization of various interest groups). Menem's successful quest to acquire special legislative powers, delegated from Congress, allowed for the expeditious passage of many economic reforms, including in the tax area. In retrospect, however, it is clear that Argentina's collective action quandary was not confronted successfully. Menem's firm decisionism turned out to be, in many ways, a pyrrhic victory. As "politics as usual" returned to the scene in 1992/3, and particularly from the time the drawbacks of the Convertibility Plan were revealed (around 1994–1995), long-standing collective action dilemmas came back to haunt Argentine politics.

Party System Institutionalization

An institutional variable of much importance when explaining the relative coherence of tax policy through time is the level of party system institutionalization. Political parties matter for the quality of policymaking because they can provide predictable economic choices to voters, link government to civil society, impose order on legislative processes, and discipline politicians. The Chilean party system is highly institutionalized (parties with deep roots in society, clear programmatic agendas, reasonably stable economic ideologies, a predictable pattern of interaction among parties, etc.). By contrast, Argentina displays a rather inchoate party system, comparatively speaking. Historically, Peronism and Radicalism qualify as movements rather than modern parties and that legacy has not been surmounted. These parties' respective economic agendas are undefined, including fiscal matters. This means that whatever tax reform initiatives are approved in Congress do not correspond to a societal compromise among competing ideas and material interests. An institutionalized party system implies that a spectrum of different interests and ideas are given representation. Every tax reform involves a political choice: a choice between efficiency and equity, between levying capital or labor, between emphasizing direct or indirect taxes, and so on. Because tax policy affects everyone in society and inevitably entails tradeoffs along with different distributional outcomes, *durable* tax policies are forged when society has an effective political voice in their enactment. In Argentina, the political exchanges inherent in any economic reform are pervaded by political clientelism. Clientelism, an informal institution that subverts democratic representation and the fiscal contract between state and society, has thus undermined fiscal state-building. In a clientelist political context, the voices of fiscal conservatives (even when they come from the Ministry of Economy) often drown in a sea of spending debauchery. The limitations encountered when trying to rationalize public finances in Argentina's clientelistic body politic are well exemplified by the failed attempt of Finance Minister Ricardo Lopez Murphy to "put the fiscal house in order" immediately upon being sworn into office. Murphy attempted to enact much-needed far-reaching structural changes in public expenditure. The proposal was dead on arrival and Murphy was forced to resign after a week in office!

Autonomy of State Institutions and Personnel Stability

Stability in top government personnel also separates Chile from Argentina. A factor fostering constant, damaging change in tax policy and administration has been the high turnover in top government posts. In Chile, finance ministers of the economy, tax agency chiefs, directors of the budget, and other top-ranking officials usually complete their statutory terms in office. Alejandro Foxley, Eduardo Aninat, and Nicolas Eyzaguirre completed their terms without a problem, as did their top lieutenants, while Javier Etcheberry headed the nation's tax bureau for over ten years. In Argentina, stability is an elusive commodity in any of its forms. Finance Ministers Rapanelli, Gonzalez, and Machinea were fired after a few months in office, Cavallo did not complete his second term, and Lopez Murphy lasted one week. Similarly, Raul Cuello did not last long as secretary for public revenues, while a remarkable public servant such as Carlos Tacchi resigned when he saw his autonomy encroached upon. The federal tax bureau (DGI) saw five different directors come and go during the thirteen-year span analyzed (1989–2001). To be sure, this instability in top-level personnel speaks to broader political and economic instability but, in no small part, it is also a reflection of the degree to which economic decision-making is politicized. The managers of the economy are made to serve their political masters in ways that would be considered unacceptable in Chile. Even the almighty Domingo Cavallo lost his job in part because he refused to yield to questionable political designs (pushed by Ministers Corach and Balza, Menem's inner circle). Reflecting Menem's desire for greater control over economic policy at a given juncture, tax policy and administration became excessively politicized during the latter half of the 1990s, with damaging consequences for tax stability, extractive capacity, and overall economic rationality. Both formal and informal institutions prevent Chile's president from politicizing tax policy in similar ways. As concerns tax administration, the Chilean head of the tax bureau (SII) enjoys substantial independence backed by law. Etcheberry persecuted tax evaders in any way he saw fit within the law, unencumbered by directives from any of the three presidents under whom he served.

Consensus and Rules Concerning Macroeconomic Stability

The relative stability of the macroeconomic environment has inevitably had implications for differences in tax system coherence and permanence. External economic shocks (Mexico's Tequila contagion in 1995, Russia's default in 1997, Brazil's devaluation in 1998) hit the Argentine economy with unusual force because economic authorities lacked the adjustment tool of monetary policy. In addition, fiscal profligacy by governors and the federal government alike magnified those crises, and generated home-grown ones. Argentine politicians did not invest in institutions that could alleviate macroeconomic instability. Again, an institutional setting that hinders collective action and heavily discounts the future accounts for the dearth of progress in this and other areas. A national debate surrounding this critical issue was (and continues to be) conspicuous by its absence. Faced with long-standing institutional and political structures that constrain economically rational policies, Argentines have demonstrated a penchant for magic formulas and "quick fixes," as these and other measures reveal. The periodic *impuestazo* packages (abrupt tax hikes) applied in succession by Ministers Cavallo, Roque Fernandez, and Machinea can be included in this "quick-fix" category. All of them failed in their objectives, and all undermined the state's fiscal rapport with taxpayers.

Again, the comparison with Chile on this count yields a striking contrast. The Chilean political class has consistently supported policies and institutions that place economic stability as the overarching objective (such as the creation of stabilization funds, etc.). Collective political learning from traumatic periods in its economic history have galvanized Chilean politicians to enshrine economic stability as an absolute value (not unlike Germany's obsession with price stability in reaction to its hyperinflationary experience). The implications for the tax system have been most beneficial. Economic and tax stability go hand in hand, because a stable macroeconomy is a sine qua non for tax policy long-term planning. In line with this healthy obsession with economic stability, the Chilean political class has shown a commitment to endow taxation policy with institutional credibility and predictability, with a view toward lengthening the decision-making horizon of economic agents—particularly that of the business sector. This commitment reflected a broad political consensus on the priority of investment formation and GDP growth. This, in turn, has had a number of virtuous corollaries: the executive has consciously sought broad legislative support for tax changes; the business community has always been a party to important tax policy innovations; political parties and candidates have been explicit about taxation during electoral campaigns; and finally, an informal interparty consensus has been forged around the need to avoid frequent tax policy changes.

Rules for Fiscal Discipline: "Tax and Spend" versus "Spend First and (Maybe) Tax later" Models

The two countries took very different paths regarding the "Washington Consensus" tenet of fiscal discipline. Notwithstanding a few exceptions, the Argentine political class showed no commitment to fiscal balance. Electoral or political factors regularly prodded the executive to stray from the path of fiscal discipline. In fact, there was abundant fiscal profligacy from the very start of convertibility. Most of the stock of debt to cover fiscal gaps was accumulated at both the national and provincial levels during the highly expansionary years, from 1991 to 1994 (Teijeiro 2001). Argentina, in contrast to Chile, clearly displayed a *spend and tax* model. No Argentine politician was bounded by the informal rules of the game (informal institutions) to explicitly account for how expenditure was to be financed *before* being spent. Politicians gorged on public spending with little concern about the way in which it was to be financed—any source, including external borrowing, was valid. Consolidated public spending in Argentina rose by 160 percent during the 1990s, while the economy only grew by 100 percent (ibid.). This gap was bridged via borrowing, leading to a burgeoning government debt that rose up to an unsustainable 41 percent of GDP by 1998 (*Economist* 2004). Some of the excess spending stemmed from Menem's attempt to buy his way into an (unconstitutional) third term in office by delivering pork to constituents and allied governors. It goes without saying that such dynamics cannot be understood without reference to a populist setting dominated by patronage politics, as well as a federal fiscal system that makes it extremely difficult to rein in provincial spending. In the 1990s, as throughout most of its history, Argentina proved unable to maintain fiscal discipline on a consistent basis. Unsurprisingly, economic authorities often found themselves scrambling to craft "magic bullet" laws to comply with the fiscal expectations of foreign investors and the IMF.

The Argentine tax story also shows that Cavallo's currency board itself posed a basic policy dilemma between competitiveness and fiscal rectitude. The one-peso-one dollar exchange rate arrangement rendered Argentine exports uncompetitive (because the peso became grossly overvalued), enticing authorities to engage in "fiscal devaluations," a supply-side measure that involved selective tax reductions to enhance export competitiveness. Indeed, Minister Cavallo enacted supply-side measures both when he served Menem and later when he tried to rescue de la Rua's doomed presidency. This policy, however, necessarily ate away tax revenues.

Chileans, on the other hand, forged a strong, unwavering political commitment to fiscal balance dating back to the 1980s. The reason this consensus was built across party lines lies in their recognition of the harmful consequences of fiscal deficits in the past and the measurable benefits that fiscal rectitude brought, particularly in terms of its contribution to macroeconomic stability. No Chilean political party was oblivious to this logic, as fiscal discipline turned into the "Chilean economic advantage" within Latin America. Fiscal discipline became a political weapon that Chilean politicians used to demolish expenditure projects of uncertain or dubious financial backing. The resolute measures taken by the Lagos administration spoke volumes about the sacred status of fiscal discipline in Chile. To signal its firm intention to continue this tradition of fiscal rectitude—and address investors' restlessness surrounding the Socialist party spending proclivities of the past—the Lagos government (a Socialist-led coalition) took great pains to institute a structural fiscal surplus of 1 percent. The country's unwritten political pact around fiscal discipline had two important repercussions with respect to tax policy. First, every increase in public spending was automatically fully financed with an increase in domestic tax levels. The direct link established between taxes and spending privileged the revenue objective of taxation above all. Revenues were not sacrificed in the pursuit of other important tax objectives—whether simplicity, economic efficiency, or horizontal equity. (Yet, these objectives were hardly ignored, as previous chapters have shown.) Second, every change in tax policy that was revenue-decreasing was compensated by another tax policy change elsewhere that raised revenue to fully offset the former. Proposals that were not fiscally compensated faced certain political defeat.

Informal Institutions: Ideational Framework

In Chile both interests and ideas (economic rationality) influence political decision-making. In Argentina, short-run particularistic and corporative interests usually rule supreme—and ideas are most often simply used to cloak interests. To this respect it is pertinent to note that while much ink was spilled over Menem's presumed ideological conversion to neoliberalism upon taking office, political developments throughout the 1990s revealed such "conversion" as purely instrumental, and moreover partial and short-lived. Menem's decade in power exemplified an enduring Argentine reality: the logic of political patronage regularly trumps economic rationality. In the long run, the logic of populist politics triumphs over the law of scarce resources. Economic theory teaches that "there are no free lunches," but Argentine politicians appear to stray from that lesson with vexing regularity. In Chile, ideas have had a more decisive influence on economic outcomes—not least on the shape of the tax system. A broad agreement exists on many (though not all) of the important characteristics of an optimal tax system—namely, a simple structure characterized by few taxes of broad bases (and high yields), horizontal equity (disregard for vertical equity), high economic efficiency, and easy administration. These ideas have delimited the Chilean tax policy debate. No such clear demarcations exist in the Argentine "debate," if there is indeed such a thing among the political class. In tax policy, as in most other economic issues, the policy stances of political parties and individual politicians are undefined. Tracking the average politician's policy stance on taxation through time would reveal major self-contradictions, as positions are not guided by basic principles or ideas. In short, there is no political debate in the strict sense of a structured, ideas-based discussion of the tradeoffs and advantages or disadvantages of different tax structures.[1]

Chile's political class underwent remarkable political learning during the 1980s and 1990s (Cavarozzi 1999), not least as regards economic affairs. The country witnessed a process of convergence in economic viewpoints that narrowed the range of what is acceptable in economic policy and what is not. There is a normative framework that informs decision-making. Such a framework is diffuse in Argentina, if it exists at all. The longtime ruling *Concertación* coalition of parties was guided by a belief in a larger and better functioning state and a larger and better functioning market (Marfan, interview). The practical consequence is that successive *Concertación* governments endeavored to increase public and social spending—in a financially responsible manner, via increased domestic taxes. Similarly, there emerged a reasonable political consensus on the need to aggressively reduce tax evasion by augmenting administration capacity, closing loopholes in the tax law, and improving the taxpayer service and image of the *Servicio de Impuestos Internos* (Sanchez 2011b). Such translation of party (or coalition) principles and ideas to economic policies is difficult to track in Argentina.

Informal Institutions: The Role of Technocracy

Another essential difference between the two neighbors is the role that technocracy plays in politics. A comparatively large proportion of Chile's political class comes from professional circles (whether economists, lawyers, scholars, etc.). In particular, the role of professional economists in Chilean politics is pervasive. The Chicago boys spearheaded a technocratization of government. As a consequence, "the economist's methods, language, myths, and their ideology of rationality became institutionalized conventions" (Montecinos 1998a, 130). To be sure, the ascent of economists to top positions of power is ubiquitous throughout Latin America. But to an extent rare in other countries, in Chile political parties' platforms and the policy positions of career politicians are heavily influenced by technocratic standards, values, and practices. *Tecnicos* and technopols, to use Jorge Dominguez's (1997) term, exercise a moderating influence on the public position of political parties; that is, they push parties toward a less ideological stance. Inevitably, a number of internal battles have ensued in the midst of Chilean parties between *politicos* and *tecnicos*. Chile's technocratic political culture gives technocrats the upper hand in such disputes. The Socialist party's internal squabbles during Frei's term (1994–1999) provide one example among many. In the internal feud between the traditional politicians and party economists over whether to attend to social deficits (in health, education, and housing) via increased spending or to withhold such spending in the name of fiscal discipline, it was the latter (technocratic) stance that easily won the day.

The Elusive Quest for Tax Reform Consolidation in Latin America

There are important insights to be extracted from Argentine and Chilean experiences that can be fruitfully applied to Latin America's struggles with tax reform consolidation. Perhaps the most important is the role played by political organizations that mediate conflicts between interest groups, classes, and coalitions. Because no other institution links state and civil society as fundamentally as political parties do, parties are essential to provide the necessary political support to legitimate state tax policies. Insofar as political parties are inchoate (and weakening) in much of the region, the prospects for consolidating transformative changes in tax policy are imperiled. Relatively few countries in the region count with political parties with deep roots in society and a stable vote share through time. The inchoate party systems increasingly plaguing Latin America (Mainwaring, Bejarano, and Leongomez 2006; Sanchez 2008) are unable to act as effective societal interlocutors vis-à-vis the state. As a consequence, tax policy reforms are often imposed from above with little or no societal dialogue. Tax reforms often unravel when they are enacted by governing parties lacking social rootedness or whose electoral support (and parliamentary strength) drops substantially. Such reforms can more easily be scrapped or undermined by subsequent governments. To be sure, the initial passing of reform may be easier in the absence of a socially rooted party opposition. However, what is ultimately more decisive for building a tax state is that the long-term *consolidation* of such reforms is undermined by the chaotic political landscapes that accompany inchoate party systems—or even party nonsystems (Sanchez 2009b). A regional background of feeble party constellations matters for another important reason: underinstitutionalized parties in power possess less political capital and are less willing to spend the capital at their disposal than more institutionalized ones. It is often said that the absence of important tax reforms in Latin America reflects the absence of genuine political will on the part of governments. Governing parties, however, often simply lack the political capital to undertake such a politically sensitive reform initiative. It stands to reason that, ceteris paribus, comprehensive tax reform bills are less likely to be introduced by inchoate parties than by institutionalized ones. And in cases where inchoate governing parties are able to enact them, such reforms face a lower probability of becoming consolidated over time.

The Argentine case distills another lesson. While executive dominance of the decision-making process can help developing nations escape severe economic crisis by dint of rapid, muscular reforms, it ultimately undermines democratic governance and reform consolidation. As Haggard and Kaufman (1992a, 19) have argued, the *consolidation* of reform "demands a somewhat different balance between state autonomy and the representation of interests" than its initiation. All too often, the final contours of taxation reforms in Latin America approximate not the resulting vector in the distributional battle among societal groups. Rather, executive fiat or petty short-term political exchanges among a few players determine those taxation contours. This undermines the legitimacy, ease of implementation, and durability of taxation codes. The potential of democratic institutions and interest groups to provide a much firmer political and institutional grounding for reforms has been obviated by many presidents in the region not least because of intractable problems of governability, tilting incentives toward unilateralism. Executive dominance, however, is not necessarily or only the result of the usurpation of legislative authority by the president, but can also stem from the weakness of the legislative process. Latin America is no stranger to such institutional deficiencies. If Argentine lawmakers have been called "amateur legislators and professional politicians," much the same could be said for the lawmakers of most legislative bodies in the region. To become effective policymakers, Latin American legislatures need to develop levels of technical capacity somewhat comparable to the technocratic economic ministries in the executive branch.

The discussion of party systems cannot be disassociated from a well-known bias afflicting taxation structures in the region: the meager presence of direct taxes in the overall tax intake. Latin American nations collect much less in direct taxes than is the global norm for countries at their level of income. If Latin American taxation systems are to become more progressive (i.e., redistributive), so as to contribute to ameliorate the region's abysmal income inequities, direct taxes need to become a greater source of revenue than is currently the case. It is difficult to envision how this can happen unless tax policy becomes deliberately politicized: that is, thrust into center-stage of political discourse and debate in electoral campaigns and discussion among political parties. Yet, for this important debate to transpire and yield fruit, some reasonable degree of party system stability and institutionalization is a sine qua non. A chaotic and ever-changing party universe does not lend itself to the politicization of this or other economic policy issues. Direct taxation is among the most politically sensitive of issues, as it directly impinges on the material interests of the middle classes and the rich. Well-rooted parties with a claim to broad societal representation can face down the veto power of rich taxpayers and business (or bring them to the negotiating table) more effectively than inchoate ones. In the absence of institutionalized parties, traditional forms of power relations tend to prevail.

Absent institutionalized parties that interact through time and forge an interparty consensus on the objectives of tax policy, one avenue to lessen tax policy volatility lies in the advent of an independent federal tax bureau. Professionalized tax administration agencies can acquire independent political weight through time. In such cases, they can become lobbies for a particular orientation in tax policy. Few tax agencies in Latin America, however, have acquired such status and clout vis-à-vis politicians. Determined political leaders continue to regularly encroach upon the workings of tax bureaus. (Even encroachments upon the independence of seemingly untouchable Central Banks have occurred in recent times in countries such as Venezuela and Argentina, among others.) Could fiscal policy eventually follow the route of monetary policy in attaining a significant degree of autonomy from politicians? It is highly unlikely, due to the fundamentally political nature of both the spending and taxation dimensions of fiscal policy. This renders most proposals to endow fiscal policy with autonomy politically unviable. Here, there exist inevitable tradeoffs between the technocratic vision of the rational management of the macroeconomy and the democratic vision of a macroeconomy shaped by popularly elected governments. Because taxes are so fundamentally political in nature, tax reform consolidation is unlikely to ever come via an institutional setup whereby tax decisions are beyond the reach of elected politicians. What is more sensible and more democratic is to strive toward building a social consensus regarding fiscal policy, which in turn necessitates reworking the entire fiscal pact between state and society. Therefore, rather than deliberate depoliticization, the opposite avenue is perhaps the only one available: the purposeful politicization and forging of a political consensus regarding overarching taxation objectives and orientation.

Yet, forging anything resembling a social consensus proves elusive amid high levels political polarization. The Chilean case also shows that a political context that aids reform consolidation is a process of convergence in economic worldviews. That ideational convergence allows for a normative framework to develop that delimits the range of what is regarded as virtuous policy in taxation and other policy realms. In this regard, Latin America has shown divergent processes in the past decade or two. The disappointing results of the Washington Consensus package of reforms have been seized by some political leaders to advocate a radical break with those reforms. The climate of political polarization engulfing countries such as Ecuador, Venezuela, Bolivia, or Nicaragua precludes any possibility for consensus on policy matters. In other countries, however, a process of convergence on economic policy viewpoints has taken place. Other than Chile, where convergence dates to the 1980s, Brazil and Peru are more recent examples of this latter trend.

The autonomy of state institutions is feeble in much of Latin America. Precisely because the custom of professional civil servants is rare (the Central Banks are generally an exception), changes in government translate into wholesale changes in personnel up and down the hierarchical ladder of public administration. This practice reveals the high degree of politicization of the state apparatus. Frequent turnover among the highest-level decision makers disrupts continuity in tax policymaking, particularly in settings where policymaking is nonconsensual, which is the case in most countries in Latin America. Finance ministers or tax agency directors bring to the job different views, ideologies, and priorities about fiscal policy and tax administration, often undermining what their predecessors have barely began to build and precluding the forging of a strong state-society fiscal compact upon which a solid tax system is necessarily based. If the economy that top fiscal policymakers inherit has been molded more by executive fiat than Congressional debate and societal input (which is most likely where party systems are inchoate), such decision-makers are not as constrained by the tax code and existing rules of the economic game, and are thus freer to chart new pathways in tax policy. The result is the intertemporal inconsistency observed in the design of taxation policy throughout much of the region. In very few Latin American countries do political parties have their own cadres of *tecnicos* and economists. In the absence of such cadres, new political administrations coming to office recruit economists in an ad hoc manner, in accordance with the perceived politico-economic necessities of each temporal juncture. In sum, tax policy volatility is fostered by the combination of high turnover rates in top civil servants, nonconsensual policymaking, and the absence of institutionalized parties endowed with cadres of economic experts of their own.

One arena impinging upon taxation that has changed in Latin America is that of the overall macroeconomic environment. The decades of the 1990s and, in particular, the 2000s have witnessed a notable improvement in the quality of macroeconomic policy management, most visibly regarding fiscal discipline. Latin American policymakers have become more cognizant of the virtues of fiscal rectitude. Indeed, a marked improvement in most countries' public finances is part of the reason the region weathered the 2008 global financial crisis quite well. If sustained, this spells well for lessened tax policy hyperactivity. If fiscal policy becomes a source of overall economic stability—rather than instability, as has historically been the case—the recurrent need to enact ad hoc changes in the tax code as a response to fiscal crises could abate. Institutions and rules that promote a countercyclical fiscal policy can aid tax stability by reducing the frequency of fiscal gaps and emergencies. In the past decade, there are some encouraging signs of political learning with respect to the importance of enhancing macroeconomic stability via home-made instruments and policies. Few countries in the region, however, exhibit anything approaching Chile's "tax and spend model," whereby proposals of additional government expenditures need to be financed via taxes before being spent. In particular, states that substantially finance themselves via rents from natural resources (such as Venezuela, Bolivia, Ecuador, etc.) are far from such a virtuous model of fiscal rectitude, not least because of the damaging political economy dynamics most rent-seeking countries generate.

The two-country comparison provided in this book showcases how efforts to ameliorate the tax system and enhance its extractive capacity are bound to fail if the broad institutional setting reinforces counterproductive norms and incentives. Economic reforms in most of Latin America have historically been permeated by rampant political clientelism, and thus final public policy outcomes leave much to be desired from the standpoint of normative economics. Systemic corruption, political clientelism, the arbitrary imposition of tax rules, and an absence of accountability mechanisms undermine the rule of law such that neither the public nor the governments expect themselves to abide by formal tax law. In such an environment, changes in tax policy and tax administration often do not yield hoped-for results. In short, enhancing the extractive capacity of tax systems goes well beyond a technical exercise of devising the "right" tax instruments or fashioning the "right" tax code. Enhancing the overall institutional fortitude of the state and strengthening the rule of law lie at the core of the taxation quandary.

Appendix: Elite Interviews

Chile

All interviews took place in Santiago de Chile between July 10 and August 27, 2002.
   Manuel Marfan Lewis, , former undersecretary of finance: July 10
   Oscar Landerretche, former minister of economics: August 5, 4:30 p.m.
   Manuel Marfan: August 9, second interview 10 a.m.
   Jose Pablo Arellano, former director of the budget: August 26

Chilean newspapers consulted:
El Mercurio,
La Tercera,
La Nacion (Santiago),
La Epoca,
La Segunda

Argentina

All interviews took place in Buenos Aires between November 23, 2002, and January 27, 2003.
   Horacio Piffano, Agencia Federal de Ingresos Publicos (AFIP): November 23
   Gomez Sabaini, former undersecretary of public finances: December 13

Argentine newspapers consulted: *Ambito Financiero, Clarín, Cronista Comercial, La Nacion,* and *La Prensa*

Notes

1 Post-Pinochet Chilean Tax Policy (1989–1995): Finding Resources to Build a Social Democracy

1. The first forward-looking economic development plan, developed in 1961 under the influence of Kennedy's *Alliance for Progress*, contained a list of economic goals, but without a description of the policies and policy instruments that would be used to attain it.
2. As center-left economists Jose De Gregorio and Oscar Landerretche (1998, 156–157) write, "For the most representative adherents of neoliberal thought [in Chile], the discussion about the redistribution of income makes no sense. Income distribution is the result of household income determined by market forces. The fundamental goals of policy must be oriented towards ensuring high rates of economic growth, better targeting social expenditure, transferring to the private sector the management of all public activities as it is possible, and increase, and increasing the efficiency of state activities."
3. In fact, it has been said that the *Concertación* has always been governed by a *partido transversal* (horizontal party), a network of like-minded politicians, economists, and social scientists who had cooperated in think tanks during the authoritarian period, and whose primary loyalty is to the "mission of the state," rather than to their respective parties.
4. The CPC is composed of the following business associations: the *Sociedad Nacional de Agricultura*, made up of traditional agricultural entrepreneurs; the *Sociedad Nacional de Mineria*, which gathers the producer trade unions and large firms; the *Sociedad de Fomento Fabril*, representing the industrial sector, the *Camara Nacional de Comercio* (National Chamber of Commerce); and the *Asociacion de Bancos e Instituciones Financieras*, defending the interests of the banking community. All of these associations represent "big businesses" or large firms. There is an enormous difference in the degree of organization and interest representation between the associations mentioned here and those representing medium and small enterprises, such as CONUPIA.
5. In sum, the supply-side-cum-trickle down arguments rest on shaky grounds. As Yale-trained economist Manuel Marfan (PS) pointed out: "It is a fallacy, or at least there is an element of voluntarism in thinking that the lower the

tax burden the higher the growth of an economy. The market economy is shown to work best in countries with a rather high tax level. In Chile, a tax reform was undertaken that allowed for the conciliation of a social program with macroeconomic stability, guaranteeing that this equilibrium could be reached. The scene we would have in 1994 with this change would be one of economic insecurity and instability. And that is the worst context in which to make long term business plans. It is naïve to think that those countries with the highest fiscal deficit can grow the most" (*El Mercurio*, March 21, 1993).
6. Some entrepreneurs suggested that privatizations could cover the resources that would not be had in a soon-to-be reduction in taxes (if the 1990 accord was kept), and that this could cover the deficit for 1994, while the economic growth of subsequent fiscal years would keep public finances in balance. Predictably, this idea did not sit well with the government.
7. For instance, the common UDI assertion that the overall tax burden stood at 26.2 percent of GDP was incorrect as it used the concept of *ingresos corrientes totales*, which included the contributions to the national treasury of the state-owned copper giant CODELCO. Similarly, the contention that Chile posted the highest tax burden in the region was untrue. In 1990, according to UN statistics, four countries in Latin America displayed higher tax pressures: Colombia, Panama, Brazil, and Venezuela.
8. This position revealed its 1990 negotiating stance to be tactical, one borne out of the particular political dynamics characterizing transition to democracy junctures than one borne out of long-term political strategy.
9. However, there has always been a sector within the *Concertacion* that has put the accent on issues of management and spending efficiency (Arellano, interview).

2 Chilean Tax Policy Tested by New Political and Economic Conditions: 1996–2001

1. In pushing the goal of redistribution, Minister Aninat was reacting to the information of the latest *Encuesta CASEN* that showed that no improvement had been made on the inequality front under the *Concertación* governments, in spite of decisive wins against poverty.
2. An econometric study by three noted Chilean economists (Engel, Galetovic, and Raddatz, 1998) shows that a substantial increase in the tax rates levied on the richest socioeconomic strata would have a very marginal effect on Chilean income distribution, whereas better targeted and more effective social spending can have a considerable effect. In summary, they find that it is the overall tax level that has an important impact upon redistribution, rather than the structure of the tax system per se.
3. The use of the term *autoflagelantes* is not necessarily an endorsement about the appropriateness of this term to describe the left-wing factions within the Socialist party. In a country with great income inequalities, where 70%

of Chileans earn too little to pay income tax and the bottom 30% lack any type of health insurance, the label may at face value appear uncharitable and unjustified. However, the term is relevant insofar as it is commonly used, revealing something important about economic policy views in Chile: the substantial degree of convergence among the political elite as to what constitutes "good" economic policy, including the consensus on what package of policies are de facto redistributive in nature. The autoflagelantes' call for progressive-minded changes in the tax system (sidelining efficiency or other considerations) along with major increases in overall public spending without much regard to fiscal balance, placed this sector on the margins of the mainstream economic debate in Chile. The redistribution debate revolved largely around the issue of how to increase the efficiency of social spending by targeting it better. In sum, the use of the label is simply meant to underscore the intellectual and political marginalization (whether justified or not) of this Socialist faction as concerns economic policymaking.
4. This did not mean that the budget would result in a surplus every year or that there would never be fiscal deficits. It simply meant that the maintenance of an appropriate level of structural surplus would only permit temporary fiscal deficits up to desired levels. Preparing the budget under this policy rule, the government would have to determine the maximum growth of structural spending compatible with a structural surplus of 1 percent of GDP. For that, economic authorities would have to make a projection of structural revenues during the period, which depended on the projected gaps between potential and actual GDP and between short- and long-term copper prices. "Structural" here means that the policy is adjusted for the business cycle and fluctuations in the price of Chile's main export commodity (and large source of government revenue), copper. For an in-depth analysis and description of the methodology used to calculate "structural balance" as well as the theoretical economic benefits of the rule, see: Mario Marcel, Marcelo Tokman, Rodrigo Valdes, and Paula Benavides, "Balance Estructural: La Base de la Nueva Regla de Politica Fiscal Chilena," *Economia Chilena* Vol. 4 (3), December 2001.
5. Those taxpayers earning up to 450,000 pesos monthly (hitherto levied with a 5 percent tax rate) would also be tax exempt. Before the reform, 3,353,000 Chileans were exempt from income taxes.

3 Argentine Tax Policy under Menem I (1989–1994): The "Tax Revolution"

1. In comparative terms, the Argentine tax collection agency fares poorly vis-à-vis homologue agencies in other countries. As a percentage of the total tax revenues it produces, the budget of the DGI is four times that of the United States and twice that of Chile, underscoring a very inefficient use of resources (FIEL 1991, 306–308).
2. Rare efforts to reform the agency along the lines of a Weberian-type bureaucracy (meritocratic recruitment and promotion formulas, flexibility in hiring

and firing, etc.) have been opposed by a powerful union, the Association of Employees of the DGI (AEDGI) (World Bank 1993, 15).
3. Quite the contrary, retrospectively one can say that Menem was the utmost political pragmatist: he went along with the neoliberal model as long as it allowed him to escape the country's economic morass, endowed his government with economic and political support from international financial institutions, and endeared him to the markets. Menem, ever an astute political Machiavellian, was ready to jump along whatever economic wagon served his short- and medium-term political purposes, and was quite ready to jump off when he deemed that a given economic agenda no longer served his political purposes. His decade-long stint in office clearly ascertains this pattern of behavior.
4. The fact that Cossio and Cuello had collaborated in government for dictatorial, repressive regimes was no coincidence: it said much about their right-wing political inclinations and working methods.
5. These perceptions were honed during his Congressional interlude. As Cavallo (1989, 176) wrote in his *Economia en Tiempos de Crisis*, "One of the first things I noticed as a member of Congress is that the budget, the supposed 'law of laws'... is handled with very little seriousness. In part, this is due to the legislators' lack of interest, but in large measure, to the lack of respect on the part of the executive power to the role that corresponds to Congress."
6. From the standpoint of economic theory, Argentina was far from being a natural or ideal candidate for a currency board, as it was not a small economy with an overwhelming amount of trade oriented to a single economy. In fact, exports to the United States amounted to only 15 percent of total Argentine exports. Only Hong Kong, Panama, and a myriad of microstates had currency boards around this time.
7. Strictly speaking, supply-siders hold that there is a tax burden level for every economy beyond which revenues will decrease as the incentive to produce is stifled. Thus, if the prevailing tax level is beyond this critical level, a decrease in taxes will augment that tax intake. The relationship between tax revenues and tax levels is presumed to be delineated by the famous Laffer Curve, named after U.S. economist Arthur Laffer.
8. These reductions would begin to take effect in those regions or sectors most affected by the inherent distortions created by these taxes.
9. Ironically, the DGI's actions were defended by many independent and even Radical party economists. Future minister of the economy under de la Rua, Jose Luis Machinea opined that "while it is probable that the DGI may have committed some excesses in the past, it is necessary to preserve the achievements of this government in matters of tax collection, in large measure due to the fact that the tax agency is now feared by many" (*La Prensa*, February 18, 1994).
10. Article 2 of the law stipulated that closures could be undertaken when: (i) There was proof of fiscal evasion that was damaging to fair competition; (ii) business did not give out receipts in legally specified ways; and (iii) a business was caught red-handed in commercial operations where taxes were evaded.

11. It must be remembered that because the post-1990 tax system was overwhelmingly on indirect taxation (about 80 percent of total collection), its revenue performance was perforce very tightly linked to the business cycle.

4 Argentine Tax Policy under Menem II and De La Rua (1995–2001): Politicization, Firefighting, and Decay

1. Cavallo would later declare: "Tacchi conceives of this issue as a matter of principles. He considers that there are legislative initiatives that we have not vetoed for political reasons which are perforating the tax base and eroding efficiency in the battle against evasion" (*Clarin*, August 2, 1995). Indeed, Tacchi, in his zealous pursuit of evaders, was not willing to compromise because of political concerns or political timing. His abrasive personality, personal inflexibility, and his outspoken nature—including direct allegations involving cabinet members—increasingly created a tense political standoff between the Federal Tax Bureau and Menem's trusted political operatives. Tacchi's intuition that, in the long term, he was involved in a losing political battle is very likely to have prompted his resignation, as many analysts coincided in pointing out. His utter lack of political and interpersonal skills certainly contributed to his undoing. Yet, he had an independent source of political capital insofar as he was regarded very highly by Argentines generally, who saw him as an unusually honest and high-principled figure. (In fact, the Ucede party seriously entertained the prospect of postulating Tacchi for mayor of Buenos Aires.)
2. Indeed, government operatives privately met with leading economists (including Roberto Aleman and Ricardo Lopez Murphy) to ask them about the possible repercussions of Cavallo's destitution. (The response was generally that the market-driven fallout would be potentially serious and would threaten to unravel the economy.) The government also made overtures to a handful of these economists to gauge their interest in serving as minister of the economy.
3. Economist Carlos Perez (Banco Quilmes) summed up the gist of these objections well: "I think it is dangerous to think that the problem is unidimensional and has to do with fiscal equilibrium. [It is dangerous] to ignore the level of economic activity. If the fiscal deficit is reduced only via greater tax pressure we would be looking at the economic picture only from a static viewpoint, not from a dynamic perspective" (*La Nación*, August 12, 1996).
4. Penalties for clients without payments receipts ranged from 20 to 2,500 pesos, but required the ex ante sanctioning of the seller. Penalties for later ranged from 300 to 30,000 pesos and closures from three to ten days. According to Undersecretary for Tax Policy Guillermo Rodriguez, this would be an effective tool only once "a real and adequate administration of taxes has been put in place."

5. Penalties ranged from two to six years in jail for evasion charges in excess of 100,000 pesos, and between one and six years in case of fraudulent receipt of fiscal benefits. For evasion sums in excess of 1 million pesos the penalty ranged from three to nine years in prison.
6. To be sure, this argument, as many originating in the Argentine Congress, was intellectually simplistic and wrong. The truth of the matter is that not long after Cavallo introduced the labor tax reduction the Tequila crisis erupted and the country saw its GDP growth come to a stop, with obvious effects upon employment. Again, Argentine lawmakers were displaying either political irresponsibility or plain ignorance (or both).
7. In a candid moment, a deputy confessed the true reason for his party's intransigence: "we [Peronists] are going to provoke the rejection of all journalist enterprises when the elections are just around the corner" (*La Prensa*, July 2, 1998).

5 Institutional Correlates of Tax Reform Consolidation: Success in Chile and Failure in Argentina

1. The UDI's official declaration of principles reads as follows: "The UDI postulates an open economy open to internal and external competition, where the market is the preferred allocation mechanism of resources...Experience shows that economic systems that foster the individual's ability to generate welfare, obtain greater economic and social welfare than economies with significant roles for the state." Moreover, toeing the Chicago school, it asserts that "economic and political liberties are interdependent and the subsistence of one without the other can only be had precariously, in exceptional or transitory fashion" (www.udi.cl).
2. In the entrepreneurial sector, other peak associations have played effective roles. The export-oriented associations ASEXMA and SOFOFA deserve mentioning in this respect.
3. The CUT is much overshadowed in political strength by the business community, but its viewpoints and interests are to some extent represented within left-wing sectors of the *Concertación*.
4. The Central Bank can voice its fiscal policy preference informally to the Finance Ministry or formally via public statements. There is substantial empirical evidence that the Central Bank has helped reinforce fiscal prudence during the post-Pinochet period.
5. As onetime UCR member Ricardo Lopez Murphy has explained, "the principled stance of the UCR never pertained to economic questions. When some party members refer to the 'party's tradition' in economic matters I ask myself: which tradition, the liberal and progressive policies of Alvear's government, or those of Alfonsin, the conductor of an omnipresent state?" (Lopez Murphy 2003, 143).

6 Conclusion

1. An additional observation bears mentioning here. Argentina political public discourse is, by any standard, opaque and misleading in the sense that the true reasons that motivate politicians to adopt or defend given policy stances are rarely revealed and bogus rationales are often offered. The distance between political rhetoric and political practice often reaches staggering dimensions in Argentina. Much of the Argentine political game is conducted in the shadows, not in the public arena. In Chile, by contrast, public discourse approximates political reality fairly well.

Bibliography

Abal Medina, Juan and Julieta Suarez Cao. 2002. "La Competencia Partidaria en la Argentina: sus implicancias sober el Regimen Democratico," in Marcelo Cavarozzi and Juan Abal Medina (eds.), *El Asedio a la Politica: Los Partidos Latinoamericanos en la era Neoliberal*. Buenos Aires: Ediciones Homo Sapiens.

Acuna, Carlos. 1994. "Politics and Economics in the Argentina of the Nineties," in William Smith, Carlos Acuna, and Eduardo Gamarra (eds.), *Democracy, Markets and Structural Reform in Latin America*. New Brunswick: Transaction Publishers.

———. 1998. "Political Struggle and Business Peak Associations: Theoretical Reflections on the Argentine Case," in Francisco Durand and Eduardo Silva (eds.), *Organized Business, Economic Change, and Democracy in Latin America*. Miami: University of Miami; North-South Center Press.

———. 2002. "Las causas político-institucionales de la actual crisis Argentina," in Celia Barbato (ed.), *Nuevas Cuestiones Sociopolíticas en el Escenario Latinoamericano*. CEPAL-Trilce-INTAL, Montevideo, Uruguay.

Acuna, Carlos and William C. Smith. 1996. "La Economia Politica del Ajuste Estructural: La Logica de Apoyo y Oposicion a las Reformas Neoliberales." *Desarrollo Economico* Vol. 36, No. 141 (April).

ADIMARK. 1990, 1992, 1996. *Estudio de Imagen Institucional del Servicio de Impuestos Internos*. Informe Final, Santiago de Chile.

Ahumada, H., A. Canavese, P. Sanguinetti, and W. Sosa Escudero. 1993. "Efectos Distributivos del impuesto inflacionario: una estimación para el caso argentino." *Economía Mexicana*, Vol. II, No. 2: 329–83.

Alesina, Alberto and Guido Tabellini. 1990. "A Political Theory of Fiscal Deficits and Government Debt." *Review of Economic Studies* Vol. 57 (July).

Alesina, Alberto, R. Hausmann, R. Hommes, and E. Stein. 1999. "Budget Institutions and Fiscal Performance in Latin America." *Journal of Development Economics* Vol. 59, No. 2.

Allamand, Andres. 1999. *La Travesia del Desierto*. Editorial Alfaguara..

Almond, Gabriel. 1988. "The Return of the State." *American Political Science Review* Vol. 82: 853–74.

Alwyn, Patricio. *Programa de Gobierno de la Concertacion*. Unpublished document. Santiago de Chile.

Andre Melo, Marcus. 2007. "Institutional Weakness and the Puzzle of Argentina's Low Taxation." *Latin American Politics and Society* Vol. 49, No. 4 (December).

Andreoni, J. B. Erard and J. Feinstein. 1998. "Tax Compliance." *Journal of Economic Literature* Vol. 35: 818–60.

Angell, Alan and Benny Pollack. 1990. "The Chilean Elections of 1989 and the Politics of the Transition to Democracy." *Bulletin of Latin American Research* Vol. 9, No. 1.

———. 1995. "The Chilean Elections of 1993: From Polarisation to Consensus." *Bulletin of Latin American Research* Vol. 14, No. 2.

———. 2000. "The Chilean Presidential Elections of 1999–2000 and Democratic Consolidation." *Bulletin of Latin American Research* Vol. 19, No. 2.

Arellano, Jose Pablo. 1995. "Politica Fiscal y Desarrollo Social," in Pizarro, Racynski, and Vial (eds.), *Politicas Economicas y Sociales en Chile*.

Arellano, Jose Pablo and Manuel Marfan. 1987. "25 Anos de Politica Fiscal en Chile." *Coleccion Estudios CIEPLAN* N.21, Santiago de Chile.

Arrate, Jorge and Paulo Hidalgo. 1989. *Pasion y Razon del Socialismo Chileno*. Santiago: Ediciones Ornitorrinco.

Arriagada Herrera, Genaro and Carol Graham. 1994. "Chile: Sustaining Adjustment during Democratic Transition," in Stephan Haggard and Steven Webb (ed.), *Voting for Reform*. New York: Oxford University Press.

Ascher, William. 1984. *Scheming for the Poor: The Politics of Redistribution in Latin America*. Cambridge: Harvard University Press.

———. 1989. "Risk, Politics, and Tax Reform: Lessons from Some Latin American Experiences," in Malcolm Gillis (ed.), *Tax Reform in Developing Countries*. Durham: Duke University Press.

Atchabahian, Adolfo. 1988. "Tax Reform Process: Argentina 1983–1987." *Bulletin for International Fiscal Documentation* Vol. 2: 65–77.

Ayuero, Javier. 2000. *Poor People's Politics. Peronist Survival Networks and the Legacy of Evita*. Durham, NC: Duke University Press.

Baldez, Lisa and John Carey. 1998. "Budget Procedure and Fiscal Restraint in Post-Transition Chile," in Stephan Haggard and M. McCubbins (eds.), *Political Institutions and Determinants of Public Policy: When Do Institutions Matter?* Princeton: Princeton University Press.

Bambaci, Juliana, Tamara Saront, and Mariano Tommasi. 2000. "La Economia Politica de las Reformas Economicas en la Argentina." *Cuadernos de Economia* Vol. 37. No. 112 (December).

Bambaci, Juliana, Pablo Spiller, and Mariano Tommasi. 2000. "Bureaucracy and Public Policy in Argentina." Mimeo, CEDI.

Banco Interamericano de Desarrollo (BID). 1995. *Reforma de la Administracion Tributaria en America Latina*. Washington, DC: BID.

———. 1997. "El Proceso de Decisiones Fiscales Democraticas a Nivel Nacional," in *America Latina Tras Una Decada de Reformas*. Washington, DC: BID.

Barrett, Patrick. 1999. "The Limits of Democracy: Sociopolitical Compromise and Regime Change in Post-Pinochet Chile." *Studies in Comparative International Development* Vol. 34, No. 3.

Barrett, Patrick. 2000. "Chile's Transformed Party System and the Future of Democratic Stability." *Journal of Interamerican Studies and World Affairs* Vol. 42, No. 3.

Barton, Jonathan and Warwick Murray. 2002. "The End of Transition? Chile 1999–2000" *Bulletin of Latin American Research* Vol. 21, No. 3.

Bates, Robert. 1989. "A Political Scientist Looks at Tax Reform," in Malcolm Gillis (ed.), *Tax Reform in Developing Countries*. Durham: Duke University Press.

Bates, Robert and Da-Hsiang D. Lien. 1985. "A Note on Taxation, Development and Respresentative Government." *Politics and Society* Vol. 14, No. 1: 53–70.

Bates, Robert, and Anne O. Krueger (eds.). 1993. *Political and Economic Interactions in Policy Reform: Evidence from Eight Countries*. Oxford: Basil Blackwell.

Berensztein, Sergio. 1998. "The Politics of Tax Reform in Mexico and Argentina." PhD dissertation, Department of Political Science. University of North Carolina.

Berensztein, Sergio, and Horacio Spector. 2003. "Business, Government, and Law," in Gerardo della Paolera and Alan M. Taylor (eds.), *A New Economic History of Argentina*. Cambridge: Cambridge University Press.

Bergman, Marcelo. 2003. "Tax Reform and Tax Compliance: the Divergent Paths of Chile and Argentina." *Journal of Latin American Studies* Vol. 35, No. 3: 593–624.

———. 2009. *Tax Evasion and the Rule of Law in Latin America*. University Park, PA: Pennsylvania State University.

Bird, Richard. 1992a. "Tax Reform in Latin America: A Review of Some Recent Experiences." *Latin American Research Review* Vol. 27, No. 1: 7–36.

———. 1992b. *Tax Policy and Economic Development*. Baltimore: Johns Hopkins University Press.

Bird, Richard, and Milka Casanegra (eds.). 1992. *Improving Tax Administration Reform in Developing Countries*. Washington, DC: IMF.

Bird, Richard, and Barbara Miller. 1989. "Taxation, Pricing and the Poor," in Richard Bird and Susan Horton (eds.), *Government Policy and the Poor in Developing Countries*. Toronto: University of Toronto Press.

Bird, Richard and Guillermo Perry. 1995. "Tax Policy in Latin America: In Crisis and After," in Ann Helwege (ed.), *The Economic Future of Latin America*. London: Lynne Ryenner.

Birdsall, Nancy, and Augusto de la Torre. 2001. *Washington Contentious: Economic Policies for Social Equity in Latin America*. Washington, DC: Inter-American Dialogue.

Bitar, Sergio (ed.). 1980. *Chile: Liberalismo Economico y Dictadura Politica*. Instituto de Estudios Peruanos.

Blutman, Gustavo. 1999. *Orden y desorden en la reforma del estado: cambios en la Argentina entre 1989–1992*. Buenos Aires: Eudeba.

Bocco, Arnaldo. "El Efecto Tacchi: Tan Lejos del Primer Mundo y tan Cerca de la Inequidad," *Oikos: Revista de Posgrado, Investigacion y Doctorado* Vol. 1, No. 2. Facultad de Ciencias Economicas, Universidad de Buenos Aires.

Boeninger, Edgardo. 1997. *Democracia en Chile: Lecciones para la Gobernabilidad.* Santiago: Editorial Andres Bello.

Boron, Atilio. 2003. "Ruling without a Party: Argentine Dominant Classes during the Twentieth Century," in Kevin Middlebrook (ed.), *Conservative Parties, the Right and Democracy in Latin America.* Washington, DC: Johns Hopkins University Press.

Borzutzky, Sylvia. 1998. "Chilean Democracy Before and After Pinochet," in Kurt von Mettenheim and James Malloy (eds.), *Deepening Democracy in Latin America.* Pittsburgh: Pittsburgh University Press.

Bosworth, Barry, Rudiger Dornbush, and Raul Laban (eds.). 1994. *The Chilean Economy: Policy, Lessons, and Challenges.* Washington, DC: Brookings Institution.

Botana, Natalio. 2002. *La Republica Vacilante: entre la Furia y la Razon.* Buenos Aires: Editorial Taurus.

Bouzas, Roberto. 2002. "La Argentina después de las reformas," in Roberto Bouzas (ed.), *Realidades nacionales comparadas: Argentina, Bolivia, Brasil, Chile, Paraguay, Uruguay.* Buenos Aires: Editorial Altamira.

Boylan, Delia M. 1996 "Taxation and Transition: The Politics of the 1990 Chilean Tax Reform." *Latin American Research Review* Vol. 31, No. 1.

———. 1997. "Evelyn Matthei: The Rise and Fall of a Technopol," in Dominguez, *Technopols.*

Brautigam, Deborah, Odd-Helge Fjeldstad, and Mick Moore (eds.). 2008. *Taxation and State-Building in Developing Countries: Capacity and Consent.* New York: Cambridge University Press.

Bresser-Pereira, Luiz Carlos. 1997. "State Reform in the 1990s: Logic and Control Mechanisms." *Documentos Debate: Estado Administracion Publica y Sociedad* No. 4 (September). Caracas, CLAD.

———. 2000. "State Reform in the 1990s: Logic and Control Mechanisms," in Leonardo Burlamaqui et al. (eds.), *Institutions and the Role of the State.* Cheltenham, UK: Edgard Elgar.

Brodershon, M. and Viviana Duran. 1990. "Crisis de la Recaudacion de Impuestos: la cara Olvidada de la Reforma del Estado," CECE, Serie de Estudios N. 2.

Buchi, Hernan. 1993. *La Transformacion Economica de Chile: del Estatismo a la Libertad Economica.* Santiago de Chile: Editorial Norma.

Burgess, R. and Nicholas Stern. 1993. "Taxation and Development." *Journal of Economic Literature* Vol. XXXI, No. 2: 762–832.

Cachanosky, Roberto. 2001. "Equilibrio Presupuestario y Sistema Impositivo." *Contribuciones,* January.

Camhi, Rosita, Rosana Costa, Tomas Flores, Eugenio Guzman, and Paulina Villagran. 1999. *Analisis del Pensamiento de la Nueva Izquierda Chilena.* Documentos Fundacion Siglo XXI. Instituto Libertad y Desarrollo. Canitrot, Adolfo. 1992. "Macroeconomia de la Inestabilidad: Argentina en los 80." *Boletin Informativo Techint* No. 272 (October/December).

Canitrot, Adolfo. 1994. "Crisis and Transformation of the Argentine State (1978–1992)," in Smith, Acuna, and Gamarra (eds.), *Democracy, Markets and Structural Reform in Latin America.*

Canitrot, Adolfo, and Silvia Sigal. 1994. "Economic Reform, Democracy, and the Crisis of the State in Argentina," in Joan Nelson (ed.), *A Precarious Balance: Democracy and Economic Reforms in Latin America*. San Francisco, CA: Institute for Contemporary Studies.
Carciofi, Ricardo. 1990. *La Desarticulacion del Pacto Fiscal*. Santiago de Chile: CEPAL. Documento de Trabajo 36.
———. 1993. *Reformas Tributarias en Argentina*. Santiago de Chile: CEPAL Serie de Reformas de Politica Publica N. 7.
Carciofi, Ricardo, and Oscar Cetrangolo. 1990. *Tax Reforms and Equity in Latin America: A Review of the 1980s and Proposals for the 1990s*. Innocenti Occasional Papers, Florence: UNICEF.
Carciofi, Ricardo, Guillermo Barris, and Oscar Centragolo. 1994. *Reformas Tributarias en America Latina: Analisis de Experiencias Durante la Decada de los Anos Ochenta*. Santiago de Chile: CEPAL.
Cauas, Jorge. 1979. "The Role of Tax Policy in National Economic Development," in Juan Carlos Mendez (ed.), *Chilean Economic Policy*. Santiago: Budget Directorate.
Cavallo, Domingo. 1993. *Volver a Crecer*. Buenos Aires: Planeta.
———. 2001. "La Lucha por Evitar el Default y la Devaluación." *La Nacion*, April 29.
Cavarozzi, Marcelo. 1984. "Los Partidos Argentinos. Subculturas Fuertes, Sistema Debil," Prepared for the seminar: *Political Parties and Redemocratization in the Southern Cone*, Woodrow Wilson Internacional Center for Scholars.
———. 1999. "Lost Opportunities and Ongoing Learning," in Jennifer McCoy (ed.), *Political Learning and Redemocratization in Latin America*. Boulder, CO: Lynne Rienner Publishers.
Cavarozzi, Marcelo, and Oscar Landi. 1992. "Political Parties Ander Alfonsin and Menem: The Effects of State Shrinking and Devaluation on Democratic Politics," in Epstein (ed.), *The New Argetine Democracy*.
Cavarozzi, Marcelo, and Juan Abal Medina. 1999. "Del Problema del Estado al Problema del Gobierno, los desafios de la nueva gestion." *Revista Sociedad* No. 15 (December). Facultad de Ciencias Sociales, UBA.
———. (eds.). 2002. *El Asedio a la Politica: Los Partidos Latinoamericanos en la era Neoliberal*. Buenos Aires: Ediciones Homo Sapiens.
Caviedes, Cesar. 1991. *Elections in Chile: The Road to Redemocratization*. Boulder, CO: Lynne Rienner Publishers.
Centeno, Miguel Angel. 1997. "Blood and Debt: War and Taxation in Nineteenth Century Latin America." *American Journal of Sociology* Vol. 102, No. 6 (May): 1582–83.
Centeno, Miguel A., and Patricio Silva (eds.). 1997. *The Politics of Expertise in Latin America*. London: MacMillan.
Centro de Estudios Publicos (CEP). 1992. *"El Ladrillo": Bases de la Poltiical Economica del Gobierno Militar Chileno*. Santiago de Chile.
CEPAL. 1991. "El Deficit Cuasifiscal: El Caso Argentino." *Serie Politica Fiscal* 27. Santiago: CEPAL/PNUD.
———. 1998. *El Pacto Fiscal: Fortalezas, Debilidades, Desafios*. Chile: Comision Economica para America Latina y el Caribe, Naciones Unidas.

CEPAL. 2002. *Seminario Regional de Politica Fiscal.* Santiago de Chile, Enero, 25–27.
Cheyre, Hernan. 1986. "Analisis de las reformas tributarias de la decada 1974–1983." *Estudios Publicos* Vol. 21, No. 1. Santiago: Centro de Estudios Publicos.
Cleaves, Peter. 1974. *Bureaucratic Politics and Administration in Chile.* Berkeley, CA: University of California Press.
Collier, Simon, and William Sater. 2003. *A History of Chile: 1808–1994.* Cambridge: Cambridge University Press.
Comentarios sobre la Situacion Economica. 1990–2000. Taller de Coyuntura. Facultad de Ciencias Economicas y Administrativas, Universidad de Chile.
Concertacion de Partidos por la Democracia. 1989. "Programa de Gobierno." Documentos La Epoca.
Corbo, Vittorio. 1989. *Public Finance, Trade, and Development: The Chilean Experience.* Washington, DC: World Bank, 49 p. (Policy, Planning, and Research Working Papers, No. 218.)
Corradi, Juan E. 1985. *The Fitful Republic: Economy, Society and Politics in Argentina.* Boulder, CO: Westview Press.
Corrales, Javier. 1997. "Why Argentines Followed Cavallo: A Technopol Between Democracy and Economic Reform," in Dominguez (ed.), *Technopols.*
———. 2001. "Technocratic Policy-Making and Parliamentary Accountability: The Argentine Case," paper presented at the XIII International Congress of the Latin American Studies Association, Washington, DC, September 6–8.
———. 2002. "The Politics of Argentina's Meltdown." *World Policy Journal* Vol. XIX, No. 3 (Fall).
———. 2003. *Presidents without Parties: The Politics of Economic Reform in Venezuela and Argentina.* Pennsylvania: Pennsylvania University Press.
Cortazar, Rene, and Joaquin Vial (eds.). 1998. *Propuestas Economicas y Sociales para el Cambio de Siglo.* Santiago: CIEPLAN.
Costa, Rosanna. 1999. "Carga Tributaria en Chile: Analisis Comparado." Serie Informe Economico. N. 105. Instituto Libertad y Desarrollo.
Cox, Gary, and Matthew McCubbins. 2001. "The Institutional Determinants of Public Policy," in Stephan Haggard and Matthew McCubbins (eds.), *Presidents, Parliaments and Policy.* New York: Cambridge University Press.
Crotty, John, Juan Toro, Benjamin Shutz, and Luis Pedroche. 2001. *Argentina: Desafios para Modernizar la Administracion Tributaria.* Departamento de Finanzas Publicas, Fondo Monetario Internacional. Washington, DC: FMI.
Cuello, Raul. 1996. "Estructura del Sistema Tributario (Un Analisis de Economia Aplicada)." *Boletin de Lecturas Sociales y Economicas* Vol. 3, No. 12.
———. 2000. "Politica Fiscal y Monetaria," in Cayetano Licciardo et al. (eds.), *Rol del Estado en la Economia.* Buenos Aires: CIEL Editorial.
Curia, Eduardo. 2002 *La Alianza y la "Convertibilidad Progresista": el Sueno Roto.* Buenos Aires: Ediciones Realidad Argentina.
David, P. 1994. "Why are Institutions the Carriers of History? Path Dependence and the Evolution of Conventions, Organizations and Institutions." *Structural Change and Economic Dynamics* Vol. 5, No. 2.
De Gregorio, Jose and Oscar Landerretche. 1998. "Equidad, Distribucion y Desarrollo Integrador," in Rene Cortazar and Joaquin Vial (eds.),

Contruyendo Opciones: Propuestas Economicas y Sociales para el Cambio de Siglo. Santiago: Editorial Dolmen.
De Riz, Liliana. 1986. "Politica y Partido. Ejercicio de Analisis Comparado: Argentina, Chile, Brazil and Uruguay." *Desarrollo Economico* Vol. 25, No. 100.
Delano, Manuel and Hugo Traslavina. 1989. *La Herencia de los Chicago Boys*. Santiago: Ediciones Ornitorrinco.
Della Parlera, Gerardo and Alan Taylor (eds.). 2003. *A New Economic History of Argentina*. Cambridge: Cambridge University Press.
DGI. 1996. *Direccion General Impositiva 1984–1995*. Buenos Aires: Republica Argentina, July.
Di Tella, Guido, and Rudiger Dornbush (eds.). 1989. *The Political Economy of Argentina (1946–1983)*. New York: Palgrave McMillan.
Diamand, Marcelo and Hugo Nochteff (eds.). 1999. *La Economia Argentina Actual: Problemas y Lineamientos de Politicas para Superarlos*. Grupo Editorial Norma.
Diaz Alejandro, Carlos. 1970. *Essays on the Economic History of the Argentine Republic*. New Haven: Yale University Press.
Dixit, Avinash. 1996. *The Making of Economic Policy: A Transaction-Cost Politics Perspective*. Cambridge: MIT Press.
Dominguez, Jorge. 1997. *Technopols: Freeing Markets and Politics in Latin America*. Pennsylvania: Pennsylvania University Press.
Drake, Paul and Ivan Jaksic (eds.). 1991. *The Struggle for Democracy in Chile 1982–1990*. Lincoln: University of Nebraska Press.
Durand, Francisco and Rosemary Thorp. 1998. "Reforming the State: A Study of the Peruvian Tax Reform." *Oxford Development Studies* Vol. 26, No. 2.
Eaton, Kent. 1998. "The Politics of Tax Refom in the Developing Countries." PhD dissertation, Yale University.
———. 2002. *Politicians and Economic Reform in New Democracies: Argentina and the Philippines in the 1990s*. Pennsylvania: Pennsylvania State University Press.
ECLA. 1998. *The Fiscal Covenant: Strengths, Weaknesses, Challenges*. United Nations: Economic Commision for Latin America (ECLA) Santiago de Chile, Chile.
Economist. 2004. "A Survey of Argentina: Becoming a Serious Country," June 3.
El Pais. 2002. "La Desaparicion de Argentina Sigue su Curso." *Seccion Economia*, April 14.
Elizondo, Carlos. 1994. "In Search of Revenue: Tax Reform in Mexico under the Administrations of Echevarria and Salinas." *Journal of Latin American Studies* Vol. 26 (January): 159–90.
———. 1995. "The Politics of Tax Reform in Latin America." Documento de Trabajo 32, Division de Estudios Politicos, CIDE.
Engel, Eduardo, and Patricio Meller. 1993. "Temporary Shocks and Stabilization Mechanisms: The Chilean Case," in Eduardo Engel and Patricio Meller (eds.), *External Shocks and Stabilization Mechanisms*. Washington, DC: Inter-American Development Bank.

Engel, Eduardo, Alex Galetovic, and C. Raddatz. 1998. "Los Impuestos y la Redistribucion del Ingreso en Chile." Departamento de Ingenieria Industrial, Universidad de Chile.

Engel, Eduardo P. Meller, and C. Bravo. 1998. "Análisis Descriptivo del Tamaño Relativo del Gasto del Gobierno Chileno." *Serie Economía* No. 43. Departamento de Ingeniería Industrial, Universidad de Chile.

Epstein, Edward (ed.). 1992. *The New Argetine Democracy: The Search for a Successful Formula*. London: Praeger.

Erro, David G. 1993. *Resolving the Argentine Paradox: Politics and Development 1966–1992*. Boulder, CO: Lynne Rienner Publishers.

Escude, Carlos. 2002. "Argentina, a 'Parasite State' on the Verge of Disintegration." *Cambridge Review of Internacional Relations* Vol. 15, No. 3.

Etchemendy, Sebastian. 2001. "Construir Coaliciones Reformistas: La Politica de las Compensaciones en el Camino Argentino hacia la Liberalizacion Economica." *Desarrollo Economico* Vol. 40, No. 160, Enero.

Evans, Peter. 1996. *Embedded Autonomy* Princeton: Princeton University Press.

Evans, Peter, Dietrich Reschemeyer, and Theda Skocpol (eds.). 1985. *Bringing the State Back In*. Cambridge: Cambridge University Press.

Eyzaguirre, Nicolas and Osvaldo Larranaga. 1990. "Macroeconomia de las Operaciones Cuasi-FIscales en Chile." *Serie Investigacion ILADES-Georgetown*, November.

Falcoff, Mark. 1989. *Modern Chile: 1970–1989*. New Brusnwick: Transaction.

Fanelli, Jose Maria. 2002. "Crecimiento, Inestabilidad y Crisis de la Convertibilidad en Argentina." *Revista de la CEPAL* Vol. 77 (August).

Fanelli, Jose Maria, Guillermo Rosewurzel, and Roberto Frenkel. 1994. "Transformacion Estructural, Estabilizacion y Reforma del Estado en la Argentina." CEDES.

Feldstein, Martin. 1986. "Supply-side Economics: Old Truths and New Claims." *American Economic Review* Vol. 76 (May): 26–30.

Ffrench-Davis, Ricardo. 1973 *Politicas Economicas en Chile 1852–1970*. Santiago de Chile: Ediciones Nueva Universidad.

———. 1991. "Desarrollo Economico y Equidad en Chile: Herencias y Desafios en el Retorno a la Democracia." *Coleccion Estudios* Vol. 31 (March): 31–50; Santiago: CIEPLAN.

———. 2001. *Entre el Neoliberalismo y el Crecimiento con Equidad. Tres Decadas de Politica Economica en Chile*. Santiago de Chile: Ediciones Dolmen.

———. 2002. *Economic Reforms in Chile: From Dictatorship to Democracy*. Michigan: University of Michigan Press.

Ffrench-Davis, Ricardo, and Oscar Munoz. 1990. "Desarrollo Economico, Insestabilidad y Desequilibrios Politicos en Chile: 1950–1989." *Coleccion Estudios* Vol. 28 (June): 121–56; Santiago: CIEPLAN.

Ffrench-Davis, Ricardo, and Stephanie Griffith-Jones (eds.). 1995. *Coping with Capital Surges: the Return of Finance to Latin America*. Boulder, CO: Lynne Rienner Publishers.

FIEL (Fundacion de Investigaciones Economicas Latinoamericanas). 1991. *El Sistema Impositivo Argentino*. Buenos Aires: Manantial.

———. 1993. *Hacia una nueva organización del federalismo fiscal en la Argentina*. Ed. Manantial.
———. 1998. *La Reforma Tributaria en la Argentina*. Ed. Manantial, November.
———. 2000. *La Economia Oculta en la Argentina*. Ed. Manantial.
———. 2001. *Crecimiento y Equidad en la Argentina: Bases de una Politica Economica para la Decada, Volumen 1*. Buenos Aires: IREAL.
Fishlow, Albert. 1990. "The Latin American State." *Journal of Economic Perspectives* Vol. 4, No. 3 (Summer): 61–74.
Fontaine, Bernardo, and Rodrigo Vergara. 1997. *Una Reforma Tributaria para el Crecimiento*. Santiago de Chile: Centro de Estudios Publicos.
———. 2000. "Analisis del Proyecto Contra la Evasion Tributaria." *Estudios Publicos* Vol. 79 (Winter).
Foxley, Alejandro. 1987. *Chile y su Futuro Posible*. Santiago: CIEPLAN.
———. 1990. "Bases para el Desarrollo de la Economia Chilena." *El Trimestre Economico* Vol. LVII, No. 226: 560–69.
———. 1993. *Economia Politica de la Transicion: El Camino del Dialogo*. Santiago: Ediciones DOLMEN.
———. 1995. "Economia Politica de la Transicion a la Democracia en Chile (1990–1994)," in C. Pizarro (ed.), *Desarrollo Social en los 90: Los Casos de Chile, Costa Rica y Mexico*. Santiago: CIEPLAN.
———. 1996 "Chile: Latin America's Middle Way." *New Perspectives Quarterly* (Fall).
———. 1999. "Financiar Politicas Sociales mediante Impuestos." *El Diario*, [Chilean newspaper], August 3.
Foxley, Alejandro, and Claudio Sapelli. 1998. "Chile's Political Economy in the 1990s: Some Governance Issues," in Guillermo Perry and Danny Leipziger (eds.), *Chile: Recent Policy Lessons and Emerging Challenges*. Washington, DC: World Bank.
Fundacion Mediterranea. 2001. *Una Reforma Tributaria Integral para el Crecimiento de la Argentina*. Buenos Aires. IREAL.
Garreton, Manuel Antonio. 1989. *Propuestas Politicas y Demandas Sociales*, Vols 1–3. Santiago: FLACSO.
———. 1995. *Hacia una Nueva Era Politica. Estudio sobre las Democratizaciones*. Santiago: Fondo de Cultura Economica.
———. 2000. "Chile's Elections: Change and Continuity." *Journal of Democracy* Vol. 11, No. 2.
———. 2002. "El Dificil Reintento de un Proyecto de Pais: La Sociedad Chilena a Comienzos de Siglo," in Roberto Bouzas (ed.), *Realidades Nacionales Comparadas*. Buenos Aires: Editorial Altamira.
Garreton, Manuel Antonio, and Malva Espinosa. 2000. "Chile: Political Learning and the Reconstruction of Democracy," in Jennifer McCoy (ed.), *Political Learning and Redemocratization in Latin America*. Miami: North-South Center Press.
Geddes, Barbara. 1994. *Politician's Dilemma: Building State Capacity in Latin America*. Berkeley: University of California Press.
Gerchunoff, Pablo, and Lucas Llach. 1998. *El Ciclo de la Ilusion y el Desencanto: Un Siglo de Politicas Economicas Argentinas*. Buenos Aires: Ariel.

Gerchunoff, Pablo. and Juan Carlos Torre. 1996. "La Politica de Liberalizacion Economica en la Administratcion de Menem." *Desarrollo Economico* Vol. 36, No. 143.

Gibson, Edward. 1996. *Class and Conservative Parties: Argentina in Comparative Perspective.* Baltimore: Johns Hopkins University Press.

———. 1999. "Electoral Coalitions and Market Reform: Evidence from Argentina," Mimeo. Department of Political Science, Northwestern University.

Gillis, Malcolm. 1989. *Tax Reform in Developing Countries.* Durham: Duke University Press.

Giraldo, Jeanne Kinney. 1997. "Development and Democracy in Chile: Finance Minister Alejandro Foxley and the Concertacion's Project for the 1990s," in Dominguez (ed.), *Technopols.*

Gomez Sabaini, Juan Carlos. 1989. *Estudios sobre el sistema tributario argentine.* Programa de Estudios sobre Politica Tributaria. Proyecto 2712/AR. Buenos Aires, October.

———. 1990. *Los Problemas Actuales de la Politica Tributaria Argentina* Instituto de Estudios Fiscales. Monografia N. 80, Madrid.

———. 1999. "La Situacion Tributaria Argentina durante el Periodo 1990–1994," in Instituto de Economia de la Universidad Argentina de la Empresa, *Ensayos sobre Politica y Gestion Tributarias: Homenaje a Carlos M. Tacchi.* IEUAE: Buenos Aires.

Gomez Sabaini, Juan Carlos, and Jorge Gaggero. 1998. "Lineamientos para una Reforma del Sistema Tributario." *Criterios Tributarios* Vol. 13 (March).

Gourevitch, Peter A. 2000. "A Comparative Perspectiva on Economic Ideas, Internacional Influences and Domestic Politics towards Policy Change in Latin America," paper prepared for Conference on Economic Doctrines in Latin America, St Antony's College, Oxford, September 28/29.

Government of Chile, Budget Deparment. 1993. "Expenditures Financed by the Tax Reform," working paper, May.

Government of Chile. Ministry of Finance. 1990a. "Analysis of the Tax Reform Bill," internal document. Santiago, Chile.

———. 1990b. "Tax Reform—Answers to Queries," internal document. Santiago, Chile.

———. 1990c. "Toward a Modern Economy of Solidarity. 1990 Tax Reform," internal document. Santiago, Chile.

Grindle, Merilee. 1995. "Building Sustainable Capacity in the Public Sector." *Public Administration and Development* Vol. 15: 441–63.

Hacienda, Ministerio de. 1994–2002. *Aspectos Macroeconomicos del Proyecto de Ley de Presupuestos del Sector Publico.* Direccion de Presupuestos, Gobierno de Chile.

Haggard, Stephan. 2000. "Interests, Institutions, and Policy Reform," In Anne Krueger (ed). *Economic Policy Reform: The Second Stage.* Chicago: University of Chicago Press.

Haggard, Stephan, and Robert Kaufman. 1992a. "The State in the Initiation and Consolidation of Market-Oriented Reform," in Louis Putterman and Dietrich

Rueschemeyer (eds.), *State and Market in Development*. Boulder, CO: Lynne Rienner Publishers.
———. 1992b. *The Politics of Economic Adjustment: International Constraints, Distributive Conflicts and the State*. Princeton: Princeton University Press.
Haggard, Stephan, and Steven Webb (eds.). 1994. *Voting for Reform: Economic Adjustment in New Democracies*. Oxford: Oxford University Press.
Halperin-Dongui, Tulio. 1994. *La Larga Agonia de la Argentina Peronista*. Buenos Aires: Eudeba.
Halpern, B. Pablo, and Edgardo Bousquet. 1992. "Percepciones de la Opinion Publica Acerca del Rol Economico y Social del Estado." *Revista de Ciencia Politica* Vol. 15, No. 1. *Universidad Pontificia Catolica de Chile*.
Helmke, Gretchen, and Steven Levitsky. 2004. "Informal Institutions and Comparative Politics." *Perspectives on Politics* Vol. 2, No. 4.
——— (eds.). 2006. *Informal Institutions and Democracy: Lessons from Latin America*. Baltimore: Johns Hopkins University Press.
Heredia, Blanca, and Ben Ross Schneider (eds.). 2002. "The Political Economy of Administrative Reform: Building State Capacity in Developing Countries," in Blanca Heredia and Ben Ross Schneider (eds.), *Reinventing Leviathan*. Miami: North-South Press.
Hettich, W., and S. L. Winer. 1988. "Economic and Political Foundations of Tax Structure." *American Economic Review* Vol. 78: 701–12.
Hite, Katherine. 2000. *When the Romance Ended: Leaders of the Chilean Left, 1968–1998*. New York: Columbia University Press.
Hojman, David. 1993. *Chile: The Political Economy of Development and Democracy in the 1990s*. London: Macmillan.
———. 1994. "The Political Economy of Recent Conversions to Market Economics in Latin America." *Journal of Latin American Studies* Vol. 26: 191–219.
———. 1995. "Chile Under Frei (Again): The First Latin American Tiger or Just another Cat?" *Bulletin of Latin American Research* Vol. 14, No. 2.
Horowitz, Michael, Manuel Marfan, Bernardo Fontaine, and Alvin Rabushka. 1994. "Sistema Tributario Chileno: Mesa Redonda." *Estudios Publicos* Vol. 53 (Summer).
Huber, Evelyne. 2000. "Assessments of State Strength," in Peter H. Smith (ed,), *Latin America in Comparative Perspective*. San Francisco: Westview Press.
Huneeus, Carlos. 1997. "Technocrats and Politicians in the Democratic Politics of Argentina (1983–1995)," in Centeno and Silva (eds.), *The Politics of Expertise in Latin America*.
———. 2000a. "Los Cambios Institucionales al Sistema Economico Durante la Transicion a la Democracia en Chile: del Neoliberalismo a la Economia Social de Mercado." *Revista de Ciencia Politica* Vol. XX, No. 2.
———. 2000b. *El Regimen de Pinochet*. Santiago de Chile: Editorial Sudamericana.
Iaryczower, Matias, Sebastian Saiegh, and Mariano Tommasi. 1998. "Algunas Consideraciones sobre Diseno Optimo de Instituciones Fiscales Federales." *Economica* Vol. XLIV, No. 3.

Inter-American Development Bank (IADB). 1997. *Economic and Social Progress in Latin America: Latin America After a Decade of Reforms.* Washington, DC: IDB.
———. 2005. *The Politics of Policies.* Rockefeller Center for Latin American Studies, Harvard University.
Jones, Mark. 1997. "Evaluating Argentina's Presidencial Democracy: 1983–1995," in Scout Mainwaring and Matthew Soberg Shugart (eds.), *Presidentialism and Democracy in Latin America.* New York: Cambridge University Press.
Jones, Mark, Sebastian Saiegh, Pablo Spiller, and Mariano Tommasi. 2001. "Amateur legislators-Professional Politicians´: The Consequences of Party-Centered Electoral Rules in a Federal System." *American Journal of Political Science* Vol. 43, No. 3: 656–69.
Jones, Mark, Pablo Sanguinetti, and Marianno Tommasi. 2000. "Politics, Institutions and Fiscal Performance in a Federal System: An Analysis of the Argentine Provinces." *Journal of Development Economics* Vol. 61: 305–33.
Jorrat, Michel. 2000. "Diagnostico del Sistema Tributario Chileno," Documento de Trabajo. Servicio de Impuestos Internos (www.sii.cl).
Jorratt, Michel, and Pablo Serra. 2000. "Estimacion de la Evasion en el Impuesto a las Empresas en Chile," Documento de Trabajo, Serie de Economia N. 72, Centro de Economia Aplicada, Depto de Ingenieria Industrial, Universidad de Chile.
Kahler, Miles. 1992. "External Influence, Conditionality and the Politics of Adjustment," in Stephan Haggard and Robert Kaufman (eds.), *The Politics of Economic Adjustment.* Princeton: Princeton University Press.
Kaldor, Nicholas. 1963. "Taxation for Economic Development." *Journal of Modern African Studies* No. 1.
Kitschelt, Herbert, and Steven Wilkinson (eds.). 2007. *Patrons, Clients and Policies: Patterns of Democratic Accountability and Political Competition.* New York: Cambridge University Press.
Lagos, Gustavo. 1999. *Analisis de la Tributacion de las Empresas Mineras del Cobre en Chile.* Centro de Mineria. Universidad Catolica de Chile.
Lahera, Eugenio, and Mabel Cabezas. 2000. "Governance and Institutional Development of the Chilean Economy," ECLAC, unpublished document.
Lahera, Eduardo, and C. Toloza (eds.). 1998. *Chile in the 1990s.* Santiago: Dolmen.
Larrain, Felipe. "Public Sector Behavior in a Highly Indebted Country: The Contrasting Chilean Experience," in Larrain and Selowsky (eds.), *The Public Sector and the Latin American Crisis.*
Larrain, Felipe, and Marcelo Selowsky (eds.). 1991. *The Public Sector and the Latin American Crisis.* San Francisco: ICS Press.
Larrain, Felipe, and Rodrigo Vergara. 2000. "Un Cuarto de Siglo de Reformas Fiscales," in Felipe Larrain and Rodrigo Vergara (eds.), *La Transformacion Economica de Chile.* Santiago: Centro de Estudios Publicos.
Larranaga, Osvaldo. 1994. Casos de Exito de la Politica Fiscal en Chile: 1980–1993," paper presented at the sixth CEPAL seminar, Santiago, Chile, January.

Lascano, Marcelo. 2000. *La Economia de los 90: Aspectos Significativos, Consecuencias Previsibles.* Buenos Aires: Ediciones Macchi.

——— (ed.). 2001. *La Economia Argentina Hoy.* Buenos Aires: Editorial El Ateneo.

Levi, Margaret. 1988. *Of Rule and Revenue.* Berkeley: University of California Press.

Levitsky, Steven. 2003a. *Transforming Labor-Based Parties in Latin America: Peronism in Comparative Perspective.* New York: Cambridge University Press.

———. 2003b. "Argentina: From Crisis to Consolidation (and Back)," in Jorge Domínguez and Michael Shifter (eds.), *Constructing Democratic Governance in Latin America.* Johns Hopkins University Press.

———. 2007. "From Populism to Clientelism? The Transformation of Labor-Based Party Linkages in Latin America," in Kitschelt and Wilkinson (eds.), *Patrons, Clients and Policies.*

Levitsky, Steven, and Maria Victoria Murillo. 2009. "Variation in Institutional Strength." *Annual Review of Political Science* Vol. 12: 115–33.

Llach, Juan Jose. 1997. *Otro Siglo, Otra Argentina: Una Estrategia para el Desarrollo Social Nacida de la Convertivilidad y su Historia.* Buenos Aires: Ariel.

———. 1999. "El Sistema Impositivo y el Gasto Social en la Argentina: Pasado y Futuro," in Instituto de Economia de la Universidad Argentina de la Empresa, *Ensayos sobre Politica y Gestion Tributarias: Homenaje a Carlos M. Tacchi.* IEUAE: Buenos Aires.

Lopez Murphy, Ricardo. 2003. *Lopez Murphy: Razon o Demagogia.* Buenos Aires: Editorial Planeta.

Lopez Murphy, Ricardo, G. Kippes, and N. Lew. 1981. "Regimenes de Promocion en la Argentina," 14 Jornadas de Finanzas Publicas, Cordoba.

Loveman, Brian. 2001. *Chile: The Legacy of Hispanic Capitalism.* Oxford: Oxford University Press.

Macon, Jorge. 1985. *Las Finanzas Publicas Argentinas: 1950–1980.* Buenos Aires: Ediciones Maachi.

———. 2000. "El Sistema Tributario y el Deficit Fiscal," *Enoikos: Revista de la Facultad de Ciencias Economicas* Universidad de Buenos Aires, Vol. V, No. 12.

Mahon, James E. 2001. "Global Finance, State-Building, and the Fiscal Contract," unpublished paper.

———. 2004. "Causes of Tax Reform in Latin America, 1977–95." *Latin American Research Review* Vol. 39, No. 1.

Mainwaring, Scott, and Timothy Scully (eds.). 1995. *Building Democratic Institutions: Party Systems in Latin America.* Stanford: Stanford University Press.

Mainwaring, Scott, Ana Maria Bejarano, and Eduardo Pizarro Leongomez. 2006. *The Crisis of Democratic Representation in the Andes.* Stanford: Stanford University Press.

Mallon, Richard, and Juan V. Sourouille. 1975. *Economic Policymaking in a Conflict Society: The Argentine Case.* Cambridge: Harvard University Press.

Manzetti, Luigi. 1993 *Institutions, Parties, and Coalitions in Argentine Politics.* Pittsburg: University of Pittsburgh Press.
———. 2002. "The Argentine Implosion," *The North-South Agenda,* paper 59. Miami: North-South Center, University of Miami.
Marcel, Mario. 1986. "Diez Anos del IVA en Chile." *Coleccion Estudios Cieplan* No. 19 (June).
———. 1991. "El Financiamiento del Gasto Social." *Coleccion Estudios Cieplan* No. 31. Santiago: CIEPLAN.
———. 1994. "Effectiveness of the State and Development Lessons from Chilean Experience," in Barry Bosworth, Rudiger Dornbush, and Raul Laban (eds.), *The Chilean Economy: Recent Challenges and Policy Lessons.* Washington, DC: Brookings Institution.
———. 1995 "Political Economy of Implementing Social Reforms: The 1990 Tax Reform in Chile, in Antonio Silva (ed.) *Implementing Policy Innovations in Latin America.* Washington, DC: Inter-American Development Bank.
———. 1997. "Politicas Publicas en Democracia: El Caso de la Reforma Tributaria de 1990 en Chile." *Coleccion Estudios CIEPLAN* No. 45 (June).
———. 1998. "Indicadores de desempeño como instrumentos de modernización del Estado en Chile." *Perspectivas en Política, Economía y Gestión* Vol. 2, No. 1.
Marcel, Mario, and Jaime Andres Crispi. 1991. "Administracion Estatal y Finanzas Publicas: la Transformacion del Estado en Chile." *Cuadernos del CLAEH* Vol. 16, No. 58–59.
Marcel, Mario, and Manuel Marfan. 1988. "The Tax Question," *CIEPLAN Review,* Santiago, Chile.
Marfan, Manuel. 1984. "Una Evaluacion de la Nueva Reforma Tributaria." *Coleccion Estudios CIEPLAN* No. 13 (June).
———. 1985. "El Conflicto entre Recaudacion de Impuestos e Inversion Privada. Elementos Teoricos para una Reforma Tributaria." *Coleccion Estudios CIEPLAN* No. 13. Santiago, Chile.
———. 1998. "El Financiamiento Fiscal en los Anos 90," in Rene Cortazar and Joaquin Vial (eds.), *Construyendo Opciones: Propuestas Economicas y Sociales para el Cambio de Siglo.* Santiago: Dolmen.
———. 2001 "The Chilean Tax Reform of 1990: A Success Story," Social Equity Forum, Political Dimension of Structural Reforms, Santiago, March 16–17.
Margheritis, Ana. 1997. "Politica Economica y Capacidades de Gobierno: Como se Construye la Viabilidad de un Programa de Ajuste (Argentina 1983–1993)," in Oszlak (ed.), *Estado y Sociedad.*
———. 2000. "Institutions, Political Dynamics and Human Agency: The Impact of Presidencial Leadership on Economic Policy Making in Argentina and Mexico," paper delivered to the Latin American Studies Association Congress, Miami, March.
Martner Fanta, Ricardo. 1996. "Indicators of Fiscal Policy: Design and Applications for Chile." *CEPAL Review* Vol. 58 (April).
———. 1998a. Volatilidad y ciclo en América Latina: debates, implicancias de política e instrumentos. Santiago: ILPES, 110 p.

Martner Fanta, Ricardo. 1998b. Política fiscal, ciclo y crecimiento. *Revista de la CEPAL* No. 64 (April): 73–90.

———. 2000. Los estabilizadores fiscales automáticos en América Latina. Santiago: ILPES, 47 p. CEPAL.

Maurich, Mario R., and Gabriela Liendo. 1997. "Reforma del Estado y Estilo Decisionista del Gobierno: Un Estudio del Caso Argentino," in Oszlak (ed.), *Estado y Sociedad.*

McGuire, James W. 1995. "Political Parties and Democracy in Argentina," in Mainwaring and Scully (eds.), *Building Democratic Institutions.*

———. 1997. *Peronism without Peron: Unions, Parties and Democracy in Argentina* Stanford: Stanford University Press.

Meller, Patricio. 1996. *Un Siglo de Economia Politica Chilena (1880–1990).* Santiago de Chile: Editorial Andres Bello.

———. 1984. "Los Chicago Boys y el Modelo Economico Chileno: 1973–1983." *Apuntes CIEPLAN* No. 43.

Menem, Carlos, and Roberto Dromi. 1990. *Reforma del Estado y Transformacion Nacional* Editorial Ciencias de la Administracion. Buenos Aires.

Migdal, Joe. 1988. *Strong Societies, Weak Status: State-Society Relations and State Capabilities in the Third World.* Princeton: Princeton University Press.

Ministerio de Economia. 1996. *Proyecto de Ley de Presupuesto General de GAstos y Calculo de Recusos de la Administracion Nacional. Mensaje.* Gobierno de la Republica Argentina.

———. 2000. *EL Programa Economico del Gobierno Nacional.* Buenos Aires.

Ministerio de Economia y Obras y Servicios Publicos. 1995. *Argentina en Crecimiento, 1995–1999.* Buenos Aires.

Ministerio de Economia. 1990. "Hacia una economia solidaria y moderna: Reforma tributaria 1990," internal document, Subsecretaria de Ingresos Publicos, March.

Ministerio de Hacienda. 1990–2000. *Exposicion sobre el Estado de la Hacienda Publica.* September.

Moe, Terry. 1990. "Political Institutions: The Neglected Side of the Story." *Journal of Law, Economics and Organization* Vol. 6: 213–55.

Montecinos, Veronica. 1998a. "Economists in Party Politics: Chilean Democracy in the Era of the Markets," in Miguel A. Centeno and Patricio Silva (eds.), *The Politics of Expertise in Latin America.* London: McMillan Press.

———. 1998b. *Economists, Politics and the State: Chile, 1958–1994.* Latin American Studies, No. 80. Thela thesis.

Montero, Cecilia. 1993. "El Actor Empresarial en Transicion." *Coleccion Estudios CIEPLAN* 37 (June).

Morales, Juan Antonio, and John MacMahon. 1993. *La Politica Economica en la Transicion a la Democracia: Lecciones de Argentina, Bolivia, Chile y Uruguay.* Santiago: CIEPLAN.

Morales Sola, J. 2001. *El Sueno Eterno: Ascenso y Caida de la Alianza.* Buenos Aires: Planeta.

Mora y Araujo, Manuel. 1991. *Ensayo y Error: la Nueva Clase Politica que Exige el Ciudadano Argentino.* Buenos Aires: Planeta.

Morriset, Jacques, and Alejandro Izquierdo. 1993. "Effects of Tax Reform on Argentina's Revenues," World Bank working paper WPS 1192, September. Washington, DC: World Bank.

Most, Benjamen. 1991. *Changing Authoritarian Rule and Public Policy in Argentina, 1930–1970.* Boulder, CO: Lynne Rienner Publishers.

Moulian, Tomas. 2002. "El Sistema de Partidos en Chile," in Marcelo Cavarozzi and Juan Manuel Abal Medina (eds.), *El Asedio a la Politica: Los Partidos Latinoamericanos en la Era Neoliberal.* Buenos Aires: Homo Sapiens Ediciones.

Moulian, Tomas, and Pilar Vergara. 1984. "Estado, Ideologia y Politicas Economicas en Chile: 1973–1978," Serie, Politicas de Estabilizacion en America Latina.

Munoz, Oscar. 1988. "El Estado y los Empresarios: Experiencias Comparadas y sus Implicaciones para Chile." *Coleccion Estudios* Vol. 25 (December): 5–53; Santiago: CIEPLAN.

——— (ed.). 1990. *Transicion a la Democracia. Marco Politico y Economico.* Santiago: CIEPLAN.

———. 1994. *Los Inesperados Caminos de la Modernizacion Economica.* Santiago: Editorial Universidad Santiago.

Murillo, Ana Victoria. 2001. *Labor Unions, Partisan Coalitions and Market Reform in Latin America.* Cambridge: Cambridge University Press.

Musgrave, Richard. 1987. "Tax Reform in Developing Countries," in David Newberry and Nicholas Stern (eds.), *The Theory of Taxation in Developing Countries.* New York: Oxford University Press.

Mussa, Michael. 2002. *Argentina y el FMI: Del Triunfo a la Tragedia.* Buenos Aires: Ediciones Planeta.

Mustapic, Ana Maria. 2000. "Oficialistas y Diputados: Las Relaciones Ejecutivo-Legislativo en la Argentina." *Desarrollo Economico* Vol. 39, No. 156.

———. 2002. "Del Partido Peronista al Partido Justicialista: las Transformaciones de un Partido Carismatico," in Cavarozzi and Medina (eds.), *Asedio a la Politica.*

Mustapic, Ana Maria, and Matteo Goretti. 1992. "Gobierno y Oposicion en el Congreso: La Practica de la Cohabitacion Durante la Presidencia de Alfonsin (1983–1989)." *Desarrollo Economico* Vol. 32, No. 126 (July–September).

Navia, Patricio. 2001. "La Concertacion como Partido Politico." *Revista de Critica Cultural.* Online. http://homepages.nyu.edu/~pdn200/papers/criticacultural2001.PDF. Accessed April 14, 2003.

Nelson, Joan. 1990. *Economic Crisis and Policy Choice: The Politics of Adjustment in the Third Worl.d* Princeton: Princeton University Press.

N'Haux, Enrique. 1993. *Menem-Cavallo: El Poder Mediterraneo.* Buenos Aires: Ediciones Corregidor.

Nino, Carlos. 1996. "Hyper-presidentialism and Constitutional Reform in Argentina," in Arend Lijphart and Carlos Waisman (eds.), *Institutional Design in New Democracies.* Boulder, CO: Westview.

Nochteff, Hugo (ed.). 1998. *La Economia Argentina a Fin de Siglo: Fragmentacion Presente y Desarrollo Ausente.* Buenos Aires: FLACSO.

Nordlinger, Eric. 1968. "Political Development: Time Sequences and Rates of Change." *World Politics* Vol. 20 (April): 494–521.
North, Douglas. 1981. *Structure and Change in Economic History*. New York: W.W. Norton.
———. 1990. *Institutions, Institutional Change and Economic Performance* Cambridge: Cambridge University Press.
Novaro, Marcos (ed.) 2002. *El Derrumbe Politico en el Ocaso de la Convertibilidad*. Buenos Aires: Grupo Editorial Norma.
Nowak, Norman. 1970. *Tax Administration in Theory and Practice: The Case of Chile*. New York: Praeger Publishers.
O'Donnell, Guillermo. 1976. *Estado y Alianzas en la Argentina, 1966–1976*. Documentos Centro de Estudios y Sociedad.
———. 1986. *El Estado Burocratico-Autoritario*. Buenos Aires: Editorial de Belgrano.
———. 1999. Polyarchies and the Unrule of Law in Latin America," in Juan Mendez and Guillermo O'Donnell (eds.), *The (Un)Rule of Law and the Underpriviledged in Latin America*. Notre Dame, IN: University of Notre Dame Press.
Olson, Mancur. 1982. *The Rise and Decline of Nations*. New Haven: Yale University Press.
Ominami, Carlos. 1991. "Promoting Economic Growth and Stability," in Joseph Tulchin and Augusto Varas (eds.), *From Dictatorship to Democracy: Rebuilding Political Consensus in Chile*. Boulder, CO: Lynne Rienner Publishers.
Oppenheim, Lois Hecht. 1985. "Democracy and Social Transformation in Chile: The Debate Within the Left." *Latin American Perspectives* Vol. 12, No. 3 (Summer).
Orlansky, Dora. 1994. "Crisis y Transformacion del Estado en la Argentina (1960–1993)." *Ciclos: en la Historia, la Economia y la Politica* Vol. IV, No. 7 (2 Semestre de).
Oszlak, Oscar. 1994. "El Estado Deseable y el que Supimos Conseguir." *Perspectiva y Dialogo Internacional*. Buenos Aires: Fundacion Andina, Vol. 6, No. 7.
———. 1997a. *La Formación del Estado Argentino: Orden, Progreso y Organización Nacional*. Buenos Aires: Planeta.
——— (ed.). 1997b. *Estado y Sociedad: Las Nuevas Reglas del Juego, Vol. 1*. Universidad de Buenos Aires.
———. 1999. "Quemar las Naves: O Como Lograr Reformas Estatales Irreversibles." *Aportes para el Estado y la Administracion Gubernamental* Vol. 6, No. 14, Primavera.
Palermo, Vicente. 1995. "Reformas Estructurales y Regimen Politico. Argentina 1989–1994." *America Latina Hoy* No. 11–12 (December).
———. 2002. "El Enemigo del Pueblo," in Novaro (ed.), *El Derrumbe Politico*.
Palermo, Vicente, and M. Novaro. 1996. *Politica y Poder en el Gobierno de Menem*. Buenos Aires: Grupo Editorial Norma.
Paredes, Ricardo, Jose Miguel Sánchez, Ricardo Sanhueza, Leonardo Letelier, and Jose Yáñez. 1997. "Autonomía de las Instituciones Gubernamentales

en Chile." Documento de Trabajo No. 152. Departamento de Economía, Universidad de Chile.

Pastor, Manuel, and Carol Wise. 1999. "Stabilization and its Discontents: Argentina's Economic Restructuring in the 1990s." *World Development* Vol. 27, No. 3.

Peralta-Ramos, Monica. 1992. *The Political Economy of Argentina: Power and Class since 1930*. Boulder, CO: Westview Press.

Perez, Andres. 1991. "Legitimacy and the Administrative Capacity of the State: Public Administration in Developing Countries." *International Review of Administrative Sciences* Vol. 4: 641.

Perkins, Dwight. 1991. *Reforming Economic Systems in Developing Countries*. Cambridge: Harvard University Press.

Perry, Guillermo. 1994. "Fiscal Reform, Structural Adjustment and the New Role of the State in Latin America," in Colin Bradford (ed.), *Redefining the State in Latin America*. Paris: OECD.

Perry, Guillermo, and A. M. Herrera. 1994. *Public Finances, Stabilization and Structural Reform in Latin America*. Washington, DC: Inter-American Development Bank.

Perry, Guillermo, John Whalley, and Gary McMahon (eds.). 2000. *Fiscal Reform and Structural Change in Developing Countries*. London: St Martin's Press.

Peters, Guy. 1991. *The Politics of Taxation: A Comparative Perspective*. Cambridge: Basil Blackwells.

Pizarro, Crisostomo, Dagmar Racynski, and Joaquin Vial (eds.). 1995. *Politicas Economicas y Sociales en el Chile Democratico*. Santiago: CIEPLAN-UNICEF.

Pollack, Marcelo. 1999. *The New Right in Chile, 1973–1997*. London: MacMillan Press.

Porterba, James M., and Jurgen von Hagen. 1999. *Fiscal Institutions and Fiscal Performance*. Chicago: The University of Chicago Press.

Porto, Alberto, and Pablo Sanguinetti. 1998. *Federalismo Fiscal en America Latina: El Caso Argentino*. CEPAL: Serie Politica Fiscal 45.

Puryear, Jeffrey. 1994. *Thinking Politics: Intellectuals and Democracy in Chile, 1973–1988*. Baltimore: Johns Hopkins University.

Putnam, Robert. 1993 *Making Democracy Work: Civic Traditions in Modern Italy*. Princeton: Princeton University Press.

Quinn, Dennis, and Robert Shapiro. 1991. "Business Political Power: The Case of Taxation." *American Political Science Review* Vol. 85, No. 3 (September): 851.

Racynski, Dagmar. 1994. "Politicas Sociales y Programas de Combate a la Pobreza en Chile: Balances y Desafios." *Coleccion Estudios* CIEPLAN 39 (June): 9–73. Santiago: CIEPLAN.

Racynski, Dagmar, and Pilar Romaguera. 1993. "Chile: Poverty, Adjustment and Social Policies in the 1980s," in Nora Lustig (ed.), *Coping with Austerity: Poverty and Inequality in Latin America*, pp. 320–38. Washington, DC: Brookings Institution.

Randall, Laura. 1978. *An Economic History of Argentina in the Twentieth Century*. New York: Columbia University Press.

Rapoport, Mario (ed.). 2000. *Historia Economica, Politica y Social de la Argentina 1880–2000*. Ediciones Macchi.
Rehren, Alfredo. 1995. "Empresarios, Transicion y Consolidacion Democratica en Chile." *Revista de Ciencia Politica* Vol. XVII, No. 1–2.
Resse, Thomas. 1980. *The Politics of Taxation*. Westport: Quorum Books.
Rey, Mabel Thwaites. 2001. "Technocrats versus Punteros: Nueva Falacia de una vieja dicotomía." *Encrucijadas* No. 6 (April).
Roberts, Kenneth. 1998. *Deepening Democracy? The Modern Left and Social Movements in Chile and Peru*. Stanford: Stanford University Press.
Rodrik, Dani. 1989. "Promises, Promises: Credible Policy Reform via Signaling." *The Economic Journal* Vol. 99 (September).
Rodriguez, Carlos A. 2000. *Argentina en Transicion. La Recesion 1998–2000*. Temas Grupo Editorial.
Rodriguez, Guillermo. 2000. "Pautas para la Formulacion de un Sistema Tributario Justo, Eficiente y Equitativo." *Criterios Tributarios* Vol. XII, No. 113.
Romero, Jose Luis. 2002. *Breve Historia Contemporanea de la Argentina*. Buenos Aires: Fondo de Cultura Economica.
Rozenwurcel, Guillermo. 1994. "Fiscal Reform and Macroeconomic Stabilization in Argentina," Documento CEDES 103, Serie Economia.
Sabaini, Juan Carlos G. 1993. Quien Paga los Impuestos en la Argentina?" in Alberto Minujin (ed.), *Desigualdad y Exclusion: Desafios para la Politica Social en la Argentina*. Buenos Aires: UNICEF.
Saiegh, M. Sebastian. 1998. "Las Instituciones Politicas Argentinas y su Reforma: Una Agenda de Investigación," CEDI, Documento 1.
Saiegh, M. Sebastian, and Mariano Tommasi. 1999. "Why is Argentina's Fiscal Federalism so Inefficient? Entering the Labyrinth." *Journal of Applied Economics* Vol. II, No. 1 (May).
Sanchez, Omar. 2006. "Tax System Reform in Latin America: Domestic and International Causes." *Review of International Political Economy* Vol. 13, No. 5 (December).
———. 2008. "Transformation and Decay: The De-Institutionalization of Party Systems in South America." *Third World Quarterly* Vol. 29, No. 2: 315–37.
———. 2009a. "Tax Reform Paralysis in Post-Conflict Guatemala." *New Political Economy* Vol. 14, No. 1 (March).
———. 2009b. "Party Non-Systems: A Conceptual Innovation." *Party Politics* Vol. 15, No. 4: 487–520.
———. 2011a. "Collective Action Dilemmas: Argentine Fiscal Federalism in the 1990s." *Latin American Policy: A Journal of Politics and Governance* Vol 2, No. 2.
———. 2011b. "Fighting Tax Evasion in Latin America: the Contrasting Strategies of Chile and Argentina." *Third World Quarterly* Vol 32.
Sanguinetti, Pablo. 2001. "Determinantes Politicos e Institucionales Ligados al Desempeno Fiscal: el Caso de las Provincias Argentinas." *Revista Internacional del Presupuesto Publico* No. 46.
Santoro, Daniel. 1996. *Los Intocables (los verdaderos): Una Investigacion que Revela Por Que Cobrar Impuestos en Argentina es una Mision Imposible*. Buenos Aires: Editorial Planeta.

Schamis, Hector. 2002. "Argentina: Crisis and Consolidation." *Journal of Democracy* Vol. 13, No. 2 (April).

Schedler, Andreas, Larry Diamond, and Marc Plattner (eds.). 1999. *The Self-Restraining State: Power and Accountability in New Democracies*. Boulder, CO: Lynne Rienner Publishers.

Schvarzer, Jorge. 1990. *Promocion Industrial en Argentina: Caracteristicas, Evolucion y Resultados*. Buenos Aires.

Schattschneider, E. 1960. *The Semi-Sovereign People*. New York: Holt, Rinehart, and Wiston.

Sebreli, Juan Jose. 2002. *Critica de las Ideas Politicas Argentinas*. Buenos Aires: Editorial Sudamericana.

Shepsle, Kenneth. 1998. "The Political Economy of State Reform—Political to the Core," lecture presented at the Seminar for State Reform, Bogota, Colombia, April.

Shome, Parthasarathi. 1995a. "Recent Tax Policy Trends and Issues in Latin America," in Andre Lara Resende (ed.), *Policies for Growth: The Latin American Experience*. Washington, DC: IMF.

Shuggart, Matthew, and Stephan Haggard. 2001. "Institutions and Public Policy in Presidential Systems," in Stephan Haggard and Mathew McCubbins (eds.), *Presidents, Parliaments and Policy*. New York: Cambridge University Press.

Siavelis, Peter. 1997. "Executive-Legislative Relations in Post-Pinochet Chile: A Preliminary Assessment," in Scott Mainwaring and Matthew Shuggart (eds.), *Presidentialism and Democracy in Latin America*. Cambridge: Cambridge University Press.

———. 2000. *The President and Congress in Postauthoritarian Chile: Institutional Constraints to Democratic Consolidation*. Pennsylvania: Pennsylvania State University Press.

———. 2002. "Exaggerated Presidentialism and Moderate Presidents: Executive-Legislative Relations in Chile," in Scott Morgernstern and Benito Nacif (eds.), *Legislative Politics in Latin America*. New York: Cambridge University Press.

———. 2006. "Accomodating Informal Institutions and Chilean Democracy," in Helmke and Leviskty (eds.), *Informal Institutions and Democracy*.

Sidicaro, Ricardo. 2001. *La Crisis del Estado: Los Actores Politicos y Socioeconomicos en la Argentina (1989–2001)*. Libros del Rojas. Universidad de Buenos Aires.

———. 2002. *Los Tres Peronismos: Estado y Poder Economico*. Siglo Veintiuno Editores.

Sikkink, Kathryn. 1991. *Ideas and Institutions: Developmentalism in Brazil and Argentina*. Ithaca: Cornell University Press.

———. 1993. "Las capacidades y la autonomia del Estado en Brasil y la Argentina: un enfoque neoinstitucionalista." *Desarrollo Economico* Vol. 32, No. 1: 543–74.

Silva, Eduardo. 1996. *The State and Capital in Chile: Business Elites, Technocrats and Market Economics*. Colorado: Westview Press.

———. 2002. "Capital and the Lagos Presidency: Business as Usual?" *Bulletin of Latin American Research* Vol. 21, No. 3.

Silva, Patricio. 1994. "State Capacity, Technocratic Insulation and Embeddedness," Government-Business Relations in South Korea and Chile.
———. 1995. Empresarios, neoliberalismo y transicion democratica en Chile. *Revista Mexicana de Sociologia* Vol. 57, No. 4: 3–25.
———. 1996. "Technocrats and Politics in Chile: from the Chicago Boys to the CIEPLAN Monks." *Journal of Latin American Studies* Vol. 23: 385–410.
Slemrod, Joel. 1992. *Why People Pay Taxes? Tax Compliance and Enforcement.* Ann Harbor: University of Michigan Press.
Smith, William C. 1989. *Authoritarianism and the Crisis of the Argentine Political Economy* Stanford: Stanford University Press.
Smith, William C., Carlos Acuna, and Eduardo Gamarra (eds.). 1994. *Democracy, Markets and Structural Reform in Latin America.* New Brunswick: Transaction Publishers.
Snow, Peter, and Luigi Manzetti. 1993. *Political Forces in Argentina* (Third Edition). London: Praeger.
Soifer, Hillel David. 2008. "State Infrastructural Power: Conceptualization and Measurement." *Studies in Comparative International Development* Vol. 43, No. 3–4: 231–51.
Solimano, Andres, Eduardo Aninat, and Nancy Birdsall (eds.). 2001. *Distributive Justice and Economic Development: The Case of Chile and Developing Countries.* Ann Arbor: University of Michigan Press.
Spiller, Pablo, and Mariano Tommasi. 2003 "The Institutional Foundations of Public Policy: A Transactions Approach with Application to Argentina." *Journal of Law, Economics and Organization* Vol 19, No. 2: 281–306.
Spiller, Pablo, Ernesto Stein, and Mariano Tommasi. 2003. "Political Institutions, Policymaking Processes and Policy Outcomes: An Intertemporal Transactions Framework." Princeton Conference on Comparative Analysis of Political Institutions. March 28.
Stallings, Barbara. 1989. "Political Economy of Democratic Transition: Chile in the 1980s," in Barbara Stallings and Robert Kaufman (eds.), *Debt and Democracy in Latin America.* Boulder, CO: Westview Press.
Starr, Pamela. 1997. "Government Coalitions and the Viability of Currency Boards: Argentina under the Cavallo Plan." *Journal of Inter-American Studies and World Affairs* Vol. 39, No. 2.
Steinmo, Sven. 1993. *Taxation and Democracy: Swedish, British and American Approaches to Financing the Modern State.* New Haven: Yale University Press.
Talavera, Arturo Fontaine. 2000. "Chile's Elections: The New Face of the Right." *Journal of Democracy* Vol. 11, No. 2 (April).
Tanzi, Vito. 1991. *Public Finance in Developing Countries.* London: Edward Elgar.
———. 1992. "Fiscal Policy and Economic Reconstruction in Latin America." *World Development*, Vol. 20, No. 5: 641–57.
———. 1994. "The IMF and Tax Reform," in Amaresh Bagchi and Nicholas Stern (eds.), *Tax Policy and Planning in Developing Countries.* Oxford: Oxford University Press.

Tanzi, Vito. 2003. "Taxation Reform in Latin America in the Last Decade," in Corbo Gonzalez and A. Krueger (eds.), *Latin American Macroeconomic Reform*. Chicago: University of Chicago Press.
Taylor, Michelle. 1992. "Formal versus Informal Incentive Structures and Behavior." *Journal of Politics* Vol. 54, No. 4: 1055–73.
Teichman, Judith. 1997. "Mexico and Argentina: Economic Reform and Technocratic Decision-Making." *Studies in Comparative International Development* Vol. 32, No. 1: 31–55.
———. 2001. *The Politics of Freeing Markets in Latin America: Chile, Argentina and Mexico*. Chapel Hill, NC: The University of North Carolina Press.
Teijeiro, Mario. 2001. "Una vez mas...La Politica Fiscal," in Marcelo Lascano (ed.), *La Economia Argentina Hoy*. Buenos Aires: Ateneo.
Thirsk, Wayne (ed.). 1997. *Tax Reform in Developing Countries*. World Bank Sectoral and Regional Studies. Washington, DC: World Bank.
Tilly, Charles. 1975. *The Formation of National States in Western Europe*. Princeton: Princeton University Press.
Toloza, Cristian and Eugenio Lahera (eds.). 1998. *Chile en los Noventa*. Santiago de Chile: Ediciones Dolme.
Tomassi, Mariano. 2000. *Las Fuentes Institucionales del Desarrollo Argentino: Hacia una Agenda Institucional*. Buenos Aires: Universidad de Buenos Aires.
Tommasi, Mariano, and Andres Velasco. 1996. "Where Are We on the Political Economy of Reform?" *Journal of Policy Reform* Vol. 1, No. 1.
Toro, Juan. 1994. "Aspectos Exitosos y Lecciones de Reformas Tributarias en Chile," paper presented at the sixth annual CEPAL Seminar, Santiago, Chile, January.
Torre, Juan Carlos. 1993. "Conflict and Cooperation in Governing the Economic Emergency: The Alfonsin Years," in Colin M. Lewis and Nissa Torrents (eds.), *Argentina in the Crisis Years (1983–1990)*. London: Institute of Latin American Studies.
———. 2002 "La Crisis de la Representacion Partidaria en Argentina," Universidad Torcuato di Tella, unpublished manuscript.
Valdes, Juan Gabriel. 1995. *Pinochet's Economists: The Chicago School in Chile*. Cambridge: Cambridge University Press.
Valenzuela, Arturo. 1984. "Parties, Politics and the State in Chile," in Ezra Suleiman (ed.), *Bureaucrats and Policymaking: A Comparative Overview*. New York: Holmes and Meier.
———. 1999. "Chile: Origins and Consolidation of a Latin American Democracy," in Larry Diamond, Jonathan Hartlyn, Juan Linz, and Seymour Martin Lipset (eds.), *Democracy in Developing Countries: Latin America*. Boulder, CO: Lynne Rienner Publishers.
Valenzuela, Samuel, and Timothy Scully. 1997. "Electoral Choices and the Party System in Chile: Continuities and Change at the Recovery of Democracy." *Comparative Politics* Vol. 29, No. 4.
Velasco, Andres. 1994. "The State and Economic Policy: Chile 1952–1992," in Bosworth, Dornbush, and Laban (eds.), *The Chilean Economy*.

Velasco, Andres. 2002. "Institucionalidad, credibilidad y manejo macroeconómico en Chile." *Estudios Públicos* No. 77 (Summer): 37–67.
Vellinga, Menno (ed.). 1999. *The Changing Role of the State in Latin America*. New York: Westview Press.
Vergara, Pilar. 1985. *Auge y Caida del Neoliberalismo en Chile*. Santiago: FLACSO.
———. 1996. "In Pursuit of 'Growth with Equity': The Limits of Chile's Free-Market Social Reforms." *NACLA Report on the Americas*, May/June.
Vergara, Rodrigo. 2001 "Politica Tributaria, Ahorro y Crecimiento," in Harald Beyer and Rodrigo Vergara (eds.), *Que Hacer Ahora? Propuestas Economicas para Chile*. Santiago de Chile: Centro de Estudios Publicos.
Vial, Joaquin. 2001. "Institucionalidad y Desempeno Fiscal: Una Mirada a la Experiencia de Chile en los 90." *Serie Estudios Socio/Economicos* N. 5, CIEPLAN, October.
Vial Ruiz-Tagle, Joaquin. 1997. *Aspectos Macroeconomicso del Proyecto de Ley de Presupuestos del Sector Publico del Ano 1998*. Ministerio de Hacienda. Direccion de Presupuestos. October.
Waisman, Carlos H. 1987. *Reversal of Development in Argentina*. Princeton: Princeton University Press.
———. 1999. "Capitalism and Democracy in Argentina," in Larry Diamond, Jonathan Hartlyn, and Juan J. Linz (eds.), *Democracy in Developing Countries: Latin America*. Boulder, CO: Lynne Rienner Publishers.
———. 2003. "El Default Argentino: Sus Causas Institucionales." *Politica y Gobierno* Vol. X, No. 1.
Walker, Ignacio, and Juan Gabriel Valdes (eds.). 1986. *Democracia en Chile: Doce Conferencias*. Santiago: CIEPLAN.
Walter, Hettich, and Stanley Winer. 1988. "Economic and Political Foundations of Tax Structure." *American Economic Review* Vol. 78, No. 4 (September): 701–12.
Weyland, Kurt. 1997. "Growth with Equity in Chile's New Democracy." *Latin American Research Review* Vol. 32, No. 1: 37–67.
———. 1999. "Economic Policy in Chile's New Democracy." *Journal of Interamerican Studies and World Affairs* Vol. 41, No. 3.
Whitehead, Laurence. 1996. "Chronic Fiscal Stress and the Reproduction of Poverty and Inequality in Latin America," in Victor Bulmer-Thomas (ed.), *The New Economic Model in Latin America and Its Impat on Income Distribution and Poverty*. London: Palgrave MacMillan.
———. 1998. "State Organization in Latin America since 1930," in Leslie Bethell (ed.), *Latin America: Economy and Society since 1930* (The Cambridge History of Latin America). Cambridge: Cambridge University Press.
Williamson, John. 1990. *Progress of Policy Reform in Latin America*. Washington, DC: Institute for International Economics.
Wise, Carol. 2000. "Argentina's Currency Board: The Ties that Bind?" in Carol Wise and Riordan Roett (eds.), *Exchange Rate Politics in Latin America*. Washington, DC: The Brookings Institution.

World Bank. 1990a. *Chile: Consolidating Economic Growth*. Washington, DC: World Bank.

———. 1990b. *Argentina: Tax Policy for Stabilization and Recovery*. A World Bank Country Study. Washington, DC: World Bank.

———. 1993. *Argentina: From Insolvency to Growth*. Washington, DC: World Bank.

———. 1998. *Argentina: The Fiscal Dimension of the Convertibility Plan*. Washington, DC: World Bank.

Yanez, Jose. 1991. "Las Reformas Tributarias en Chile 1974–1990." Mimeo, Departamento de Economia, Universidad de Chile.

Index

Administracion Federal de Impuestos Publicos (AFIP, Federal Public Revenue Administration) 147, 153–154
Administracion General de Aduanas (National Customs Office) 139
Agenda pro-crecimiento (Pro-Growth agenda plan) 78, 79
Alfonsin, Raul 14, 89, 93–96, 100, 102, 105, 184
Alianza government 149, 150–151, 153, 154, 157, 160, 161, 162
Allende, Salvador
  government of, 20, 71
  period 28, 36, 65, 167, 176
Alvarez, "Chacho" 143, 152
Aninat, Eduardo 49, 51, 52, 55, 57, 58, 60, 61, 62, 71, 72, 85, 195
Arellano, Pablo 22, 44, 173
Autocomplacientes (self-complacent) 65
Autoflagelantes (self-flagellants) 65, 71, 81
Aylwin, Patricio 17, 25, 26, 30, 31, 32, 38, 39, 41, 46, 48, 53, 60, 89, 174

Bates, Robert 5, 8
Bauza, Eduardo 129, 131–133
Bergman, Marcelo 9
Bitar, Sergio 50, 77, 175
Boeninger, Eduardo 34, 77
  Foxley-Boeinger tax initiative 80, 83, 86
Boron, Atilio 179
Buchi, Hernan 24, 25, 27, 28, 34, 36

Candessus, Michel 127
Canitrot, Adolfo 95
Cardoso, Fernando H. 25
Cauas, Jorge 19, 22
Cavallo, Domingo 14, 103–112, 114
  as minister under De la Rua 155–161, 192, 195, 196, 198
  as minister under Menem 116–121, 125, 128–137, 140, 144, 147, 151
Central Bank
  Argentina 103, 111, 128, 135, 153, 156
  Chile 63, 67, 70, 79, 82, 171
  Latin America 203, 204
Central Unitaria de Trabajadores (CUT, Central Workers Union) 38, 170
Centro de Estudios Macroeconomicos (CEMA) 134, 151
Chicago boys
  And Argentine economy 134
  And Chilean economic policy 174
  And CIEPLAN monks 30
  Economic thought 21
  And technocracy 200
  Trade regime 60
Christian Democratic Party (*Partido Cristiano Democrata*) 27, 49, 65, 70, 72, 167, 174, 175
CIEPLAN 30, 31, 174
  Monks 30
Clientelism 183, 184, 185, 188–190, 194, 205

Collective action 6, 7, 163
  Dilemma 12, 169, 178, 190, 192–194, 196
Concha, Andres 61
Confederacion de Produccion y Comercio (CPC) 34, 35, 41, 42, 45, 57, 61, 79, 170
Convertibility Law (*Ley de Convertibilidad*) 103, 111, 112, 114, 116, 119, 122, 123, 125, 130, 133, 134, 135, 146, 148, 157, 158, 161, 194, 197
Copper Stabilization Fund 36, 173
Corach, Carlos 129, 133, 195
CORFO 18
Cossio, Ricardo 99, 100, 116, 121, 122, 129, 131, 132, 138
Cuello, Raul 99–101, 110, 195

De Castro, Sergio 22
De Gregorio 71, 81
De la Rua, Fernando 143, 148–150, 152, 153, 155–157, 162, 198
Direccion General Impositiva (DGI, Argentina Tax Bureau) 89, 91–93, 98–101, 109, 110, 115, 118, 119, 121–123, 125, 129, 130, 131, 132, 133, 137, 138, 139, 140, 143, 145, 153, 195
Dominguez, Jorge 200

Economic crisis
  In Argentina, 102, 193, 202
  In Chile 63, 66, 72, 86
Economic reform
  in Argentina 95, 98
  and Carlos Menem 194
  in Chile 13, 20, 36
  and clientelism 190, 194
  and the *Concertacion* 34
  in Latin America, 205
  liberal, in Argentina, 156
  and party systems 184
  and president De la Rua, 157
  and *Renovacion Nacional* 168
  Structural 4
  and transition in Chile 31

Etcheberry, Javier 74–75, 195
Eyzaguirre, Nicolas 70, 74, 76, 77, 78, 80, 81, 82, 84, 167, 195

Federal fiscal system 187–188, 198
Fernandez, Roque 133–137, 140–142, 144–146, 148, 151, 161, 196
Ffrench-Davis, Ricardo 18, 68, 126
Fiscal discipline
  In Argentina 147, 148, 149, 198
  In Chile 22, 38, 40, 55, 59, 65–66, 73, 85, 163, 172–173, 197–198, 201
  In Latin America 205
Fiscal pact 3, 6, 12, 13, 92, 94, 96, 106, 122, 123, 150, 151, 166, 182, 190, 203
Fiscal policy 15, 17, 55, 57, 59, 63, 64, 66, 67, 73, 79–82, 84, 85, 167, 188, 203, 204, 205
Fishlow, Albert 1
Foxley, Alejandro 28, 30, 31, 32, 34, 36, 38, 39, 42, 44, 45, 46, 68, 76, 77, 166, 174, 195
  Foxley-Boeinger tax initiative 80, 83, 86
Frei, Eduardo 49, 50, 53, 57, 58, 63, 66, 71, 75, 81, 85, 86, 200
FREPASO 142, 143, 155, 157, 183
Fundacion de Investigaciones Economicas Latinoamericanas (FIEL, Argentine think tank) 156
Fundacion Mediterranea (Argentine think tank) 103–104, 107

Geddes, Barbara 180, 181
Grondona, Mario 134
'Growth with Equity' 17, 18, 26, 44, 48, 53, 54, 55, 67, 68, 170

Hyperinflation 14, 96, 97, 102, 103, 106, 111, 114, 171, 196

IEPE (*Impuesto sobre el Excedente Primario de las Empresas*) 113–114

Inflation 17–21, 36, 37, 41, 48, 49, 51, 53, 54, 59, 71, 94, 95–97, 100, 102, 103, 106, 108, 109, 111, 113, 123, 134, 160, 171, 196
Informal institutions 4, 12–13, 15, 173, 177, 188–190, 191, 196, 197, 199–200
Inter-American Development Bank 3
International Monetary Fund (IMF) 71, 98, 100, 112, 118, 125, 127, 128, 129, 136, 137, 140, 142, 143, 145, 152, 155, 158, 159, 161, 171, 198

Kaldor, Nicholas 1–2
Kohler, Horst 159

Lagos, Ricardo 70–74, 76, 78, 79–80, 82, 83, 85–86, 166, 167, 173, 175, 198
Landerretche, Oscar 81
Lavandero, Jorge 64, 65
Lavin, Joaquin 69, 70
Law of Fiscal Responsibility 147, 148, 150
Ley de Abastecimientos 115, 121, 122, 138
Lopez Murphy, Ricardo 156, 157, 159, 195
Los Intocables (The Untouchables) 119, 130–131, 138, 139

Machinea, Jose Luis 149–152, 154–157, 195, 196
Macri, Francisco 130–131
Mahon, James 7
Marcel, Mario 72, 74, 82
Marfan, Manuel 30, 31, 44, 50, 56, 66, 175
Massad, Carlos 67
Menem, Carlos 14, 89, 96, 97, 99–102, 103, 105, 114, 118, 120, 123, 130–133, 135, 136, 137, 139, 140, 141, 142, 143, 144, 152, 154, 160, 184, 189, 193, 194, 195, 197, 198, 199

Military regime
  In Argentina 89, 90, 103, 180, 181, 182
  In Chile 17, 25, 26, 28, 29, 30, 34, 35, 36, 164, 165, 168, 172, 173, 174
Mora y Araujo, Carlos 106
Moyano, Hugo 153
Munoz, Oscar 174

Neoliberal
  Economics 17, 24, 26, 65, 72, 81, 104, 174, 199
  Reform 5

OECD 141
Olivera-Tanzi effect, 18, 96, 111, 122, 126
Olson, Mancur 169
Ominami, Carlos 34, 43, 44, 76, 81, 83, 175
Oszlak, Oscar 93

Partido por la Democracia (PPD, Party for Democracy) 31, 56, 65, 70, 85, 175
Partido Socialista Chileno (PS, Chilean SOcialist Party) 31, 70, 71, 73, 78, 80, 81, 82, 85, 166, 167, 175, 198, 200
Party system
  In Argentina 177, 183–185, 194
  In Chile 15, 163, 166–169, 170
  In Latin America 201–204
Pena, Luis Maria 130, 139
Peron, Juan Domingo 180, 184
Peronist party (*Partido Peronista*) 14, 94, 95, 101, 108, 109, 114, 116, 130, 142, 143, 149, 151, 152, 179, 180, 183, 184, 186, 187, 189
Pinera 33, 83
Pinochet, Augusto 13, 20
  detention in London 66
  and economic growth 40
  economic legacy 36, 168, 174
  economic team, 22, 23, 172
  ideological confrontations 175

Pinochet, Augusto—*Continued*
  regime 24–27
  and social debt 44
  and tax agency 89
  and tax reductions 43
Politicas de Estado 4, 149, 163, 173, 184
Pou, Pedro 156
Public goods 7, 8, 106, 190

Radical party (*Union Civica Radica*, UCR) 95, 97, 101, 105, 109, 113, 143, 150, 180, 183, 184
Rapanelli, Nestor 100, 102, 104, 195
Renovacion Nacional (RN, National Renovation party) 32, 33, 35, 38, 40, 44, 45–48, 51, 52, 54, 56, 58, 59, 61, 68, 69, 77, 83, 84, 167
Riesco, Walter 57, 66
Rodriguez, Guillermo 138, 141, 142
Rodriguez, Hector 154
Rodriguez Saa, Afolfo 160
Rodrik, Dani 97
Rule of law
  In Argentina 182
  In Chile 15, 191
  In Latin America 7
  And taxation 205, 206

Sanchez, Carlos 119, 159
Servicio de Impuestos Internos (SII, Chilean Central Tax Bureau) 74, 75, 196, 200
Silva, Patricio 30
Silvani, Carlos 137–139, 141, 145–146, 152–153, 161
SOFOFA 61, 78, 79
Soros, George 148
Spend and tax model 161, 197
State-building 2, 5, 163, 191, 194
State-society fiscal relations
  In Argentina 92, 103, 122–123, 190
  In Chile 34
  In Latin America 177, 204
  And tax reform consolidation 163

Steinmo, Sven 10
Supply-side economics 24, 27, 40, 66, 77, 83, 86, 87, 111, 112, 116, 137, 155, 160, 198

Tacchi, Carlos 106–108, 110, 112–116, 119–122, 125, 126, 129, 130–132, 138, 139, 151, 161, 195
Tanzi, Vito 100, 137, 141, 142, 151
Tax administration
  1990 Chilean tax reform 29
  In Argentina, historical trend 89
  Argentina's Penal Tax Law 101
  And Argentina's tax code 91
  And argentine state-society relations 92
  And Boeninger-Foxley initative 77
  And Carlos Menem reforms 99, 140, 160–161
  In Chile, historical trend, 89
  And Chile's SII 196
  And Clientelism in Argentina 190
  And Domingo Cavallo 13, 104, 109
  During minister Rapanelli 104
  And federal fiscal system 161
  and inflation in Chile 20
  In Latin America 204, 206
  Reforms by Etcheberry 75
  Under Carlos Silvani 138
  Under Carlos Taachi 108, 110, 113, 118, 122–126, 131
  Under Hector Rodriguez 154
  Under president Frei 51
  Under president Lagos 70
  Under the Concertacion governments 54
Tax and spend 38, 44, 63, 72, 85, 172, 175, 197, 205
Taxation
  Cascading 21
  on global sales 147
  On income 5, 18, 23, 29, 42, 46, 47, 53, 58, 59, 62, 63, 65, 66, 74, 77, 78, 80, 81, 83, 84, 86, 91, 98, 104, 112, 113, 114, 117, 118, 128, 130, 132, 136, 137, 138,

139, 141, 143, 145, 147, 150, 159, 166, 176
loopholes 5, 10, 50, 54, 70, 75, 76, 90, 91, 138, 200
on luxury 62, 120, 128, 141
moratorium 119, 129, 152, 156
noncompliance 12, 89, 161
progressive 20, 161
regressive 36, 126, 144
Tax avoidance
In Argentina 138, 182, 188
In Chile 29, 50, 51, 54, 70, 75, 76
Tax culture
In Argentina 89, 110, 122, 123
In Chile 65
Tax evasion
in *Administracion General de Aduanas* 139
in Argentina in 1980s 96
and Argentine income tax 139
and Carlos Menem 136, 139
in Chile, consensus on combat 169
and clientelism in Argentina 190
and Concertacion governments 200
and criticism of anti-evasion effort 115
effort to combat by SII's Etcheberry 74
effort to combat under president Lagos 70, 78
and federal fiscal system in Argentina 188
and Felipe Cavallo 104
and fiscal rebellion 153
increase in Argentina 129
and inflation in Argentina 106
level in Argentina in 1996 133
level in Argentina in 2001 159
and lowering marginal tax rates in Chile 77
in pre-Pinochet Chile 19
reduction under Aylwin 60
and state-society pact in Argentina 182

and Taachi anti-evasion campaign 119–120
Tax exemptions
In Argentina 157, 158
In Chile 19, 22, 50, 76
Tax state 15, 201
Technocrats
In Argentina 98, 103, 124, 134, 140, 156, 185, 191
In Chile 64, 65, 90, 166, 173, 176, 200
Tecnicos (technocrats)
In Chile 167, 168, 175, 200
In Latin America 204
Terragno, Rodolfo 148, 152, 153, 154
Thirsk, Wayne 10
Trickle-down economics 20, 27, 30, 40, 48, 71, 169

Union Democratica Independiente (UDI, Independent Democratic Union party) 28, 32, 33, 36, 38, 40, 43, 45, 48, 54, 56, 67, 68, 69, 70, 72, 77, 83, 84, 166, 167, 168, 170
Union Industrial Argentina (Argentine Industrial Union) 113, 145, 186

Value Added Tax (VAT)
In Argentina 90, 98, 100, 101, 104, 106, 107, 109, 113, 117, 118, 119, 120, 122, 125, 126, 128, 129, 130, 136, 137, 139, 140–147, 150, 159, 160
In Chile 21, 23, 24, 29, 31, 36, 41, 47, 50, 52, 56, 59, 62, 65, 83, 84
Vergara, Rodrigo 62
Vial, Joaquin 59, 66
Villarzu, Juan 63, 64

World Bank 97, 98, 109